Musée de l'Orangerie

Catalogue of the
Jean Walter and Paul Guillaume Collection

# Musée de l'Orangerie

# Catalogue of the Jean Walter and Paul Guillaume Collection

By Michel Hoog,
Conservateur en chef

With the collaboration of
Hélène Guicharnaud, Conservateur
and Colette Giraudon, Documentaliste

Translated by Barbara Shuey

Ministère de la Culture et de la Communication
Éditions de la Réunion des musées nationaux
Paris, 1987

Cover: Renoir, *Claude Renoir in Clown Costume*
No. 97 in the catalogue

ISBN 2-7118-0.262-0 (French edition, RMN)

ISBN 2-7118-2.076-9 (English edition, RMN)

© Editions de la Réunion des Musées Nationaux,
 Paris, 1987
 10, rue de l'Abbaye, 75006 Paris
© ADAGP, Paris, 1984
© SPADEM, Paris, 1984

# Introduction

After playing host to so many temporary exhibitions, the Musée de l'Orangerie will henceforth be housing the Walter-Guillaume collection as a permanent feature. This double name designates the works collected by the great art dealer Paul Guillaume, which were added to by his widow and by her second husband, Jean Walter. This collection, which was bequeathed to the French government under particularly generous conditions, will share the premises with Claude Monet's *Water Lilies* paintings, which, until 1984, had constituted the museum's only permanent exhibit. This museum, whose contents bear witness to the tastes of great art lovers, fulfills a mission that is complementary to systematic, methodical collections; such museums had already existed in Paris for earlier artistic periods. None of them was devoted to the particularly glorious moment of artistic creativeness in Paris that ranges from Impressionism to the 1930s.

Is it because Paul Guillaume died young, and because his gallery vanished with him, that he has tended to fall into oblivion today and that various errors have prevailed concerning him? His premature demise prevented him from drafting the memoirs that have enabled other dealers to leave a legacy of self-portraits that are flattering to greater or lesser degrees. This "Introduction" does not claim to constitute the detailed study that is deserved by such an individual: the extremely sketchy reference literature available today does not make this possible.

De Chirico, *Portrait of Paul Guillaume*. Grenoble, Museum of Painting and Sculpture.

Paul Guillaume was born on 28 November 1891 in Paris, where he died on 1 October 1934. Little is known about his background, although he doubtless came from an affluent family; his parents were Parisians, and the Guillaume name was not a pseudonym.

During Paul Guillaume's adolescence, Paris experienced the impact of Fauvism and Cubism, as well as that of Sergei Diaghilev's Ballets Russes and of abstract art, which was beginning to emerge. Guillaume kept abreast of these developments, which were highly controversial at the time, and for his initial exhibits, he selected certain artists who, because of their originality, had been the most exposed to these movements. It is fascinating to realize that it was a twenty-three-year-old man who inaugurated his gallery in 1914 with a show featuring "Madame Natalie de Gontcharowa, the designer of the sets for *Le Coq d'Or,* and Mr. Michel Larionov, the leader of the modern movement in Russia." They were succeeded in 1916 by Derain, in 1918 by Matisse and Picasso in a group show — a rare occurrence that would seldom be repeated — and, later on, by a Van Dongen show and group shows (for example, in 1918, again, Matisse, Picasso, Derain, de Chirico, Vlaminck, de La Fresnaye, Modigliani, Utrillo).

Guillaume had been exempted from military service for health reasons, and was one of the individuals who managed to maintain an artistic life in Paris during World War I. Although his later choices attest to his independence of mind, he by no means consigned his earlier choices to oblivion.

Probably none of the other great "diviner-dealers" of his time opted for such a varied range of choices. It is a continuing matter for admiration to realize that amid indifference and sarcasm (which tend to be forgotten about today), a handful of individuals like Paul Guillaume were sufficiently discerning to make selections that were subsequently ratified by posterity.

By and large, the many works published in those days devoted to the artistic trends of the time, whether general treatises or collections of articles, disregarded the roles played by individuals and institutions[1]. Admittedly, their authors describe the polemic context amid which modern art developed. But they seemingly ignored the efforts of a few dealers (Paul Guillaume having been one of the most active, although of course not the only one), the role of the galleries, the indifference of French officialdom — whereas foreign museums were acquiring works and staging exhibitions — all the combats that the artists could never have waged by themselves... All this seems to have been largely overlooked.

Modigliani, *Portrait of Paul Guillaume*. Toledo Museum of Art, Toledo, Ohio.

Paul Guillaume benefited from the advice of Guillaume Apollinaire, with whom he became acquainted around 1910 and whom he requested, on several occasions, to write the forewords to his catalogues. Apollinaire's intellectual voracity and his qualities as an animating spirit could not have failed to find a kindred soul in Paul Guillaume. However, it was also necessary to remain receptive to the suggestions of a volatile, demanding temperament; others had been more circumspect, and Guillaume did not always share all of the poet's admirations and commitments.

After 1918, Guillaume became interested in Robert Delaunay, who, after brilliant beginnings, which had been celebrated by Apollinaire, was experiencing difficulties. It may have been Delaunay, a great admirer of the Douanier Rousseau, who helped to arouse Guillaume's interest in the latter. He was also enthusiastic about artists who had been unknown before 1914, including Modigliani, one of whose very rare supporters was Guillaume, along with Zborowski and Soutine, whome he discovered and launched. Guillaume was a discreet art patron who espoused the cause of several different painters, and his action was especially meritorious in view of the fact that after 1929, he himself was hit by the depression. His activity further included the preceding generation, with Renoir, Cézanne and the Douanier Rousseau. In 1920, these artists, especially the latter, had not won general acceptance and recognition.

Guillaume's taste for African art looms as even more venturesome. It would seem to be as precocious, or nearly so, as his interest in living art. We are indebted to first-hand accounts gathered by Jean Laude[2] from Alice

1. One of the rare exceptions was G. Turpin's work (*La Stratégie Artistique*, Paris, 1929), in which the role of Waldemar George (designated by his initials) with regard to Paul Guillaume is clearly described.

2. Jean Laude, *La peinture française (1905-1914) et "l'art nègre"*, Paris, 1968, pages 117 and 364.

Halicka, the wife of the painter Marcoussis, and from Charles Ratton, the African art specialist, for details concerning the awakening of his interest, as follows: "In about 1910, Paul Guillaume frequented the company of artists and writers who gathered around Guillaume Apollinaire (...). The Czechoslovakian sculptor Brummer had called his attention to the Fang figures." Young Paul Guillaume's cleaning woman, who also worked for Marcoussis, had a son who was doing his military service in what were then the French overseas colonies; this son sent her Negro art objects. The tire dealer by whom he was employed, near the Place de l'Etoile, also owned certain examples of African art.

By the dawn of the century, the Parisian and German avant-gardes had already become interested in what, thus far, had been merely ethnographic curiosity. In these objects, they discerned a repertory of forms that were *different*. But Paul Guillaume was one of the first to recognize them as works of art. In a way, this act of recognition provided the assurance that artists were looking for in African art, which constituted a manner of representation of volume and space that was independent from the rules handed down by the Italian Renaissance. Guillaume devoted several articles and two books to African sculpture.

Paul Guillaume never dissociated his activity as a gallery manager from his work as a writer and publisher. With his very first exhibition, devoted to Larionov and Gontcharova, he issued a carefully compiled catalogue, for which Apollinaire drafted the foreword. This was the first of a long series. At the time, such an occurrence, which today is common practice, was exceptional, and it offers yet another example of Guillaume's pioneering qualities. In 1918, he began publishing a magazine entitled *Les Arts à Paris*, in whose pages young critics had a chance to voice their opinions.

In 1929, one of those critics, Waldemar George, published a volume devoted to the glory of his "employer" and of the latter's collections, under the significant title of *La Grande Peinture Contemporaine à la Collection Paul Guillaume*; part of this was published in one of Guillaume's independent magazines, *La Renaissance de l'Art et des Industries de Luxe*, a title with the value of a manifesto that he would surely have supported. In some instances, for example against Camille Mauclair, he was not above personally engaging in controversy.

Guillaume also became a propagandist abroad for artists whom he liked, turning out articles and lectures, making loans to exhibitions, selling works to collectors and museums. In this regard, his meeting with Dr. Albert C. Barnes was a decisive event. A great deal has been written about the extraordinary personality of the American doctor who had amassed a fortune in the drug industry and who earmarked his money for the assembling of one of the largest collections of nineteenth- and twentieth-century French art. He housed his collection in a structure whose building stones, on Guillaume's advice, were imported from France, which constitutes a foundation known for its extremely original pedagogical orientations. The character of this man, his insistent educational theories, his irritation over the mitigated appreciation aroused by his collection, the strict regulations governing visits thereto triggered passions and legends. There remains the

Anthropomorphic mask, Gabon.
Paris, Musée de l'Homme.
(Gift of Mrs. Paul Guillaume, 1941.)

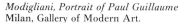

*Modigliani, Portrait of Paul Guillaume*
Milan, Gallery of Modern Art.

prodigious array still on view in Merion, in the suburbs of Philadelphia, for which Guillaume was the principal supplier. It was through the French dealer's enthusiasm that Barnes acquired his own enthusiasm for Modigliani and Soutine and, doubtlessly, for Negro art also. In addition, it was the Barnes Foundation that sponsored the publication of the English translation of the book by Paul Guillaume and Thomas Munro on African sculpture (*Primitive Negro Sculpture*, 1926, whose French edition did not appear until 1929). Clearly, Paul Guillaume was one of the most effectual propagandists for the French art of his time in the United States. Today, it even seems faintly ironic that the letter written by Edouard Herriot, then France's minister of education, recommending Guillaume as a candidate for the Legion of Honor award (24 January 1928), stressed his role as a "supplier" for American museums. Since those days, the trend has been rather to decry the foreign exodus of French art works. However, it should be borne in mind that the painters who were defended by Guillaume, and whose works he induced his foreign clients to purchase, were, except for Renoir, either suspect or totally unknown.

However, Herriot's letter, which was surely inspired by Paul Guillaume, does contain obvious exaggerations, asserting, for example, that the Barnes collection had been "wholly constituted by Paul Guillaume." Even if he did serve Barnes as an adviser, it was not Guillaume who sold him all the works on display at Merion today. But this must have seemed a sound argument, and Guillaume, who was already a foreign trade consultant, received the Legion of Honor award in 1930 ; it was conferred upon him by a man whom he could view as his model in many respects, Ambroise Vollard. In 1920, Guillaume married Juliette Lacaze, who has remained famous for her beauty and elegance. By 1930, Paul Guillaume, a dashing society figure, had become a personality in the Parisian art world; the couple entertained frequently and had friends in political circles. Thus it was that Albert Sarraut, with whom they enjoyed a close friendship, delivered an address in 1929 at the presentation of the collection at the Galerie Bernheim Jeune; the text of this address was subsequently published in book form under the title of *Variations sur la Peinture Contemporaine*. The support given by influential politicians to persons with committed tastes, like Paul Guillaume, points an even more sharply accusing finger at the gap between these official positions and the negligence of the incumbent public authorities vis-à-vis the art of their time. Not until the advent of Louis Hautecœur and Jean Cassou and the preparations for the 1937 world's fair in Paris was there the emergence of the initial valid steps taken in this direction.

Paul Guillaume considered his own collection as a kind of museum placed freely at the disposal of artists and specialists. He planned to ensure its conservation, but, whether he had felt that the time was not yet ripe or whether his premature decease prevented him from carrying out his plans, in 1934 nothing had been decided on. Mrs. Walter's decision clearly implements Paul Guillaume's intention. This is specifically indicated by statements in various articles that, even if they were not inspired by him, had his approval; for example, an article by Jacques Villeneuve reads as follows: "Over the past few years, Paul Guillaume has travelled extensively abroad.

Anthropomorphic statue, Gabon.
Paris, Musée de l'Homme.
(Gift of Mrs. Paul Guillaume, 1941.)

Ritual mask, Gabon.
Paris, Musée de l'Homme.
(Gift of Mrs. Paul Guillaume, 1941.)

Admittedly, these were fact-finding journeys, but they were journeys during which his covetous quest for masterpieces underwent trying ordeals. He had sufficient decisiveness and good sense — and also the good luck — to acquire a number of capital works by masters such as Manet, Cézanne, Renoir, etc., which will be added to his vast private collection once his planned museum-home has been built. This museum-home, which will be open to the public and which may eventually be donated to the State — if the latter proves worthy thereof — will constitute, according to its planners, the world's most brilliant representation, second only to that of the Barnes Foundation, and a considerable distance away from it, to be sure, of the great French paintings of the past fifty years."[1]

During his lifetime, Paul Guillaume made several donations to museums, including the following: to the Musée de Grenoble, Giorgio de Chirico's *The Married Couple*, in 1927, and Derain's *Mestizo in White Shirt*, in 1932; to the Algiers Fine Arts Museum, Derain's *Girl with Coral Necklace*; to the Colonial Museum in Paris (now the Musée des Arts Africains et Océaniens), seven major ancient bas-reliefs from Madagascar; and, in June 1934, shortly before his death, to the Musée du Luxembourg in Paris, Edouard Goerg's *The Pretty Flower Vendor*.

However, the descriptions available in the memorialists' chronicles are scanty and far from reliable, such as the one given by Maurice Sachs

De Chirico, *The Married Couple*.
Grenoble, Museum of Painting and Sculpture.
(Gift of Paul Guillaume, 1927.)

1. *Les Arts à Paris*, X-27, No. 14, page 2, "Echos Actualités," by Jacques Villeneuve.

Madagascan bedstead carvings. Paris, Musée des Arts Africains et Océaniens. (Gift of Paul Guillaume, 1932.)

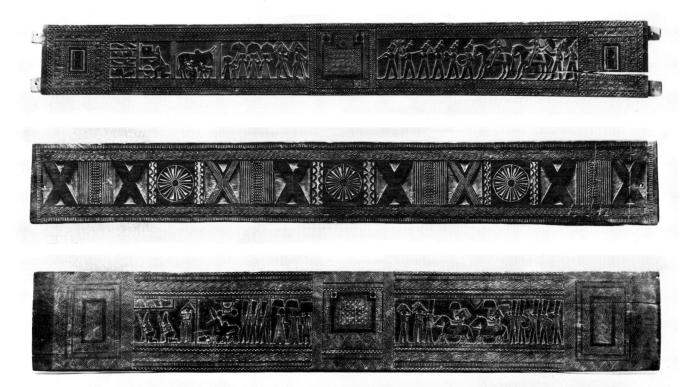

*(Chronique Joyeuse et Scandaleuse)*, in which Paul Guillaume is mercilessly depicted under the pseudonym of Hector Frédéric.

But the emotion caused by his death affords some idea of the place that he enjoyed, and the names of the founding members of the Société des Amis de Paul Guillaume speak for themselves, including those of artists, gallery owners, ethnologists, statesmen, writers and critics: Georges Braque, Josse Bernheim, Francis Carco, André Demaison, André Derain, Roland Dorgelès, A. Fauchier-Magnan, Andry-Farcy, baron Gourgaud, Maximilien Gauthier, Edouard Goerg, Max Jacob, Stéphane Manier, Henri Matisse, Pablo Picasso, Professor Rivet, Georges-Henri Rivière, André Salmon, Albert Sarraut, Ambroise Vollard, and Waldemar George.

After Paul Guillaume's death (1934), his gallery was closed and a few months later, the magazine entitled *Les Arts à Paris* ceased publication. On 25 September 1941, Mrs. Paul Guillaume married Jean Walter, an architect and industrialist who was also an art patron and art lover. It is not possible to designate in every case the specific provenance of each of the works that are conserved in the Musée de l'Orangerie today. Although the great majority of them unquestionably came from Paul Guillaume's collection, certain of them were purchased by Mrs. Jean Walter. We are indebted to her for various works by painters of the Impressionist generation, including the Sisley, several Renoirs, and most of the Cézannes, specifically the two great later landscapes. The purchase of *Apples and Cakes* (No. 5) at the famous Cognacq sale (Galerie Charpentier, 14 May 1952) for the sum of thirty-five million francs of that time — a record price — created a special stir because of the fact that Mrs. Walter personally attended as a bidder, thereby attracting attention to a collection that had formerly been known to only a handful of art lovers.

Mrs. Walter continued to devote interest to the art of her time, sponsoring several different artists and purchasing certain of their works that are not in the Orangerie collection. She even wrote an article in defense of one of her favorite painters, Bernard Lorjou (*Combat Arts*, No. 63, May 1954).

Paul Guillaume's home was furnished in a resolutely modern style, as far as can be judged from a few photographs. Apparently, it was not until after his death that his widow purchased some antique furniture, of which she owned a handsome collection, displayed to advantage, as well as an array of first-edition books. Certain items of furniture were included in her bequest. Pursuing Paul Guillaume's efforts, as is attested, notably, by Pierre Loeb (*Voyages à travers la peinture*, Paris, 1945, page 35), she concerned herself with finding frequently sumptuous antique frames for her paintings. She had wanted to donate to the Musée de l'Homme in Paris the African and Oceanic art items left her by her husband. However, the negotiations failed to work out satisfactorily, and eventually, in 1941, this museum received only sixteen Gabonese works, all of them of fine quality, of course. The others were auctioned off at the Drouot auction hall (on 9 November 1965).

Did Jean Walter play a part in the assembling of the collection? He may have personally purchased certain of the Renoir and Rousseau paintings. The records reveal nothing more specific on this matter. It was with his agreement that Mrs. Walter conserved and enriched the collection, and it

Anthropomorphic statue, Gabon.
Paris, Musée de l'Homme.
(Gift of Mrs. Paul Guillaume, 1941.)

Ritual mask, Gabon.
Paris, Musée de l'Homme.
(Gift of Mrs. Paul Guillaume, 1941.)

was in keeping with the intentions of both Paul Guillaume and Jean Walter that she decided to propose it to the French government in order to constitute a museum that would bear the names of both men.

The year 1957 ushered in the negotiations that led to two successive deeds of gift in 1959 and 1963. The collection was willed to the French national museums under exceptionally generous conditions, with the participation of *Les Amis du Louvre*, with the provision that after the decease of the donatrix, it be displayed in an independent museum, the Musée de l'Orangerie des Tuileries. In 1966, an exhibition was organized by Mrs. Hélène Adhémar, and the works were returned to Mrs. Walter, who agreed to lend certain of them again, notably for the Cézanne exhibition held by the French national museum authority and housed in the Musée de l'Orangerie in 1974.

Mrs. Walter passed away on 30 June 1977, only a short while before cracks began to appear in the structure of the Musée de l'Orangerie, threatening the building's very existence and jeopardizing the safety of Monet's *Water Lilies*. The construction of the Orangerie had been ordained by a decree of 25 May 1852, and the building had undergone sundry transformations, during the course of which it had received only summary foundations. Since it was materially impossible to move the *Water Lilies*, it was necessary to rebuild the entire edifice from its foundations and to install micro-piles. This project was carried out with utmost care under the supervision of Mr. Jean-Claude Daufresne, architect in chief, and under the authority of the Musées de France. It provided an opportunity for enhancing the Orangerie with vitally needed service facility areas.

The present catalogue endeavours to supply a detailed survey of the paintings. In certain cases, however, gaps in the records (for example, concerning the history of certain works) and the lack of exhaustive research material on certain artists made it impossible for us to be as precise and complete as we would like to be.

Michel Hoog

*Acknowledgments*

The authors of the catalogue wish to acknowledge with thanks the assistance of all those who aided them in their undertaking, including in particular the following:

Mrs. Sylvia Blatas, Mr. Alain Bouret, Mrs. Yvelyne Cantarel-Besson, Mrs. Judith Cousin, Miss France Daguet, Mr. Guy Patrice Dauberville, Mrs. Anne Distel, Mr. Charles Durand-Ruel, (†) Mrs. Caroline Godfroy, Mrs. Jacqueline Henry, Mrs. Claude Laugier, Mr. Daniel Marchesseau, Miss Laurence Marceillac, Mr. Daniel Meyer, Mr. John Rewald, Mr. Olivier Rouart, Maître Dominique Tailleur, Mrs. Nicole Tamburini, Miss Nicole Villa.

# Catalogue

# Paul Cézanne

Aix-en-Provence, 1839-1906

---

## 1

## *The Luncheon on the Grass*

(Le déjeuner sur l'herbe)

Oil on canvas. H. 21 cm.; W. 27 cm.
Unsigned.
RF 1963-11

In the series of *Les Bacchanales* and *Les Pastorales*, dated generally from 1873 to 1878, some of them perhaps from an earlier period, this is one of the quietest paintings. The brushstroke is staccato and legible; the design of the composition, which at first glance appears difficult to decipher, is actually quite calculated, the summarily brushed-in figures being distributed on either side of a vertical axis described by a standing woman, whose silhouette is extended by a church spire. It is possible to identify this tower with the steeple of a church in Aix-en-Provence (St. John of Malta church?).

Should this theme, which Cézanne handled on several occasions, be viewed as an ironical allusion to the painting by Manet that had sparked a public outcry, with Cézanne, in the present picture, repeating the "reducing" operation he had achieved in *A Modern Olympia* (Musée d'Orsay)? However, although the subject (people conversing amid a verdant setting) is indeed that of Manet's and Monet's paintings, there is no certainty that the title of this picture originated with Cézanne himself. The arrangement is also reminiscent of that in a *Bacchanale* by Poussin. There may also be an allusion to the pleasant outings in the countryside around Aix enjoyed by Cézanne and his friends, described in the writings of Emile Zola, who took part in them as a young man. M.H.

*Collections:*
E. Fabbri, Florence; P. Rosenberg, Paris; Mrs. Jean Walter.

*Exhibitions:*
1920, Venice, No. 3; 1966, Paris, No. 2 (reproduction); 1974, Tokyo, No. 14; 1974, Paris, No. 18 (reproduction); 1983, Centre Georges-Pompidou, Musée National d'Art Moderne, Galeries Contemporaines, *Bonjour Monsieur Manet* (reproduction); 1984, Madrid, Spanish Museum of Contemporary Art, *Paul Cézanne*, No. 9 (color repr.).

*Literature:*
L. Venturi, 1936, volume 1, No. 238 (reproduction); M. and G. Blunden, *Le Journal de l'Impressionnisme*, Geneva, 1970, page 81; *Tout l'œuvre peint*, No. 258 (reproduction); *L'Impressionnisme*, Paris, 1971, page 112 (reproduction and detail, page 113); J. Arrouye, "Le Dépassement de la nostalgie," *Cézanne ou la peinture en jeu*, Limoges, 1982, pages 117-120; Y. Le Pichon, *Les peintres du bonheur*, Paris, 1983, fig. 2, p. 99; J. Rewald, No. 258.

Cézanne, *Bathers*, Paris, Musée d'Orsay.

# Paul Cézanne

## 2

## *Landscape with Red Rooftop,* or *Pine-tree at L'Estaque*

(Paysage au toit rouge, *ou* Le Pin à l'Estaque)

Oil on canvas. H. 73 cm., W. 60 cm.
Unsigned.
RF 1963-7

If, as Venturi states, this scene represents L'Estaque, it was probably painted by Cézanne during his stay there in 1876. The thick, broad brushstroke, very similar to the one used in his Auvers landscapes, foreshadows the advent of the Fauve painters, who saw Cézanne's works at the 1904 Salon des Indépendants. In this painting, he broke away from the arrangements of classical landscapes and those of the Barbizon School: there is no background, but there is a highly dissymmetrical foreground constituted by the hill slope and the pine-tree, analogous examples of which recur in certain views of the Montagne Sainte-Victoire.

Cézanne paid frequent visits to L'Estaque, near Marseille, and this site provided the inspiration for most of his seascapes. His mother had a house here, in which he took refuge during the Franco-Prussian war, and also in order to conceal his liaison from his father (cf. No. 8).

A letter dated 1876 from Cézanne to Pissarro provides insight into his pattern of procedure: "It's like a playing card. Red roofs against a blue sea. If the weather cooperates, I might be able to carry them through to an extreme level... There are motifs that will require three or four months of work, which it would be possible to find, because the vegetation doesn't change." The essential role of observation is thus affirmed, but the comparison with playing cards is also suggestive: the playing card was one of the rare forms of stylization, i.e. of systematic distortion —or, in the vocabulary of the time, of "synthesis"— that was then being accepted, and this comparison was frequently employed during that period, notably in connection with Manet.

This painting is probably the one that the French government was planning to purchase in 1904. Except on one occasion, thanks to his friend Guillemet, Cézanne was consistently barred from exhibiting in the official Salon. In 1904, the new Beaux-Arts director, Henri Marcel, decided to liberalize the purchasing system, and dispatched representatives to the Salon d'Automne. Among them was Roger Marx, and it was doubtlessly thanks to him that special attention was drawn to "the exhibit of the painter Cézanne, with the recommendation that one of his works be acquired, specifically the picture depicting a white house in a landscape." The administrative decision was negative: "Since this painting belongs to Mr. Vollard, it is better to await an opportunity to deal directly with the artist." M.H.

*Collections:*
A. Vollard, Paris; Mrs. Henry P. Newman, nee von Duering, Hamburg; Wildenstein Galleries, Paris, London, New York; purchased by Mrs. Jean Walter in 1953.

*Exhibitions:*
1904, Paris, Salon d'Automne, No. 904; 1921, Berlin, Paul Cassirer, *Cézanne*, No. 27; 1934, Hamburg, Kunsthalle, *Das Bilder Landschaft*, No. 87 (repr.); 1966, Paris, No. 3 (repr.); 1974, Paris, No. 19 (color repr.); 1980, Athens, No. 4 (color repr.); 1981, Tbilisi-Leningrad, No. 4 (repr.).

*Literature:*
A. Vollard, *Paul Cézanne*, 1914, pl. 44; L. Venturi, 1936, vol. 1, No. 163 (repr.); Michel Hoog, "La direction des Beaux-Arts et les Fauves," *Art de France*, 1963, p. 364; *Tout l'œuvre peint*, No. 160 (repr.); Michel Hoog, *L'Univers de Cézanne*, Paris, 1971, p. 81; J. Rewald, No. 241.

# Paul Cézanne

## 3
## *Flowers in a Blue Vase*

(Fleurs dans un vase bleu)

Oil on canvas; H. 30 cm.; W. 23 cm.
Unsigned.
RF 1963-12

In addition to the still lifes in which Cézanne carefully arranged a fairly variegated array of objects, there are others in which he limited himself to a very small number of elements. The still life shown here displays extreme simplicity of design and great delicacy of coloring. The pale pink blossoms, the exact species of which is hard to identify (possibly paper flowers, of which Cézanne occasionally did make use) are done with a precious paint substance that is thicker than the rest of the canvas. By their simplicity and by the quality of their matter, these flowers are closely similar to those in Manet's last *Bouquets* (1881-1883), which were roughly contemporary. This marked a fresh encounter between Manet and Cézanne in the art of the still life. Back in the 1860s, both of them had painted still lifes from the same dark, naturalistic approach.

Like J. Rewald (written statement), Venturi dates this painting at circa 1880. Only the manner in which the flowers and vase emerge as if laid on with blunt force against the wall, which displays a suggestion of a wallpaper design, might point to a later date.　　　　M.H.

---

*Collections:*
M. Gangnat, Paris; Gangnat auction, Paris, 25 June 1925, No. 164 (catalogue repr.); E. Vautheret, Lyon; Vautheret auction, 16 June 1933, No. 3 (catalogue repr.); Reid and Lefevre Gallery, London; E. Bignou, New York; Mrs. Paul Guillaume (in 1931).

*Exhibitions:*
1934, Ottawa, Galerie Nationale; Toronto, Galerie d'Art; Montreal, Association d'Art; Glasgow, McLellan Gallery, *French Painting in the Nineteenth Century*, No. 10; 1934, London, Reid and Lefevre Gallery, *Renoir, Cézanne and their Contemporaries*, No. 6; 1934, London, Reid and Lefebvre Gallery, *Cézanne*, No. 1; 1946, Paris, Galerie Charpentier, *Tableaux de la vie silencieuse*, No. 13; 1966, Paris, No. 9 (repr.); 1974, Tokyo, No. 26 (repr.); 1974, Paris, No. 28 (repr.); 1980, Marcq-en-Barœul, Septentrion, *Impressionnisme*, No. 6 (repr.); 1981, Tbilisi-Leningrad, No. 7 (repr.).

*Literature:*
*Amour de l'Art*, 1925, No. 2, p. 55 (repr.); C. Zervos, "Renoir, Cézanne, leurs contemporains et la jeune peinture anglaise," *Cahiers d'Art*, 1934, Nos. 5-8, (repr. p. 136); L. Venturi, 1936, vol. 1, No. 362 (repr.); *Tout l'œuvre peint*, No. 490 (repr. p. 109); J. Rewald, No. 435.

# Paul Cézanne

## 4
## *Flowers and Fruits*

(Fleurs et fruits)

Oil on canvas; H. 35 cm.; L. 21 cm.
Unsigned.
RF 1963-6

This still life can be compared with the one shown under No. 3, on the preceding page: it displays the same simplicity of design and the same delicacy of coloring. The vase holding the flowers and leaves is also the same in both paintings, but is represented in a different size, in accordance with a procedure other examples of which exist. The fruits, whose surfaces have lost their sensual appearance and their texture, are arranged in order of size, and, curiously, are also arranged in the order of occurrence of the colors in the spectrum, describing an orange, yellow, green and blue rainbow. Noteworthy is a survival from Impressionism in the reflection of the green fruit on the lemon.

It is not easy to date this painting. The flowers and foliage in the upper part appear to be relatively early. In contrast, the flatter brushwork on the fruits and the light ring surrounding them suggest a date definitely posterior to 1880. Venturi situates this work in the 1879-1882 sequence, J. Rewald dates it at circa 1880 or shortly after, and C. Sterling (1936 catalogue) at circa 1886.

This unfinished canvas may possibly be a painting that Cézanne had abandoned, only to take it up again after several years. M.H.

*Collections:*
Paul Guillaume (in 1931); Mrs. Jean Walter.

*Exhibitions:*
1935, Springfield, Mass.; 1936, Paris, No. 69; 1946, Paris, Galerie Charpentier, *Tableaux de la vie silencieuse*, No. 12; 1966, Paris, No. 8 (repr.); 1974, Paris, No. 31 (repr.); 1981, Tbilisi-Leningrad, No. 8 (repr.).

*Literature:*
*Les Arts à Paris*, July 1931, p. 34 (repr.); L. Venturi, volume 1, No. 359 (repr.); *Tout l'œuvre peint*, No. 486 (repr.); J. Rewald, No. 436.

# Paul Cézanne

## 5

### *Apples and Biscuits*
(Pommes et Biscuits)

Oil on canvas. H. 45 cm.; W. 55 cm.
Unsigned.
RF 1960-11

This is one of the purest still lifes produced by Cézanne at the peak of his maturity, an example of those that most felicitously sum up the essential features of his artistry during his most serene period. It suffices for him to have a plate and a few apples arranged on a chest in order to create a composition of perfect coherence. The delicacy of the tones (pink and pale blue, on the right) with their overtones of watercolors, the feigned simplicity of the arrangement that subtly employs empty spaces around a few everyday objects are not to be found elsewhere except in works by Baugin or Zurbarán, and it is unlikely that Cézanne ever viewed the latter's still lifes.

Clearly, in his quest for stylization of forms and the rendering of volumes by color, Cézanne viewed apples as a particularly suitable medium, and this fact has been recognized for some time. Nor does it rule out the likelihood that his repeated choice of this fruit may have a deeper meaning. Meyer Schapiro has devoted extensive analysis to this aspect of Cézanne's thematic material. Quite apart from what one may venture to describe as their banal, conventional erotic symbolism, apples were a basic element in the expression of the artist's pictorial combat. His childhood relationships with the young Zola had been established on the basis of the future painter's providing protection for the future novelist, who was slightly younger than he. It all began with a few apples given by Zola to his elder friend as a token of appreciation for a service rendered him by the latter at school. Cézanne provided a brotherly, not to say fatherly protection for Zola, whose father's death had left him a half-orphan. In later years, Cézanne painted a large number of still lifes with apples, at a time when still lifes were a fairly minor, neglected genre. Cézanne restored this art to its eminent dignity, and was eager, as he put it, "to conquer Paris with an apple," i.e. to acquire a reputation as a painter handling a subject that was both commonplace and fraught with poetic meaning through the whole background of its tradition (*Eve, The Judgment of Paris*, with the involuntary pun on the name of Paris) and that, for him, was also replete with childhood recollections.

To Meyer Schapiro's lengthy demonstration, there should be added a further detail. During the time when Cézanne, Zola and their friends were actively waging their combat against the official Salon, whose juries refused nearly all their paintings, one young artist committed suicide because of his rejection by the judges (1867). This painter's name was Holzappfel, meaning "wooden apple." Cézanne could not have failed to learn of this incident, the import of which was heightened by the coincidence between names. (Cf. Emile Zola, collection entitled *Génies et Réalités*, Paris, 1969, page 197.)          M.H.

*Collections:*
A. Kahn, Saint-Germain-en-Laye; Marczell de Nèmes, Budapest; auction of the de Nèmes collection, Paris, 18 June 1913, No. 87 (cat. repr.); Biermann; baron M. de Herzog, Budapest; P. Rosenberg, Paris; Durand-Ruel, Paris and New York; G. Cognacq, Paris; Cognacq auction, Galerie Charpentier, 14 May 1952, No. 28 (cat. pl. XXVI), knocked down to Mrs. Jean Walter.

*Exhibitions:*
1910, Budapest, Fine Arts Museum, *Impressionists*, No. 15; 1911, Budapest, Fine Arts Museum, *Exhibition of the de Nèmes Collection*; 1912, Düsseldorf, Staedtische Kunsthalle, *Exhibition of the de Nèmes Collection*, No. 114 (repr.); 1918, Budapest, Museum, *First Exhibition of Socialized Art Treasures*, No. 5; 1931, Paris, Galerie Paul Rosenberg, *Grands Maîtres du XIXᵉ siècle, au profit de la Cité Universitaire*, No. 3 (repr.); 1936, Paris, No. 54; 1937, Paris, *Chefs-d'œuvre de l'art français*, No. 250; 1939, Paris, Galerie Paul Rosenberg, *Cézanne*, No. 7 (repr.); 1939, London, No. 23; 1945, Paris, Galerie Charpentier, *La vie silencieuse*; 1949, Lyon, *Les grands courants de la peinture contemporaine*, No. 20 (repr. Figure 6); 1950, Paris, Galerie Kaganovitch, *Œuvres choisies du XIXᵉ siècle*, No. 6; 1957, Paris, Galerie Charpentier, *Cent chefs-d'œuvre de l'art français, 1750-1950*, No. 9 (repr.); 1966, Paris, No. 5 (repr.); 1974, Paris, No. 30 (repr.); 1983, Paris, unnumbered.

*Literature:*
*Kunstchronik und Kunstmarkt*, "Die Sammlung Nemes," 17 January 1973; E. Bernard, *Sur Paul Cézanne*, Paris, 1925, p. 109 (repr.); M. Müveszet, 1927, No. 4, p. 205 (repr.); L. Venturi, 1936, No. 343 (repr.); *L'Art et les Artistes*, 1936, p. 337; *L'Art sacré*, May 1936, figure 11; *Amour de l'Art*, May 1936, p. 178 (repr.); A. Barnes and V. de Mazia, *The Art of Cézanne*, New York, 1939, pp. 214, 340, 341 (repr.); R. Cogniat, *Cézanne*, Paris, 1939, pl. 50; B. Dorival, *Cézanne*, Paris, 1948, pp. 154-155, No. 65 (color repr.); C. Sterling, *La nature morte de l'antiquité à nos jours*, Paris, 1952, p. 93 (color repr.); L. Gowing, *Burlington Magazine*, vol. XCVIII, June 1956, p. 188; W. George, *Arts*, 1959 (repr.); J. Bouret, "L'Eblouissante collection Walter," *Réalités*, No. 239, December 1965 (color repr.); M. Schapiro, "Les pommes de Cézanne," *La Revue de l'Art*, 1968, I-II, pp. 73-87; *Tout l'œuvre peint*, No. 450 (repr.); C. Bonzo, *Jardin des Arts*, January 1972, p. 64 (repr.); *L'Impressionnisme*, Paris, 1971, p. 258; M. Brion, 1972, p. 34, p. 35 (color repr.); F. Tobien, 1981, color plate 66.

# Paul Cézanne

## 6
## *Fruits, Napkin and Milk Can*

(Fruits, serviette et boîte à lait)

Oil on canvas; H. 60 cm.; W. 73 cm.
Unsigned.
RF 1960-10

Still lifes featuring only a few everyday objects on a table or chest served Cézanne as a medium for countless variations. As a slow worker, he appreciated in these fruits and utensils obedient models with simple, quasi geometrical shapes.

Although we today no longer wonder at the manner in which the objects are flattened back onto the chest, in accordance with a new system of perspective, in Cézanne's day this procedure induced shock in the art-viewing public. The chest lid should have formed a ninety-degree angle with the wall, which is adorned with wallpaper, and the apples should have been arranged one behind the other rather than rising in tiers one above the other. The two ends of the back edge of the chest do not fall into each other's prolongations. However, although the arrangement of the objects has undergone a considerable distortion with regard to the rules of traditional perspective, their forms have remained accurate and carefully modelled, in obedience to these rules. Cézanne has achieved an extraordinary balance between the strictness of the composition and the feeling that is conveyed of the presence of the humblest objects.

Scholars have endeavoured to use the wallpaper patterns in some twenty of Cézanne's still lifes as a reference basis for dating the paintings, on the assumption that these papers adorned the walls of such-and-such of the artist's domiciles. They are run-of-the-mill wallpapers, and it was entirely possible for their patterns to be retained in Cézanne's memory even after they were out of his sight. Similarly, the objects depicted in this still life and the chest that supports them recur occasionally in works of widely varying dates.

For the significance of the apple as a favored theme in Cézanne's works, refer to the description of painting No. 5.

M.H.

*Collections:*
Durand-Ruel, Paris; Brown, Baden-Baden; Mauthner-Markhof, Vienna; P. Rosenberg, Paris; Galerie Thannhauser, Lucerne; Galerie S. Rosengart, Lucerne; M. Silberberg, Breslau; S. and S. auction, Galerie Georges Petit, 9 June 1932, No. 13, cat. repr.; private collection, Holland; Mrs. Jean Walter (in 1936).

*Exhibitions:*
1922, Paris, Galerie Paul Rosenberg, *Les maîtres du siècle passé*, No. 6; 1934, New York, Galerie Durand-Ruel, *Exhibition of Important Paintings by Great French Masters*, No. 1; 1938, Amsterdam, Stedelijk Museum, *Honderd Jaar Franske Kunst*, No. 24; 1966, Paris, No. 4 (repr.); 1974, Paris, No. 29 (repr.); 1980, Athens, No. 5 (color repr.); 1981, Tbilisi-Leningrad, No. 6 (color repr.); 1982, Prague-Berlin, No. 18 (color repr.); 1983, Paris, unnumbered.

*Literature:*
G. Janneau, "Les grandes expositions: Maîtres du siècle passé chez Paul Rosenberg," *La Renaissance*, 1922, No. 5, p. 343 (repr.); G. Rivière, *Le Maître Paul Cézanne*, Paris, 1923, p. 141; E. d'Ors, *Paul Cézanne*, Paris, undated, pl. 29; *Kunst und Künstler*, October 1931 (repr. p. 11); *Bulletin de l'Art*, October 1932 (repr. p. 300); *L'Art Sacré*, May 1936, Figure 9; L. Venturi, 1936, vol. 1, No. 356 (repr.); B. Dorival, *Cézanne*, Paris, 1948, p. 154 (repr. p. 63); L. Gowing, *Burlington Magazine*, vol. XCVIII, p. 188; *Tout l'œuvre peint*, No. 447 (repr.); J. Rewald, No. 441.

# Paul Cézanne

## 7

## *Portrait of the Artist's Son*

(Portrait du fils de l'artiste)

Oil on canvas; H. 35 cm.; W. 38 cm.
Unsigned.
RF 1963-59

Paul Cézanne, Junior, born on 4 January 1872, seems to be perched on the arm of a chair whose back is visible on the right. Lack of knowledge of the model's exact age makes it difficult to date this work with any degree of accuracy. However, the date listed by Venturi (1883-1885) would seem to be an extreme limit, since the boy's face suggests a somewhat earlier date. But with Cézanne, the more familiar the model, the less individualized was the portrait; this is true for the many drawings and paintings posed for by his wife or son.

The period around 1880 witnessed this definitive abandonment of perspective and the flattening of volumes, which are so clearly marked here in the clothing, neck and forehead, and which foreshadow Gauguin. J. Rewald (written statement) proposes 1881-1882 or a bit later as the date. It is noteworthy that for the purpose of dating this picture, Cézanne scholars have relied on considerations of style rather than on the model's apparent age. There is no clearer proof of the fact that the painter's *manner* is more important than his concern with representation.

Cézanne seems to have been deeply attached to his son, whose illegitimate birth had caused serious difficulties between the artist and his own father. In his later years, Cézanne, who had apparently developed a suspicious nature and was not on the friendliest of terms with his wife, found moral assistance and support in his son.          M.H.

*Collections:*
A. Vollard, Paris (in 1931); Paul Guillaume (?); Mrs. Jean Walter.

*Exhibitions:*
1966, Paris, No. 7 (color repr.); 1966, Paris, Théâtre de l'Est Parisien, *Chefs-d'œuvre de l'Impressionnisme*, No. 7; 1974, Tokyo, No. 30 (color repr.); 1974, Paris, No. 32 (repr.); 1981, Paris, unnumbered.

*Literature:*
M. Dormoy, "Quelques tableaux de la collection particulière d'Ambroise Vollard," *Formes*, No. 17, September 1931; A. Vollard, "Souvenirs sur Paul Cézanne," *Cahiers d'Art*, Nos. 9 and 10, 1931, p. 390 (repr.); L. Venturi, 1936, vol. 1, No. 535 (repr.); J. Bouret, "L'Eblouissante Collection Walter," *Réalités*, No. 239, December 1965 (color repr.); *Tout l'œuvre peint*, No. 514 (repr. p. 110); M. Brion, 1972, p. 47, No. 3 (color repr.); "The Paradoxes of Cézanne," *Apollo*, August 1974, No. 150, p. 106, No. 15 (repr.); *Cézanne ou la peinture en jeu*, Limoges, 1982, p. 267 (repr.); J. Rewald, No. 428.

# Paul Cézanne

## 8

## *Madame Cézanne in the Garden*
(Madame Cézanne au jardin)

Oil on canvas; H. 80 cm.; W. 63 cm.
Unsigned.
RF 1960-8

Over twenty painted portraits of Cézanne's wife are known: grouping and dating them is a task fraught with problems. A. van Buren (*loc. cit.*) has undertaken to date this one on the basis of Madame Cézanne's clothing, which is in the fashion of the late 1870s. Like the appearance of the face, such a datum can provide only an approximate indication. It therefore seems preferable to conserve the margin of imprecision adopted by Venturi (1879-1882).

Among the many portraits sat for by Madame Cézanne, this one can be compared with one of the few detailed sketches, dated circa 1880 by Chappuis (1973, No. 729, former Cassirer collection). Madame Cézanne is shown seated, in a three-quarter view, busy at her sewing. On the left side of the sketch, a bedstead and a table are discernible, whereas in the painting, Madame Cézanne is posed out of doors, her elbow resting on a garden table, against an unfinished background of foliage. Such a setting is quite unusual in Cézanne's portraits, which are generally situated in an interior or against a neutral background. Not until very late in his career, specifically in the *Jardiniers Vallier* series, did he consent to use a plein air setting for his individualized portraits.

Hortense Fiquet, whom Cézanne had met in Paris in 1871, bore him a son the following year (cf. No. 7). For a long time, Cézanne had to conceal this illicit affair from his father. When the latter found out about it, there ensued a tension that continued until 1885; the following year, the painter married Hortense.

She was Cézanne's most frequent and most patient model. It is a matter of record that he subjected her to lengthy sittings. Since we know that the more familiar were the models' faces, the less Cézanne characterized them, we can draw neither stylistic nor psychological conclusions from the rather inexpressive appearance of Madame Cézanne's face.

M.H.

*Collections:*
Paul Guillaume, Mrs. Jean Walter.

*Exhibitions:*
1929, Paris, Galerie Pigalle, No. 11; 1931, Paris; 1939, London, Wildenstein Gallery, No. 24; 1939, Lyon, Palais Saint-Pierre, *Centenaire de Paul Cézanne*, No. 26; 1950, Paris, Galerie Charpentier, *Cent portraits de femmes du XVᵉ siècle à nos jours*, No. 13 (repr.); 1966, Paris, No. 6 (repr.); 1974, Paris, No. 27 (repr.); 1981, Tbilisi-Leningrad, No. 5, (repr.); 1982, Liège-Aix-en-Provence, No. 8 (repr.).

*Literature:*
*The Arts*, XIII, May 1928, p. 326 (repr.); Waldemar George, 1929, p. 47 (repr. p. 49); Waldemar George, *La Renaissance*, No. 4, April 1929, (repr. p. 174); *Les Arts à Paris*, No. 16, 1929, p. 28; L. Venturi, 1936, vol.1, No. 370 (repr.); Waldemar George, "La femme, mesure de l'art français," *L'Art et les Artistes*, February 1938, p. 173; A. van Buren, "Madame Cézanne's Fashions and the Dates of her Portraits," *Art Quarterly*, 1966, No. 2, fig. 17, p. 122; *Tout l'œuvre peint*, No. 499 (repr.), color plate XV; F. Tobien, 1981, color plate 43; J. Rewald, No. 424.

# Paul Cézanne

## 9
## *Trees and Houses*
(Arbres et maisons)

Oil on canvas; H. 54 cm.; W. 73 cm.
Unsigned.
RF 1963-8

This painting probably depicts a house located near Tholonet, between Aix-en-Provence and the Montagne Sainte-Victoire, along a road that is now called La Route Cézanne.

Cézanne frequently employed a pictorial procedure that consisted of arranging several dark-trunked trees with, on either side, a light-colored landscape. In his works from the years 1878-1885, the trees can be said to be the foreground, thereby enabling the painter to define the depth; as he gradually abandoned traditional perspective, the recognizable distinctions between the various planes (middle ground, background, etc.) became less and less sharply defined. Here, the space occupied by the line of trees, like that occupied by the facades of the houses, is strictly parallel to the plane of the canvas; between the two lies an intermediate area that has been left indeterminate. In particular, Cézanne has avoided any curve or diagonal that might have suggested depth, and only the contrast of values contributes to defining space. Light colors pre-dominate, with a very light play of greens, blues and ochres. The paint is sparingly applied, the canvas is barely covered.

However, the design of the composition remains largely traditional, involving an interplay of knowingly structured vertical, horizontal and oblique lines which, in addition to being reminiscent of the studiedly constructed orchards of his friend Pissarro, put the beholder in mind of Poussin's most structured landscapes. This work was painted circa 1885, at the end of Cézanne's serene period.

There are two other versions of this composition: the closest to it in date is the one in the Robert Lehman Foundation (New York, Metropolitan Museum, Venturi, 479). J. Rewald considers it as being anterior. In contrast with the present work, the arrangement of the trees on the right and the patterns of movement of the earth create a certain layering of the planes. The third version (Oslo, Nasjonalgalleriet, Venturi, 481) looks unfinished.     M.H.

Cézanne, *Trees and Houses*, New York
Metropolitan Museum of Art, Lehman collection.

*Collections:*
A. Vollard, Paris; A. Gold, Berlin; long-term loan to National Gallery, Berlin; Galerie S. Rosengart, Lucerne; baron E. von der Heydt, Ascona; Mrs. Paul Guillaume.

*Exhibitions:*
1966, Paris, No. 10 (repr.); 1974, Paris, No. 34 (color repr.); 1978, Paris, Grand Palais, *De Renoir à Matisse, 22 chefs-d'œuvre des musées soviétiques et français*, No. 2, (repr.); 1980, Athens, No. 7 (color repr.); 1981, Tbilisi-Leningrad, No. 9 (color repr.); 1982, Prague-Berlin, No. 19 (repr.); 1983, Paris, Grand Palais, Salon d'Automne, *De Cézanne à Matisse*, No. 8 (color repr.).

*Literature:*
A. Vollard, *Paul Cézanne*, Paris, 1914, pl. 47; E. Bernard, *Sur Paul Cézanne*, Paris, 1925, p. 32 (repr.); E. d'Ors, *Paul Cézanne*, Paris, undated, p. 79 (repr.); L. Venturi, 1936, vol. 1, No. 480 (repr.); *Tout l'œuvre peint*, No. 399 (repr.); F. Tobien, 1981, color pl. 48; J. Rewald, No. 515.

# Paul Cézanne

## 10
## *Portrait of Madame Cézanne*
(Portrait de Madame Cézanne)

Oil on canvas; H. 81 cm.; W. 65 cm.
Unsigned.
RF 1960-9

In the many portraits of Madame Cézanne, the intent to create symmetry and frontality is seldom as assertive as it is here. Without being exceptional, this arrangement is not the one most frequently used by Cézanne; it is the one that he adopted in general for major, elaborately handled works (*Portrait of Achille Emperaire, Woman with Coffeepot*, Musée d'Orsay). Despite its smaller size and its apparently unfinished condition, this picture displays the same monumental, hieratic character. The planes and volumes are distributed in space, with no concern for conventional perspective: evidence of this is in the lengthening of the left arm and the elimination of the chair's righthand armrest. Among the portraits of Madame Cézanne, this one occupies a place intermediate between the familiar portrait and the rather elaborate effigies, such as those in the Metropolitan Museum (Venturi, 569, 570), in Chicago (Venturi, 572) and Sao Paulo (Venturi, 573). It is hard to pinpoint the date of this painting with any close degree of accuracy —it was probably done sometime between 1886 and 1890. It invites comparison with the roughly sketched half-length figure in the Guggenheim Museum (Thannhauser Bequest, Venturi, 525), with the one recently acquired by the French national collections (Musée d'Orsay, Venturi, 524) and with the portrait in the Barnes Foundation (Venturi, 522). There is no known drawing that bears a direct relationship with this portrait. The most closely similar one is that in the album of the Paul Mellon collection (Chappuis, No. 1068).

The most highly structured portraits of Madame Cézanne particularly attracted the attention of the next generation of artists. Juan Gris copied them several times, and Kasimir Malevitch devoted a careful analysis to them in his book that was published under the auspices of the Bauhaus (entitled *Die gegenstandslose Welt*, Munich, 1927).                                            M.H.

*Collections:*
P. Cassirer, Berlin; Paul Guillaume (in 1927); Mrs. Jean Walter.

*Exhibitions:*
1926, Paris, No. 2869; 1929, Paris; 1929, Paris, Galerie Pigalle, No. 12 (repr.); 1930, Amsterdam, Stedelijk Museum, *Van Gogh and his Contemporaries*, No. 129; 1936, Paris, No. 65; 1939, Paris, Société des Artistes Indépendants, No. 14; 1945, Paris, Galerie Charpentier, *Portraits français*, No. 11 (repr.); 1966, Paris, No. 11 (repr.); 1974, Paris, No. 35 (repr.); 1978, Paris, No. 4 (repr.); 1980, Athens, No. 6 (color repr.); 1981, Paris, unnumbered; 1982, Prague-Berlin, No. 20 (color repr.); Madrid, Spanish Museum of Contemporary art, *Paul Cézanne*, No. 33 (color repr.).

*Literature:*
Waldemar George, "Trente ans d'art indépendant," *L'Amour de l'Art*, January 1926, No. 1 (repr. p. 90); *Les Arts à Paris*, June 1927, No. 13, p. 18; Waldemar George, undated, p. 47 (repr. p. 19); G. Charensol, "La quinzaine artistique. Cézanne à la Galerie Pigalle," *Art Vivant*, February 1930 (repr. p. 181); L. Venturi, 1936, vol. 1, No. 523 (repr.); A. Chappuis and R. Bacou, *Album de Paul Cézanne*, 1966, p. 28; A.H. van Buren, "Madame Cézanne's Fashions and the dates of her portraits," *The Art Quarterly*, 1966, pp. 119, 125 (fig. 15); *Tout l'œuvre peint*, No. 534 (repr.); M. Brion, 1972, No. 4, p. 46 (color repr. p. 47); *Goya*, mars-avril 1984, No. 179, repr. p. 307.

Cézanne, *Portrait of Madame Cézanne*, Musée Granet, Aix-en-Provence

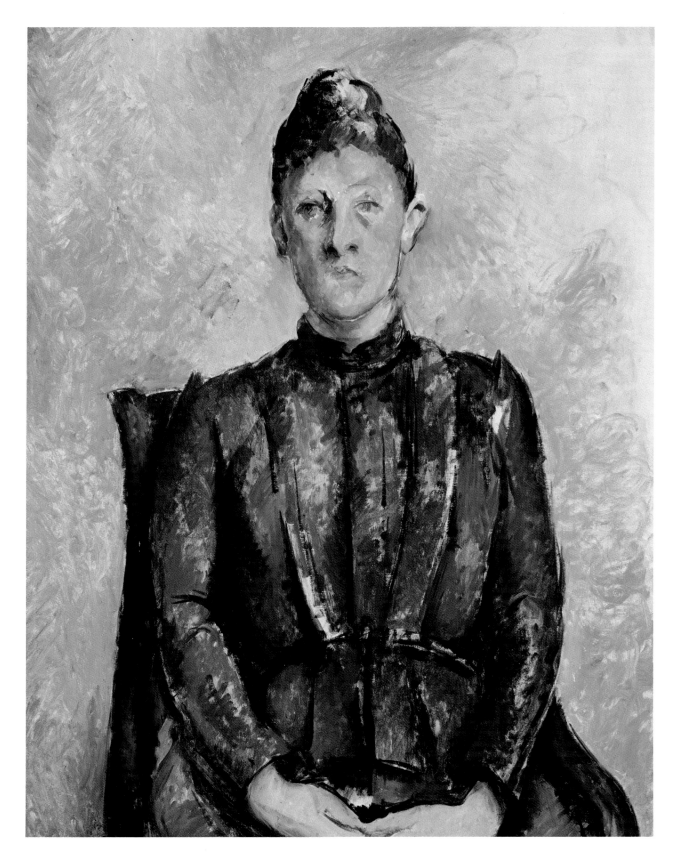

# Paul Cézanne

## 11
## *Boat and Bathers*
(La barque et les baigneurs)

Oil on canvas; H. 30 cm.; W. 125 cm.
Unsigned.
RF 1973-55 (central part); RF 1960-12 and 1960-13

This work, whose reconstitution was made possible through a purchase, is of outstanding importance. With the exception of the murals with which Cézanne, in his younger years, adorned the walls of the Jas de Bouffan, his father's property in Aix, this is the only one of Cézanne's works that was designed for a specific architectural setting. It was originally designed as an overdoor for the Paris apartment of Victor Chocquet, a collector of eighteenth-century art and of Delacroix's paintings, who was also an admirer of Impressionist art (cf. J. Rewald, *loc. cit.*). He was one of Cézanne's first —and, for a long time, one of his only— admirers and supporters, and owned thirty-one of his paintings. This was enough to induce the umbrageous Cézanne to agree to paint his portrait and to accept a commission for a most unusual format and the execution of what amounted to pendant paintings (of which there are no other examples in Cézanne's work). The pendant repre-sents a fountain in a park (Venturi, No. 315, private collec-tion, *Sept Impressionnistes* exhibition, Paris, Galerie Alex Maguy, 1974, unnumbered). The peculiar destination of this painting may also have been responsible for the rather exceptional nature of its subject (in all likelihood an alle-gory of earth and water). Although the bather theme is of frequent recurrence in Cézanne's works, his bathers were usually depicted without water, or virtually so. With the exception of his views of L'Estaque, this is Cézanne's only seascape.

G. Rivière has assigned the date of 1888 to these works, and notes that they had not been finished by the time of Chocquet's death in 1891.

As has been pointed out by M.-T. Lemoyne de Forges, the group shown on the left occurs in almost identical form, but reversed, in a watercolor (Venturi, No. 1104).    M.H.

*Collections:*
Victor Chocquet, Paris; Chocquet auction, Paris, Galerie G. Petit, 1 to 4 July 1899, No. 19; J. Bernheim-Jeune, Paris; Walter-Guillaume collection. This painting was divided into three parts; the two side fragments were in the Walter-Guillaume collection, and the central part was purchased in 1973 by the French national museum authority, enabling reconstitution of the whole.

*Exhibitions:*
1926, Paris, Galerie Bernheim-Jeune, *Rétrospective Paul Cézanne*; 1945, Galerie Charpentier, *Paysages d'eau douce*, No. 20; 1966, Paris, No. 12 and 13 (repr.); 1974, Paris, No. 40 (repr.); 1979, Paris, Musée de la Monnaie, *Vingtième anniversaire du prix Victor Chocquet.*

*Literature:*
O. Mirbeau, T. Duret, L. Werth, F. Jourdain, *Cézanne*, Paris, 1914, pl. 27; *Le Carnet des Artistes*, 1 July 1917, p. 14 (repr.); *L'Art Moderne*, Paris, 1919, vol. 1, pl. 26; G. Rivière, *Paul Cézanne*, Paris, 1923, p. 217; L. Ven-turi, No. 583; C. Roger-Marx, "Le Nu et la Mer," *Jardin des Arts*, 1955, p. 661; J. Bouret, "L'éblouissante collection Walter," *Réalités*, Décember 1965 (color repr.); J. Rewald, "Chocquet and Cézanne," *Gazette des Beaux-Arts*, 1969, pp. 68, 69 and 83; *Tout l'œuvre peint*, No. 626 (repr.); M. Brion, 1972, pp. 60 and 61 (color repr. Nos. 1 and 3); H. Adhémar, "Cézanne dans les Collections des Musées Nationaux," *La Revue du Louvre*, 1974, No. 3, p. 218 (repr. No. 2), p. 219 (repr. No. 4).

Cézanne, *Boat and Bathers*
(detail of right side).

# Paul Cézanne

## 12
## *Straw-Trimmed Vase, Sugar Bowl and Apples*

(Vase paillé, sucrier et pommes)

Oil on canvas; H. 36 cm.; W. 46 cm.
Unsigned.
RF 1963-9

This still life is one of the boldest in Cézanne's world of inventiveness. It ignores conventional perspective, and the objects are freely dispersed over the canvas in an arrangement whose coherence relates to the needs of art rather than to the need to describe. The refutation of literal representation, or at least of plausible depiction, concerns the textures and shapes of the objects as much as their positions in relation to the table surface, which itself is artfully tampered with. Moreover, in this painting Cézanne has introduced indecipherable —i.e. abstract— elements such as the vertical line that extends between the vase and the sugar bowl, the oblique black line (a knife handle?) that touches the edge of the picture on the right, and the traces of the contour of the vase in its initial position, which Cézanne refrained from erasing.

As for the apparently disequilibrated fruit-filled plate, Cézanne repeated this motif some ten times, both with and without the straw-trimmed vase, for example in the great *Still Life* at the Metropolitan Museum (Venturi, No. 793).

Maurice Denis, who was one of Cézanne's earliest admirers among the painters of his generation, and was also one of the first commentators on Cézanne's work, did a very subtle analysis of Cézanne's pattern of procedure as it emerges in this still life: "Cézanne's fruits and his unfinished figures are the best example of this working method, which may derive from Chardin: a few square brushstrokes, applied in the form of certain softly blending colors placed side by side, indicate the rounded shapes; the outline emerges only at the end, like a furious accent, a stroke denoting the essence, which emphasizes and sets off the form that has already been brought out by the gradual shadings of color.

"In this combined effect of colors aimed at achieving an effect of grand style, the planes of perspective vanish, the values (in the sense of Beaux-Arts School values), and the values of atmosphere become attenuated and are equipollent. The decorative effect and the equilibrium of the composition emerge with special sharpness because the overhead perspective has been considerably foreshortened." (*L'Occident*, September 1907, reprinted in *Théories*, Paris 1920, page 259.)          M.H.

*Collections:*
Paul Guillaume (in 1927); Mrs. Jean Walter.

*Exhibitions:*
1929, Paris; 1929, Paris, Galerie Pigalle, No. 13 (repr.); 1931, Paris; 1939, London, No. 380; 1939, Lyon, No. 32; 1966, Paris, No. 14 (repr.); 1974, Paris, No. 43 (repr.); 1974, Tokyo, No. 47 (repr.); 1982, Liège - Aix-en-Provence, No. 19 (color repr.); 1982, Saint-Germain-en-Laye, Musée du Prieuré, *L'Eclatement de l'Impressionnisme*, No. 5 (repr. 54); 1983, Paris, Grand Palais, Salon d'Automne, *De Cézanne à Matisse*, No. 11; 1984, Madrid, Spanish Museum of Contemporary Art, *Paul Cézanne*, No. 41, p. 154, color repr. p. 155.

*Literature:*
E. Tériade, "Les peintres nouveaux. La formation d'une plastique moderne," *Les Cahiers d'Art*, 1927, No. 1 (repr. p. 25); R. Huyghe, "Les origines de la peinture contemporaine," *L'Amour de l'Art*, 1933, No. 1 (repr. p. 16, fig. 14); L. Venturi, 1936, vol. 1, No. 616 (repr.); *Tout l'œuvre peint*, No. 791 (repr.); M. Costantini, "Le primitif d'un art nouveau," *Cézanne ou la peinture en jeu*, Limoges, 1982, pp. 121, 122 (repr. p. 165), p. 198.

# Paul Cézanne

## 13
## *The Red Rock*

(Le rocher rouge)

Oil on canvas; H. 92 cm.; W. 68 cm.
Unsigned.
RF 1960-14

Circa 1895, Cézanne's landscapes changed their character. They shed the serenity, the clear organization and the sun-drenched daylight of those of the previous years. In the countryside around Aix, Cézanne sought out wilderness sites in which plant life and rock formations blended into thickly wooded compositions with rugged relief features.

The interplay of lights and values determines a composition devoid of any hint of perspective. The tree mass, handled with small, regular hachures, is curiously interrupted by the reddish-orange wall of an overhanging boulder, whose coloring and brushwork make it contrast with the rest of the picture.

As John Rewald observes, "From the standpoint of composition, the totally asymmetrical and abrupt superimposition of the rock in this forest scene is a wholly unaccustomed element in Cézanne's landscapes. However, a miraculous balance is achieved by a white milestone, in the lower left, whose stability stands out from the luxuriant vegetation and whose solidity echoes that of the rock on the right" (*Catalogue*, 1978, No. 37).

Rocks of similar appearance, but occupying a far greater amount of surface area, are shown in the famous *View of the Bibemus Quarry* in Essen's Folkwang Museum. This latter canvas was sold off during the Hitler years "because such wretched painting does not deserve to hang on a German wall"; however, the Essen museum was subsequently able to repurchase it (noted by J. Rewald, *Catalogue*, 1978).

M.H.

*Collections:*
A. Vollard, Paris; Mrs. Jean Walter.

*Exhibitions:*
1933, New York, Galerie Knoedler, *Paintings from the Ambroise Vollard Collection,* No. 42; 1939, Paris, Galerie Rosenberg, No. 32 (repr.); 1966, Paris, No. 15 (repr.); 1974, Paris, No. 47 (repr.); 1977, New York, Museum of Modern Art, Houston, Museum of Fine Arts, *Cézanne, the Late Work,* No. 13 (color repr.); 1978, Paris, Grand Palais, *Cézanne, les dernières années* (No. 37, color repr.); 1982, Saint-Germain-en-Laye, Musée du Prieuré, *L'éclatement de l'Impressionnisme,* p. 57 (repr.), p. 39 (color plate).

*Literature:*
J. Rewald, *Amour de l'Art,* 1935, pp. 15-21; L. Venturi, 1936, vol. 1 ,No. 776 (repr.); *Tout l'œuvre peint,* No. 706 (repr.) and color plate LIX; T. Reff, "Painting and Theory in the Final Decade," *Cézanne, The Late Work,* New York, 1977, p. 24; F. Tobien, 1981, color plate 51.

# Paul Cézanne

## 14

## *In the Park at Château Noir*

(Dans le Parc de Château Noir)

Oil on canvas; H. 92 cm.; W. 73 cm.
Unsigned.
RF 1960-15

In *Trees and Houses* (No. 9), the landscape was broken up into two planes. Here, a single plane unifies the mineral and plant elements. This lush, overgrown, intemporal nature, whence mankind is excluded, is characteristic of Cézanne's last landscapes, of which it emerges as one of the most grandiose examples. Their poetics are not unrelated to the pantheism-tinged poetics of Monet's *Water Lilies*, which are only slightly posterior.

Never has the painter's hold over the visible world been so strong, never has nature been so subservient to the artist's "sensation," as Cézanne was wont to say; but, paradoxically enough, this determination on the part of the artist intervenes in the choice of the moment and of the motif far more than in its representation. Exactly as Monet planted a garden in the patterns in which he planned to paint it, Cézanne carefully selected the motifs that interested him in the countryside around Aix and transposed them so slightly that it has often been possible to pinpoint them precisely, as is the case with the present picture (J. Rewald and L. Marschutz, 1935).

There are three versions of this composition: the present one, in which greens and browns predominate; one in London's National Gallery (handled in a darker color range); and one in a Swiss private collection (Venturi, 788). There are a number of related drawings and watercolors (the most closely similar being the Venturi 1543, sold by Sotheby, London, on 26 June 1972) representing analogous huddles of branches and rocks depicted amid an identical setting. Here, again, the comparison with Monet is obvious: Monet's series paintings that repeated a given motif under various different effects of light were exactly contemporary. In 1891, Cézanne could have viewed the Durand-Ruel exhibition of the *Grainstacks*, or he could have attended the 1895 show of the *Rouen Cathedral* paintings. Does this mean that there was an influence? Is it not more likely, instead, that in these two strong personalities (two individuals who mutually appreciated each other), there was the same in-depth investigation and systemization of the major discoveries of Impressionism, which neither had ever disavowed?

Château Noir is an estate located between Aix-en-Provence and the Montagne Sainte-Victoire. Cézanne enjoyed painting in the wilderness grounds that surrounded the house, where for a while he rented a studio.

This painting has prompted the painter André Lhote to engage in an objective analysis of Cézanne's handling of color, as follows: "A painting can be brought to its maximum color intensity provided that the color harmony is extremely reduced. If there is the desire to apply one color in its pure state, then all the others must be diminished to an extreme point; if one decides in favor of equally saturated hues, they must consist of a cold color and a warm one which, by mutually strengthening each other, appear pure by contrast. They will have previously been altered, in so far as their opposition intensifies them. And all the other colors will become as if effaced; they will not be present or active, but will be suggested by the play of complementary fadings.

"The multiple modulations amplify the scale of the objects, just as the details that are differentiated or are sufficiently isolated from one another amplify the scale of sketched or modeled composition." (André Lhote, *Traités du paysage et de la figure*, Paris, 1958, commentary for plate 1.)

M.H.

*Collections:*
A. Vollard, Paris; G. Bernheim, Paris; Dr. J. Soubies (?), Paris; Mrs. Jean Walter.

*Exhibitions:*
1939, Paris, No. 33 (repr.); 1945, Paris, Galerie Charpentier, *Paysages de France*, No. 12 (repr.); 1950, Paris, Galerie Charpentier, *Autour de 1900*, No. 54; 1966, Paris, No. 16 (repr.); 1967, Paris, Musée de l'Orangerie, *Vingt ans d'acquisition au Musée du Louvre*, 1947-1967, No. 407; 1974, Paris, No. 48 (color repr.); 1977, New York, Museum of Modern Art, and Houston, Museum of Fine Arts, *Cézanne: The Late Work*, N°. 49 (repr.); 1978, Paris, Grand Palais, *Cézanne: les dernières années*, No. 47 (repr.); 1982, Liège - Aix-en-Provence, *Cézanne*, No. 24 (repr.).

*Literature:*
J. Rewald and L. Marschutz, "Cézanne au Château Noir," *Amour de l'Art*, 1935, No. 1, p. 20 (repr. fig. 13); E. D'Ors, *Paul Cézanne*, Paris, undated (repr. p. 17); L. Venturi, 1936, vol. 1, No. 779 (repr.); *Tout l'œuvre peint*, No. 711 (repr.); M. Brion, 1972, p. 66 (color repr.); H. Adhémar, "Cézanne dans les collections des Musées Nationaux," *La Revue du Louvre*, 1974, No. 3, p. 219 (repr. fig. 6); F. Tobien, 1981, color pl. 27; M.J. Coutagne-Wathier, "Quand Blondel manque Cézanne...," *Cézanne ou la peinture en jeu*, Limoges, 1982, p. 232 (repr.), inset color plate.

# Paul Cézanne (attributed to)

## 15
## *Still Life, Pear and Green Apples*

(Nature morte, poire et pommes vertes)

Oil on canvas; H. 22 cm.; W. 32 cm.
Unsigned.
RF 1963-10

This small canvas, which has seldom been exhibited, and to which scholars have devoted but little study, bears a fairly close relationship to certain works that have been dated from 1873 to 1877 by Venturi. However, although the extremely simple, artless arrangement is like that of several still lifes of that period, the fine, discontinuous outlines of the fruit on the left recur primarily in later paintings. This lack of consistency in execution, as well as the lackluster colors and a certain poverty of invention have caused its authenticity to be challenged. L. Venturi does not list it, but quite possibly he did not know of its existence, since during the 1930s, when he compiled his catalogue, this painting was in the custody of Paul Gachet, the son of Cézanne's doctor friend and protector of Van Gogh; it is a matter of record that Venturi omitted other irrefutably authentic works. This painting is rejected by J. Rewald.
M.H.

*Collections:*
Dr. Gachet, Auvers-sur-Oise; Paul Gachet; Mrs. Jean Walter.

*Exhibitions:*
1966, Paris, No. 1 (repr.); 1974, Paris, No. 7 (repr.); 1983, Paris unnumbered.

*Literature:*
Not listed by Venturi; J. Bouret, "L'éblouissante Collection Walter," *Réalités*, No. 239, December 1965 (color repr.); *Tout l'œuvre peint*, No. 842 (not repr.); *Cézanne ou la peinture en jeu*, Limoges, 1982, p. 281 (repr.).

# André Derain

Chatou, 1880-Garches 1954

---

## 16
## *The Game Bag*
(La gibecière)

Oil on canvas. H. 116 cm.; W. 81 cm.
Signed lower right: A. Derain.
RF 1963-38

Although Derain's Fauve and Cubist period production was largely devoted to figures and, especially, to landscapes, he also painted still lifes, which he had begun developing upon returning from travels in Spain. In the latter country, he had no doubt been impressed by the subtly insightful compositions of the *Bodegón* masters, from Sanchez Cotan to Zurbarán. His works from that period include a series of laden tables, but the manner in which they are handled reflects his sundry plastic investigations. *The Game Bag*, done in 1913, remains attached to his Cubist-trend manner, which characterized Derain's *Still Life with Pitcher*, done in 1910 (Paris, Musée d'Art Moderne), and *The Table*, from 1911 (New York, Metropolitan Museum of Art, Wolfe Fund). The elements in the composition stand out according to their individual relationships with the luminous rays emanating from a point at the upper left: the bag is modulated by a succession of triangular patches of shadow and light; the fruit dish participates in a luminous movement that envelops it while simultaneously accentuating the roundness of the woodcock's belly, echoing the inverted round of the light-colored drapery. Wherever the objects elude the direct focus of the ray of light, they are outlined in black, like the wicker basket; the latter has as its pendant the water jug, which lengthens the basket's geometrical shadow and receives from the fruit dish the reflection of two points of pinkish light. The right-angled composition is strict, and calls to mind *The Dessert*, dated 1912 (Switzerland, Bottmingen, Dr. Arthur Wilhelm Collection); the *Still Life with Basket* (Hermitage Museum, Leningrad); and *The Checkerboard* (Paris, private collection), in which a draped arrangement replaces the verticality of the game bag and the powder horns. In 1928, with a still life featuring a laden table bearing the spoils of a hunting party, Derain won a first-prize award from the Carnegie Institute in Pittsburgh.

*The Game Bag* was twice sold at auction before coming into Paul Guillaume's hands. According to the descriptions in the various sales catalogues, Derain's signature was on the back of the painting, in the upper left. After 1926, Derain began signing on the lower right of the picture surface.                                          C.G.

---

*Collections:*
Purchased from the artist by D.H. Kahnweiler, Paris; Kahnweiler auction at Drouot auction hall, 13-14 June 1921 (wartime sequestration of property), No. 43; A. Pellerin auction, Drouot, 7 May 1926, No. 8; Van Leer, Paris; Paul Guillaume; Mrs. Jean Walter.

*Exhibitions:*
1943, Paris, Galerie Charpentier, *L'Automne*, No. 220 (repr.); 1954, Paris, No. 31; 1966, Paris, No. 64 (repr.); 1967, Edinburgh-London, No. 54 (repr.); 1980, Paris (repr.); 1983, Paris, unnumbered.

*Literature:*
D. Henry (Kahnweiler), 1920 (repr.); A. Salmon, "André Derain," *L'Amour de l'Art*, October 1920, No. 6, pp. 196-199 (repr. p. 197); Waldemar Georges, "Derain," *Médecines, Peintures*, Paris, 1935, repr.; D. Sutton, 1959, fig. 37, description on p. 151; G. Hilaire, 1959, repr. fig. 105; G. Diehl, undated, pp. 53-54; N. Katalina, A. Barskaia, E. Gheorghreskaya, *André Derain dans les musées soviétiques*, Leningrad, 1976, p. 134, repr.

# André Derain

---

## 17
### *Portrait of Paul Guillaume*
(Portrait de Paul Guillaume)

Oil on canvas. H. 81 cm.; W. 64 cm.
Autographed to Paul Guillaume, signed in lower right: A. Derain.
RF 1960-40

The date of 1922 assigned by A. Salmon to this portrait is clearly wrong, since the painting had already been reproduced in D. Henry's publication (Kahnweiler), issued in 1920, and was listed as dating from 1919. This portrait is done in cold tones of blue —the model's favorite color— and the likeness stands out against a delicately wrought background of short, horizontal brushstrokes. The face, its upper part brightly lighted, presents a flattened nose and a receding forehead, in which the ray of light mordantly etches out the separation between it and the hairline. The chin, which recedes slightly into the neck, accentuates the round of the lower part of the face, revealing a certain softness in the features. The blue of the eyes, enlivened by the addition of white, conveys an impression of melancholy that is not belied by the impassive mouth. This intensity of color takes on special depth through the fact that the other shades of blue in the bow tie, the suit, and the ring's gemstone are softened by touches of yellow. In this paint-

ing, Derain broke away from the angular style and dark color range of his prewar portraits. As noted by G. Allemand-Lacambre, the mellowness of the light and the softness of the volumes, including that of the familiar gesture of the hand with the fingers clasping a half-consumed cigarette, are reminiscent of certain portraits by Renoir.

It was through Max Jacob that Derain, on Apollinaire's recommendation, met Paul Guillaume. In 1916, the latter held a one-man show of Derain's works, and invited five poets to draft the catalogue descriptions —Apollinaire, Blaise Cendrars, Max Jacob, Pierre Reverdy and Fernand Divoire. An atmosphere of perfect confidence prevailed between the two men until Guillaume's death in 1934.

Paul Guillaume sat for several painters, as is evidenced by his portraits done by Modigliani (No. 61) and by Van Dongen (No. 143). C.G.

---

*Collections:*
Paul Guillaume (in 1919); Mrs. Jean Walter.

*Exhibitions:*
1954, Paris, No. 44; 1966, Paris, No. 65 (repr.); 1967, Edinburgh-London, No. 63 (repr.); 1976, Rome, No. 25 (repr.); 1977, Paris, No. 29 (repr.); 1978, Paris, No. 33.

*Literature:*
D. Henry (Kahnweiler), 1920 (repr.); A. Salmon, 1929, pl. 7; D. Sutton, 1959, p. 36.

# André Derain

## 18
## *Rustic Still Life*
(Nature morte champêtre)

Oil on canvas. H. 58 cm.; W. 117 cm.
Unsigned.
RF 1963-34

In this painting, the objects seem to be barely resting on a base, as if they were hovering over a series of draperies in evanescent hues of black, white, green and orange. The colors shade off gently into one another. The blackness of the fipple flute gleams against the white fabric, which is warmed by yellow. All these colors succeed one another like a sequence of musical notes, and bestow upon this composition a harmonic rhythm that is of frequent occurrence in Derain's paintings.

This still life has the format and appearance of an overdoor, which, although a conventional type of work, was one that the avant-garde artists were not averse to trying. This picture was probably designed to adorn the apartment of a Norwegian collector named Halvorsen, who lived in Paris. The liberties taken by Derain in per-

spective and the seeming artlessness of the composition situate this work at circa 1921, doubtless prior to the series of great still lifes depicting kitchen implements, characterized by a more strictly organized arrangement and mordant outlines. The assemblage of these objects should perhaps be interpreted as an old-fashioned allegory illustrating the delights of country life.

This picture may be compared with Roger de La Fresnaye's overdoors, painted for the famous *Cubist House* and exhibited at the 1913 Salon d'Automne, with which Derain was familiar, and which represented, respectively, garden occupations and intellectual labor (G. Seligman, *Roger de La Fresnaye*, Neuchâtel, 1969, Nos. 167 and 169).                                        C.G.

*Collections:*
Paul Guillaume; Mrs. Jean Walter.

*Exhibitions:*
1966, Paris, No. 66 (repr.); 1980, Athens, No. 9 (repr.); 1981, Tblisi-Leningrad, No. 12 (repr.).

# André Derain

## 19
### *The Kitchen Table*
(La table de cuisine)

Oil on canvas. H. 119 cm.; W. 119 cm.
Signed on lower right: A. Derain.
RF 1960-38

From 1922 to 1925, Derain painted a series of large still lifes representing kitchen implements; they are characterized by static, monumental constructions and dark colors, with browns predominating. In these paintings, Derain, in his way, was repeating Cézanne's experiments.

*The Kitchen Table* is one of the most important in the series, and it quickly won fame. The critics saw in it reminiscences of early, classical painting. J. Guenne termed it a "museum work" (*L'Art Vivant*, May 1931); Waldemar George noted that "The names of Caravaggio and of the Bolognese painters spring to mind because of the deep accords of smoky blacks, Havana browns, whites and iron grey that form Derain's chromatic register" (*loc. cit.*). Without a doubt, this painting does harbor reminiscences; for example, the slightly slanted knife has been a commonplace accessory in still life scenes since the seventeenth century. But the extremely subtle arrangement of the objects in their interrelationships, in a seemingly casual disorder, is the trademark of Derain alone; this is likewise true of the fascinating presence that he infuses into these modest implements, a presence that verges on trompe-l'œil, a genre that was being favored by certain Surrealist painters at the time.

The surface is richly crisscrossed with horizontal and vertical lines created by the three brown shades in the background and the table in a frontal position, with its legs, in three-quarter view, cutting the entire foreground of the picture. With this composition, Derain endeavours to pinpoint the effect of light on every utensil and object on the table and, through a trompe-l'œil view, to uncover a degree of concordance therein.

The same glow radiating from a frontal source of light, represented by yellow-highlighted white, links the soup tureen to the other objects onto which this glow is projected: the grill handle and certain of its rods that have shed their original blackness, the neighboring jug highlighted by a gleam of light in its center, the inside of the sieve, of the frying pan and of the plates, the bread, the table cloth and the lettuce basket, certain parts of whose wire structure are transfigured. Similarly, a dual point of view enables Derain to reveal the interiors of the hollow forms (tureen, sieve, frying pan, plates) and also the space underneath the curves of the long forms (back of the tin spoon and of the wooden fork, interior of the metal grater and of the wooden corkscrew in the foreground). Another of the concordances that recur in Derain's works lies in the harmoniously inverted round of the spoon's shank and the back of the fork, repeated more restrainedly by the wooden fork and spoon on the right. These concordances, sprung from the painter's artistry —the play of light, inverted curves, trompe-l'œil composition— camouflage a composition designed with two opposed isoceles triangles whose apexes merge at the center of the frying pan, creating two geometrically separated worlds, with the upper triangle containing the round objects and the lower triangle containing the long objects; the grill in the upper part and the draped cloth on the table edge in the lower part are there to create a diversion from this overly rigorous composition.

The 1966 catalogue contains Madame Derain's statement situating the execution of this painting at Saint-Cyr-sur-Mer, at La Janette, a villa in which the painter lived during two summers.

C.G.

Collections:
Paul Guillaume (in 1928); Mrs. Jean Walter.

Exhibitions:
1929, Paris; 1936, New York, Brummer Gallery, No. 1; 1937, Paris, No. 28; 1939, Buenos Aires, *La peinture française de David à nos jours*, No. 152; 1941, Worcester, Mass., Art Museum, *The Art of the Third Republic*, No. 30 (repr.); 1941, Los Angeles County Museum, *The Painting of France since the French Revolution*, No. 44; 1954, Paris, No. 53; 1958, Paris, No. 3; 1966, Paris, No. 68 (color repr.); 1967, Edinburg-London, No. 73 (repr.); 1976, Rome, No. 34 (repr.); 1980, Athens, No. 10 (color repr.); 1980, Paris, *Les Réalismes*, 1919-1939 (color repr. p. 206); 1981, Tbilisi-Leningrad, No. 13 (color repr.).

Literature:
M. Raynal, *Anthologie de la peinture en France de 1906 à nos jours*, 1927, p. 121 (repr.); *Drawing and Design*, 1928, p. 280; *Les Arts à Paris*, May 1928 (repr. p. 10); A. Salmon, 1929, pl. 18; A. Basler, 1929, pl. 9; W. George, undated (repr. p. 105); *Cahiers de Belgique*, April-May 1931, p. 120; J. Guenne, "L'Art d'André Derain," *L'Art Vivant*, 1931, p. 13; W. George, "André Derain," *L'Amour de l'Art*, July 1933, No. 7 (p. 159, fig. 196), p. 162; W. George, 1935, pl. 4; D. Sutton, 1959, p. 154, No. 6; J. Bouret, "Pour un portrait de Derain," *Galerie Jardin des Arts*, March 1977, No. 167 (repr. p. 42).

# André Derain

## 20
## *The Handsome Model*
(Le beau modèle)

Oil on canvas. H. 115 cm.; W. 90 cm.
Signed on lower right: A. Derain
RF 1960-37

In 1920, Derain began painting what eventually became a series of seated nudes. In 1928, he confided to René Gimpel that he had devoted five or six months of the year to doing drawings of nudes at the rate of three or four drawings daily "in order to find a position," and that he had not yet found one. With his paintings of nudes, Derain devoted himself to an investigation of what Jacques Guenne has called "the architecture of forms," and he pursued this investigation throughout his career.

*The Handsome Model* is a particularly felicitous example of the study of a position of the body. The raised left arm, bent back above the head, determines a vertical line for the shoulder and back, whose stiffness is attenuated by a sort of quivering vibration. The vertical lines contrast with the relaxed muscles on the front part of the body, accentuated by the bent leg and the lowered arm. This study of the tissues —now stretched, now relaxed— is rendered with a loosely applied brushstroke that stands out against a dark background; it finds its fullest expression in the bluish-grey fabric on which the body is resting, and which makes this color vibrate, creating a grey worthy of Renoir's most refined tones.

This painting has been assigned the date of 1923 by D. Sutton. A similar pose occurs in a painting entitled *Nude with Cat*, from 1923, handled with a more linear graphism (G. Diehl, plate 29). Derain had posed the same woman, facing forward, with her hair falling over her shoulders, to produce *The Pretty Model*, in 1928, which was part of Paul Guillaume's collection (A. Basler, 1931, plate 22). The handling of the brushstroke, however, is compared by Sutton with that used in *The Red-Haired Model* (Waldemar George, 1929, reproduction page 97).       C.G.

*Collections:*
Paul Guillaume; Mrs. Jean Walter.

*Exhibitions:*
1946, Paris, No. 22; 1954, Paris, No. 15 (repr.); 1964, Marseille, No. 41 (repr.); 1966, Paris, No. 67 (repr.); 1967, Edinburgh-London, No. 72 (repr.); 1976, Rome, No. 32 (repr.); 1977, Paris, No. 36 (repr.); 1978, Paris, No. 34; 1981, Marcq-en-Barœul, No. 12 (repr.).

*Literature:*
W. George, undated, p. 83 (repr.); J. Guenne, "L'Art d'André Derain," *L'Art Vivant*, 1931; R. Brielle, "André Derain, peintre classique," *L'Art et les Artistes*, April 1934 (repr. p. 225); G. Hilaire, 1959, No. 136 (repr.), p. 147; D. Sutton, 1959, No. 55 (repr.), p. 153; G. Diehl, undated, p. 61; J.-P. Crespelle, *La folle époque*, Paris, 1968, p. 214, repr. p. 215.

# André Derain

## 21

## *Harlequin and Pierrot*

(Arlequin et Pierrot)

Oil on canvas. H. 175 cm.; W. 175 cm.
Signed on lower right: A. Derain
RF 1960-41

This work was commissioned by Paul Guillaume, and, according to G. Charensol, the two figures were posed for by the same person, Jacinto Salvado, a Spanish painter who, unable to earn a livelihood from his artistic profession, sat for Picasso and Derain. The painting hung in a prominent place in Guillaume's apartment together with Matisse's *The Three Sisters* (No. 50) (photographs from *Les Cahiers d'Art*, 1927, *loc. cit.*). It also looms in the background of the *Portrait of Mrs. Paul Guillaume in a Wide-Brimmed Hat* (No. 31).

Renoir, Cézanne and Picasso all three used this theme as an inspiration. The model most closely resembling that of Derain —and this resemblance appears never to have been noted— is Cézanne's *Mardi Gras* (Moscow, Pushkin Museum): the same figures, but in a reversed position, the same disequilibrium of outlines in motion, the same precipitation toward the beholder, the same impression of melancholy in a theme portraying entertainment. These two compositions are too strikingly similar for there not to have been at least an unconscious reminiscence.

The schematizing graphism, the similarity of certain accessories (the jug and the mandolin), the contrast between a wilderness landscape and a figure in fancy-dress costume recur in the Douanier Rousseau's famous *The Sleeping Gypsy* (New York, Museum of Modern Art), which had been rediscovered precisely in 1923, and of which Derain had cognizance; indeed, at first, this painting had even been attributed to Derain.

Despite the classicism of the theme and the fact that the work had been commissioned, Derain created a profoundly original painting with his *Harlequin and Pierrot*.

Amid a stark, static landscape —a background of a hill slope and a cloud mass that partially obscures the solid-color sky— on a barren, forward-tipping expanse of ground, the two figures stand out against a line of horizon which is so low that it leaves them no room for either moving backward or advancing. They are carried along in an endless motion by a dancing rhythm that Pierrot is endeavouring to express by the movement of his lips. The shadows of their feet seem to pin them down more intensely to the earth and to oppose the movement of their legs; in the same way, there is opposed to them, in their fixity, the

still life in the foreground and the planted hillock on the left, whose foliage, slanting toward the two figures, seems however to wish to join in the dance.

The grave facial expressions, the deliberate absurdity of the movements, the barren landscape account for the overall feeling of anguish that is conveyed by this picture, to which its subject matter should have lent a certain blitheness. The truth is that all the way from Watteau to Van Dongen, Picasso and Rouault, from Leoncavallo to Chaplin and Fellini, there is a long tradition devoted to highlighting the tragic destiny of professional entertainers —clowns, buffoons, strolling players.

The planning of this large canvas, which is square-shaped like the one in *The Kitchen Table* (No. 19), involved a considerable number of preliminary studies. One drawing, autographed to Paul Guillaume (Musée de Troyes, Pierre Lévy Bequest), shows Harlequin depicted alone, facing forward; the leg movement is reversed and his

Cézanne, *Mardi Gras*,
Moscow, Pushkin Museum.

# André Derain

hands clasp the mandolin loosely. The two figures appear in a drawing in the former Robert von Hirsch collection (Sotheby auction, London, 26-27 June 1978, No. 869); the rhythm of the two faces is out of time with the beat shown by the dance step. Another drawing (34 × 23 cm.), exhibited in 1981 (New York, Theo Waddington Gallery, *Paintings and Drawings*, reproduced but unnumbered) shows the two faces made up with grease paint, which is rare in the usual depictions of this subject; Pierrot, in a reversed position on the left, is holding a guitar, while Harlequin clasps a mandolin; a tambourine lies at their feet. Several of Derain's paintings attest to his persistent interest in this theme: *Harlequin with Guitar* (No. 23), in an imaginary setting with a very low horizon; *Harlequin*, half-length (National Gallery, Washington, D.C., Chester Dale collection), and *Harlequin playing a guitar* (Copenhagen, State Museum). Last but not least, there is an oil study (37 × 32 cm.) that once belonged to Paul Guillaume, showing the composition in place except for the lower foreground with the small still life consisting of the violin and jug (London, private collection, exhibited in Rome in 1976, No. 35, and in Paris in 1977, No. 38).                    M.H.

*Collections:*

Paul Guillaume (in 1927); Mrs. Jean Walter.

*Exhibitions:*
1929, Paris; 1935, Paris, No. 419; 1954, Paris, No. 51 (repr.); 1966, Paris, No. 69 (repr.); 1972, Paris, Galerie René Drouet, *André Derain*, No. 57; 1976, Rome, No. 36; 1980, Paris, Centre Georges-Pompidou, *les Réalismes, 1919-1939* (color repr. p. 206).

*Literature:*
R. Rey, "Derain," *Art et Décoration*, 1925, p. 43; J. Cassou, "Derain," *Cahiers d'Art*, No. 8, October 1926, p. 197 (repr.); E. Tériade, "Nos enquêtes. Entretien avec Paul Guillaume," *Cahiers d'Art*, No. 1, 1927, pp. 6-8; W. George, undated, p. 108, cover (color repr.), p. 109 (repr.); W. George, *La Renaissance*, No. 4, April 1929, pp. 178, 180, 181 (repr. p. 185); *L'Amour de l'Art*, July 1929 (repr. p. 274); A. Basler, 1929, pl. 11; J. Guenne, "L'Art d'André Derain," *L'Art Vivant*, 1931; W. George, "André Derain," *L'Amour de l'Art*, July 1933, No. 7, p. 160, fig. 197, p. 163; W. George, 1935, pl. 7; R. Huyghe, *Les Contemporains*, Paris, 1939, pl. 50; W. George, "André Derain ou l'apprenti sorcier," *La Renaissance*, March 1939 (color repr.); F. Carco, *L'ami des peintres*, Paris, 1953, p. 89; D. Sutton, 1959, No. 61 (repr. p. 154); G. Hilaire, 1959, p. 63 (repr. p. 139); G. Diehl, undated, p. 31; G. Charensol, "Guillaume, curieux homme and homme curieux," *Plaisir de France*, December 1966, p. 15; N. Katalina, A. Barskaia, E. Gheorghreskaya, 1976, repr. p. 20.

Derain, *Harlequin*,
Troyes,
Musée d'Art Moderne
(Pierre et Denise Lévy Bequest).

# André Derain

## 22
## *Nude with Pitcher*
(Nu à la cruche)

Oil on canvas. H. 170 cm.; W. 131 cm.
Signed on lower right: A. Derain
RF 1960-42

This monumental figure by Derain calls to mind Picasso's investigations devoted to associating female nudes with various natural elements such as sand or rock.

The setting, as conventional and simplified as the one used in *Harlequin and Pierrot* and *Harlequin with Guitar*, is handled in the same color ranges of browns and greens, accentuated here by a very pale olive green with yellow and white highlights in the background line of mountains. The blue of the sky and water disrupts the overall harmony. The sky, which takes up a considerable amount of space in the composition, bears numerous traces of alterations: originally, the mountains doubtless occupied a larger share of the background.

The scene is devoid of plant life; there is not even the stylized vegetation of the *Harlequin and Pierrot* painting, and the figure is situated in a world in which the mineral kingdom dominates. The lower part of the body in contact with the rock is straight; the low, rounded shoulders are characteristic of Derain's nudes from the 1924-1930 period (*The Blond Model*, No. 24). The face is hard, much harder than in the *Large Recumbent Nude*, and looks like a metallic mask.

Like Renoir, Derain was interested in painting nudes amid outdoor settings. The handling of the form, rendered now by color values, now by brushstrokes, recurs in a seated, full-length nude like this one, done in 1923-1924, in a small format and painted in an indoor setting (Paris, Musée d'Art Moderne de la Ville de Paris).                C.G.

*Nude Woman at the Seaside with a Jug*, Paris, Bibliothèque Nationale, Cabinet des Estampes (etching, outline drawing).

Derain, *Mask with hair on forehead*. Troyes, Musée d'Art Moderne. (Pierre and Denise Lévy Bequest).

*Collections:*
Paul Guillaume; Mrs. Jean Walter.

*Exhibitions:*
1955, Paris, No. 17; 1966, Paris, No. 70 (repr.).

# André Derain

## 23
## *Harlequin with Guitar*

(Arlequin à la guitare)

Oil on canvas. H. 190 cm.; W. 97 cm.
Signed on lower right: A. Derain
RF 1960-43

Due to a confusion with the figure in the large *Harlequin and Pierrot* and with certain drawings devoted to the same subject, this painting was called *Harlequin with Mandolin* while it was in Mrs. Walter's collection. Its original title can be restored to it unambiguously, for what the performer is holding on his knee is clearly a guitar. The same model, Jacinto Salvado, posed here for Harlequin, in a landscape that is as stark as the one in the large, square-shaped companion painting but that lacks the latter's foreground.

In the green and brown colorings of the *Nude with Jug* (No. 22), the wholly invented colored masses —neither decorative nor descriptive— lift the figure out of reality by emphasizing its lunar aspect.

On closer inspection, this figure reveals a surprising and unexpected feature: the right leg, with its pointed foot, is poised for a dance step, bringing about muscular tension on the same side up to waist height. The left leg is bent and the foot is flat on the ground, to ensure solid support for the guitar. On one side, the body is poised to dance, while on the other it is ready to play an instrument with invisible strings, carrying along in its rhythm the movement of the face with its pursed mouth and hollow cheeks; the look in the performer's eyes seems to accompany this wholly interior musical beat. The effect of strangeness is enhanced by the filtered colors, which abruptly cast an excessive amount of light on the performer's white collar and socks.

C.G.

*Collections:*
Paul Guillaume (in 1929); Mrs. Jean Walter.

*Exhibitions:*
1929, Paris; 1936, New York; 1954, Paris, No. 23 (repr.); 1958, Paris, No. 4 (repr. on cover); 1964, Marseille, No. 43 (repr.); 1966, Paris, No. 71 (repr.); 1976, Rome, No. 37 (repr.); 1977, Paris, No. 39 (repr.); 1980, Athens, No. 11 (repr.).

*Literature:*
W. George, undated, p. 33 (repr.); M. Morsell, "French Masters of the Twentieth Century in the Valentine Show," *Art News*, 11 January 1936 (repr.); A. Basler, 1931 (repr. on cover); D. Sutton, 1959, p. 155, pl. 64; G. Hilaire, 1959, pl. 153.

# André Derain

## 24
## *The Blond Model*
(Le modèle blond)

Oil on canvas. H. 100 cm.; W. 68 cm.
Signed on lower right: A. Derain
RF 1963-50

Derain used this same model from which to paint several nudes that belonged to Paul Guillaume. One of them, *Seated Nude* (Sotheby auction, London, 2 July 1975, No. 97), shows the model depicted full face, with a cloth draped over her thighs. The background is dark and the figure is centered.

In *The Blond Model*, the figure, seated sideways, forms a diagonal pattern and occupies a greater amount of space. The lower back and the cloth that delicately covers the tips of the model's knees are handled with the same loosely applied brushstroke. The back is rounded in a pose of abandonment and the head follows the curve of the body maintained by the arm bent at the elbow and resting on one knee. This pose masks all the articulations. The black outlines that define the roundness of the forms date this painting at circa 1925-1926.

The distribution of the light masses would seem to illustrate one of Derain's remarks, as follows (*loc. cit.*): "A picture is constructed by its light, no matter what the light, the light cast on the forms as well as that cast on substances or even the light of a figured atmosphere."  C.G.

*Collections:*
Paul Guillaume (in 1928); Mrs. Jean Walter.

*Exhibitions:*
1929, Paris; 1954, Paris, No. 20 (repr.); 1958, Paris, No. 14; 1966, Paris, No. 73 (repr.); 1976, Rome, No. 38 (repr.); 1977, Paris, No. 40 (repr.).

*Literature:*
*Les Arts à Paris*, May 1928, repr. p. 30; W. George, undated, repr. p. 85; A. Derain, "Notes sur la peinture," *Cahiers du Musée National d'Art Moderne*, p. 356, quoted by G. Salomon.

# André Derain

## 25
## *Still Life with Glass of Wine*
(Natre morte au verre de vin)

Oil on canvas. H. 37 cm.; W. 52 cm.
Signed on lower right: A. Derain
RF 1963-35

The small Derain still lifes in the collection range from the year 1925 to 1932. What emerges is a technique that was common to Derain's paintings during that period, whether in his nudes, landscapes or still lifes, i.e. the artist's approach to the rendering of form; he defines this in Manuscript No. 6887 of his *Notes* as follows: "Two symbols for a single idea destroy each other, and also destroy the idea. Example: color and line employed simultaneously annihilate each other and become devoid of expression." It is for this reason that certain volumes are outlined by large black or white brushstrokes: this is the case for the grapes and the forms of the wine glass; in contrast, other objects are thrown into relief by the values of the colors, which confer glow and volume upon them: the piece of bread and the pears.

This is the only painting in the collection that thus develops the shadow cast upon the table by the piece of bread and the glass. This shadow recurs in other Derain compositions: one example is a still life painted circa 1923-1925 (*Derain*, Galerie Schmit, Paris, 1976, No. 30, Van Leer-Mouradian collection, Paris) in which sundry objects rest on a table. C.G.

*Collections:*
Paul Guillaume; Mrs. Jean Walter.

*Exhibitions:*
1935, Paris, No. 422: 1939, New York, World Fair; 1958, Paris, No. 9; 1966, Paris, No. 72 (repr.); 1967, Edinburgh-London, No. 75 (repr.).

*Literature:*
A. Derain, "Notes sur la peinture," *Cahiers du Musée National d'Art Moderne*, No. 5, p. 350, quoted by G. Salomon.

# André Derain

## 26
## *Still Life with Basket*
(Nature morte au panier)

Oil on canvas. H. 58 cm.; W. 72 cm.
Signed on lower right: A. Derain
RF 1963-36

Baskets are continuously featured in the works of twentieth-century painters of still lifes. They enable the artist to space out his composition in height. The composition shown here is one of the still lifes painted from 1924 to 1927, in which light intervenes in the modelling of the volumes; this light is rendered now by white highlights, now by undulating brushstrokes or by quick brushstrokes of irregular thicknesses applied one on top of the other. The shallow dish, like the stemmed bowl, presents reliefs that are made dissymmetrical through deformations of the light.

The color range is the same as the one used in the *Reclining Nude* (No. 29) and *Nude with Jug* (No. 22): pale green for the table, plate, stemmed bowl, and water pitcher, dark brown for the background, and a lighter brown for the basket and fruit. Derain did not fail to introduce an unexpected effect into this painting: by their colored density, the two fruits behind the basket disrupt these mordantly executed forms and create an effect of surprise that foreshadows Balthus, whose style is highly evocative of Derain's art.                                          C.G.

*Collections:*
Paul Guillaume (in 1929); Mrs. Jean Walter.

*Exhibitions:*
1929, Paris; 1935, Paris, No. 420; 1954, Paris, No. 61; 1957, London, Wildenstein Gallery, *Derain*, No. 50; 1958, Paris, No. 5; 1966, Paris, No. 74 (repr.); 1981, Marcq-en-Barœul, No. 14.

*Literature:*
W. George, undated, repr. p. 94; *L'Amour de l'Art*, No. 7, July 1929, p. 254.

# André Derain

## 27
## *Melon and Fruits*
(Melon et fruits)

Oil on canvas. H. 50 cm.; W. 58 cm.
Signed on lower right: A. Derain
RF 1963-37

Derain organized this still life in accordance with a triangle whose apex occupies the upper righthand part of the picture, and one side of which lies along a diagonal. In the foreground, the grapeleaves are arranged in a garland that ripples with the folds in the cloth, which are marked by a mordant black outline. The plate of fruits is dominated by the melon, whose undulating stem reaches up in the graphic movement of a black-shadowed white line.

In this strict composition, Derain arranged his volumes after the manner of the seventeenth-century Dutch painters, by scattering white points over the light elements contrasting with the melon's shape, in which the dull coloring creates an effect of mass.

Although the objects are arranged in a pattern that is more spaced out than usual, Derain nevertheless links them together by relationships of form and color. "The artist does not create what he represents, he creates the link between the objects represented." (Derain, quoted by G. Salomon, page 359.)                    C.G.

*Collections:*
Paul Guillaume (1929); Mrs. Jean Walter.

*Exhibitions:*
1929, Paris; 1954, Paris, No. 62; 1958, Paris, No. 6; 1966, Paris, No. 75 (repr.); 1967, Edinburgh-London, No. 77 (repr.); 1976, Rome, No. 39 (repr.); 1977, Paris, No. 41 (repr.); 1981, Marcq-en-Barœul, No. 15 (repr.).

*Literature:*
W. George, undated, p. 44 (repr.); R. Brielle, "André Derain, peintre classique," *L'Art et les Artistes*, April 1934 (repr. p. 226); W. George, "André Derain ou l'apprenti sorcier," *La Renaissance*, March 1939 (repr.); G. Hilaire, 1959, p. 197, pl. 149.

# André Derain

## 28
## *The Ballerina Sonia*
(La danseuse Sonia)

Oil on canvas. H. 47 cm.; W. 34 cm.
Signed on lower right: A. Derain
RF 1963-46

In or around the year 1927, Derain, who by then had become famous, received an offer from two ballet dancers to sit for him. He saw this opportunity as a chance to do a series of paintings illustrating a universe with which he was familiar. Already, in 1919, at Sergei Diaghilev's request, he had designed for the Ballets Russes the sets and costumes of *The Fantastic Toy Shop* and, in 1926, those of *Jack in the Box*; from then on, Derain never stopped working for the theatre. This attraction for the world of entertainment, especially for ballet, was felt by many contemporary artists, and Derain additionally shared it with Paul Guillaume, who expressed his enthusiasm in an article in *Les Arts de Paris* (15 July 1918, No. 2, page 9).

In this small painting, the ballerina Sonia poses alone. The green and red wall hangings suggest a theatre stage. Instead of seeking to capture the model's gracefulness, the painter has observed the position of a dancer during a rehearsal work-out: her body is constricted, her feet are spread apart, her wrist is bent back against her waist, her neck is taut and her gaze is fixed on some distant point on the floor.

The 1929 exhibition of the Paul Guillaume collection, at the Galerie Bernheim-Jeune, included a painting entitled *Two Ballerinas* (38 × 49 cm.). This was also the title of a work on loan from the Galerie Schmit (Paris) to the Derain exhibition in Japan, in 1981 (reproduction No. 29 65 × 53 cm.). In *Les Cahiers d'Art* (*loc. cit.*), G. Gabory has reproduced a painting of *Ballerinas* that also belonged to Paul Guillaume. The two dancers are holding hands; the eyes of the one on the left are barely roughed in; the mouth of the one on the right is unfinished. At the exhibition entitled *The Stage* (New York, Jacob Seligmann, 1939), there was shown a painting called *The Two Ballerinas* (Stephen C. Clark collection, reproduction No. 32); one figure is standing, in a dancing pose, while the other is seated in front of her, her legs crossed, and her head resting on one arm; a guitar is resting against the wall hanging in the right background; on the floor lies a tambourine. The stage set is a house, in the left background.

C.G.

*Collections:*
Paul Guillaume (in 1929); Mrs. Jean Walter.

*Exhibitions:*
1929, Paris; 1966, Paris, No. 76 (repr.).

*Literature:*
W. George, undated, repr. p. 108; W. George, "André Derain ou l'apprenti sorcier," *La Renaissance*, March 1939 (repr.).

# André Derain

## 29
## *Large Reclining Nude*
(Grand nu couché)

Oil on canvas. H. 97 cm.; W. 193 cm.
Signed on lower right: A. Derain
RF 1963-49

The painting entitled *Large Reclining Nude* dates from the years 1924 to 1930, during which period Derain concentrated his attention on the posing of the female body and thereby achieved a highly elaborated plastic art. The background and the figure share the space almost equally. The stretched-out body scarcely disturbs the architecture of the landscape, composed of a line of horizon done in long, light green strokes, similar to those used for depicting the sea in a darker register. The beach develops its uniformly ochre color, interrupted by a sharply downward variation in level designed to set off the woman's bust. As is often the case in Derain's nudes, the face seems to be excluded from the artist's inspiration by being given a mask-like appearance. The body is in contact with the sand at three points; there is no abandonment of forms; at no point does their weight elude the internal tension which confers a regular roundness. The body rests in a flowing arabesque retained by the closed face, which seems indifferent to this controlled position.

Derain painted a similar nude figure amid an imaginary landscape, but this figure is in an inverted position, and her head lies on a cushion (Stockholm Museum of Modern Art). C.G.

*Collections:*
Paul Guillaume (in 1929); Mrs. Jean Walter.

*Exhibitions:*
1966, Paris, No. 77 (repr.).

*Literature:*
A. Basler, 1929 (repr.); *Formes*, No. 2, 1930 (repr.).

# André Derain

## 30
## *Black Man with Mandolin*
(Le noir à la mandoline)

Oil on canvas. H. 92 cm.; W. 73 cm.
Signed on lower right: A. Derain
RF 1963-45

In addition to his carefully individualized portraits, Derain liked to freely depict simple, fanciful figures like the one shown here. In his models' hands, he placed a musical instrument or some other accessory available in his studio. Here, he has revived the musician figures of Caravaggio's Dutch followers or of Corot. However, this type of more or less conscious reminiscence, which is frequent in Derain's work, in no way interferes with its originality. By its pose —sleeves rolled up to the elbows, open shirt collar, fingers poised for plucking the strings—the painting entitled *Black Man with Mandolin* can be compared with *The Guitar Player*, belonging to an American collection (reproduction No. 10, Cincinnati, Ohio, 1930).

On the objects, the light forms violent contrasts between browns and whites. The white touches, subtly applied to certain parts of the face, enliven its expression and infuse it with a strange life: whites of the eyes, tip of the nose, lower lip and top of the upper lip. These white touches look as if they were reflections of the light that is concentrated on the shirt, applied in the form of impasto. The face is especially luminous because of the low-keyed background. This painting is evidence of the very subdued color range used by Derain during this period: pale green, shades of brown and white. C.G.

Derain, *Mestizo in White Shirt*,
Grenoble,
Musée de Peinture et de Sculpture

# André Derain

## 31
### *Portrait of Mrs. Paul Guillaume in a Wide-Brimmed Hat*
(Portrait de Madame Paul Guillaume au grand chapeau)

Oil on canvas. H. 92 cm.; W. 73 cm.
Signed on lower right: A. Derain
RF 1960-36

This portrait of Mrs. Paul Guillaume, who later became Mrs. Jean Walter, and who made the bequest leaving her collection of paintings to the Musée de l'Orangerie, was done some ten years after that of Paul Guillaume (No. 17). According to Mrs. Derain's statement quoted in the 1966 catalogue, it was painted in the studio on the Rue du Douanier, now Rue Georges-Braque, where Derain began working in the early summer of 1928. This painting is reproduced in the work by Waldemar George, the Doucet Library's copy of which is autographed by Paul Guillaume, with the date of April 1929. It was hence painted during the autumn or winter of 1928-1929.

Its fabrics and draped effects are a concession to the fashionable society world of the time. A red wall-hanging is shown in the left background; on the right can be seen a large portion of the painting entitled *Harlequin and Pierrot* (No. 21); a folded cloth is draped over the back of the armchair; a stole frames the neckline of the dress, a scarf is knotted over the model's right shoulder, and other lengths of fabric cover the forearms, resting on her lap. Contrasting with the fluidity of all these materials is the model's majestic presence. Her gaze betrays a great, restrained strength of purpose, the power of which is rendered by the use of white paint to highlight the pupils, and its overall effect is enigmatic.

This portrait features the same handling of the brushstroke as in portrait No. 41 (*The Painter's Niece, Seated*): loosely applied, vibrant strokes to render the pigmentation of the arms and of the throat and shoulder areas, in the same coloring as the wide-brimmed hat, and long, smooth brushwork for the particularly slender hands.

Derain did another portrait of Paul Guillaume's wife, in which she is bareheaded and wearing a dark dress with a round white collar (Paris, private collection, exhibition in Tokyo, 1981, No. 26, reproduction). In this attire, she looks much more like a career woman, like an art dealer's wife, than she does in the pose of a glamorous woman of the world.                                                                C.G.

*Collections:*
Paul Guillaume (in 1929); Mrs. Jean Walter.

*Exhibitions:*
1950, Paris, Galerie Charpentier, *Cent portraits de femmes du XVᵉ siècle à nos jours*, No. 28 (repr.); 1966, Paris, No. 79 (repr.); 1980, Paris (repr.).

*Literature:*
W. George, undated, p. 106, fig. 107; W. George, *La Renaissance*, April 1929, pp. 181, 182 (cover repr.); A. Basler, *L'Amour de l'art*, July 1929, p. 252 (repr.); A. Basler, 1931, pl. 2; Roger Brielle, "André Derain, peintre classique," *L'Art et les Artistes*, April 1934, supplement to issue No. 146 (color repr.); W. George, "L'Art français et l'esprit de suite," *La Renaissance*, March-April 1937, Nos. 3-4, p. 29 (detail repr.); G. Hilaire, 1959, p. 146; G. Charensol, "Guillaume, curieux homme et homme curieux," *Plaisir de France*, December 1966.

# André Derain

---

## 32

### *Pears and Jug*

(Poires et cruche)

Oil on canvas. H. 25 cm.; W. 29 cm.
Signed on lower right: A. Derain
RF 1963-33

In this small-sized still life, the forms are exalted by the intensity of the light, rendered by white impasto and a deft brushstroke that mordantly models the roundness of the jug and the fruits, the lines of their stems and the sundry patches of light that highlight all these round forms. The only horizontal lines are those of the table, which separates the various planes and which is linked to the objects through the use of the same impastos.

What we have here is no longer the delicacy of the earlier still lifes, in which the painter investigated the rendering of light on the various volumes; rather, this is a simple, brilliantly brought-off depiction that enables him to infuse intense life into a greatly reduced space.　　C.G.

---

*Collections:*
Paul Guillaume; Mrs. Jean Walter.

*Exhibitions:*
1966, Paris, No. 80 (repr.); 1976, Rome, No. 41 (repr.); 1977, Paris, No. 43 (repr.).

# André Derain

## 33
## *The Large Tree*
(Le gros arbre)

Oil on canvas. H. 73 cm.; W. 92 cm.
Signed on lower right: A. Derain
RF 1963-41

*The Large Tree* belongs to the series of landscapes painted in Saint-Maximin, which were exhibited at the Galerie Paul Guillaume in 1931. The Renaissance art historian Hans Tietze (*loc. cit.*) appreciates the references chosen by the painter, and situates Derain's last orientations as follows: "What emerges from this exhibition is that the artist is more than ever attached to the classical ideal, to the classical form, to the classical execution, which he combines with his own qualities, those of a highly gifted painter... At the present time, he stands out as the only great artist in the Renaissance tradition."

This landscape is painted with great restraint. The vertical masses are handled with long brushstrokes. A filtered daylight is suggested by light colorings and, in certain places, with greater brilliance, by white and yellow patches on the tree. On the left, two orange-shaded lines of a meadow cast light on the whole scene, and constitute an additional borrowing from the procedures of traditional painting. C.G.

*Collections:*
Paul Guillaume (in 1931); Mrs. Jean Walter.

*Exhibitions:*
1931, Paris, Galerie Paul Guillaume, *Onze paysages de l'été*, 1930; 1931, Pittsburgh, Pennsylvania, Carnegie Institute, No. 178; 1954, Paris, No. 64; 1966, Paris, No. 81 (repr.); 1976, Rome, No. 42.

*Literature:*
J. Guenne, "L'Art d'André Derain," *L'Art Vivant*, 1931 (repr.); H. Tietze, "Les expositions à Paris et ailleurs," *Les Cahiers d'Art*, No. 3, 1931, p. 167; G. Hilaire, 1959 (repr. pl. 147).

# André Derain

## 34

## *Landscape in Provence*

(Paysage de Provence)

Oil on canvas. H. 33 cm.; W. 41 cm.
Signed on lower right: A. Derain
RF 1963-42

The unity of this small landscape is shattered by the dead tree in the foreground, which, through its aggressive brown coloring, opposes the muted pastels of the overall scene. This element may possibly have been added as an afterthought. In the composition of painting No. 35, the scattered dead trees seem to be made of the same mineral material as the houses under the effect of the sunlight, whereas here, the solitary tree strikes an eerie, almost disquieting note.

The forms and colors are all diluted by the sun's warmth. The olive trees on the right are marked by the dominant color of their leaves, which impart a colored imprint to the broad trunks. The structures of the low wall and of the other reliefs are as indistinct as the colors; the forms do not stand out. The pebbles become a rocky conglomerate, the houses are yellow and red highlights in the remote distance, and the features of the terrain emerge as movements. The impression of heat prevails. Only the sky expresses the glow of its whiteness above the burning blue.                                                                C.G.

*Collections:*
Paul Guillaume; Mrs. Jean Walter.

*Exhibitions:*
1947, Paris, Galerie Charpentier, *Beautés de Provence*, No. 35; 1954, Paris, No. 57-bis; 1958, No. 10; 1964, Marseilles, No. 45; 1964, New York, Hirsch and Adler Galleries, No. 20; 1966, Paris, No. 83 (repr.); 1967, London-Edinburgh, No. 81 (repr.).

# André Derain

## 35

### Landscape in Provence

(Paysage de Provence)

Oil on canvas. H. 33 cm.; W. 41 cm.
Signed on lower right: A. Derain
RF 1963-44

This landscape represents the same cluster of houses as in No. 34, which is of identical size, but from a different vantage point and under a different light.

The very pale sky, painted with a horizontal stroke in a light impasto, looms quite unobtrusively, enhancing the serenity of the softly brushed in forms in which no single element predominates, neither houses nor trees, neither bushes nor walls. Olive trees and shrubs are spaced out in a pattern designed to create depth. The oblique light —perhaps that of the morning sun?— makes the more numerous pebbles in the foreground look as if they were about to start rolling. Through their shadings, they mark a more sharply delineated downward declivity on the left side. They are reminiscent of certain of Corot's Italian landscapes, such as *Volterra* and *The Municipium* (Musée du Louvre). The mineral and vegetable kingdoms are closely imbricated. On the left, trees and stone walls are superimposed, but Derain is not interested in materials. He is attracted only by the encounters between the various colored surfaces, which he handles with fluid paint and a lightly-applied brush —the ochres of the earth, the studied greys of the walls and pebbles, the richly varied greens of the nearby olive trees and vegetation, the houses that blend with the forms of the ground. They emerge through a few horizontal lines, with only scarce openings, in order to provide protection from the sun. The leafless trees standing nearby look as if they were petrified.

Georges Hilaire has identified the actual site of this scene as being near Les Lecques, a small fishing port lying east of La Ciotat, near Saint-Cyr-sur-Mer. It is hard to pinpoint it accurately, however, since the depiction of the scene is characterized by great economy of detail, and this fact also makes it difficult to assign a date. C.G.

*Collections:*
Paul Guillaume (in 1933); Mrs. Jean Walter.

*Exhibitions:*
1933, Pittsburgh, Penn., Carnegie Institute, *Thirty-First International Exhibition of Paintings*, No. 183; 1947, Paris, Galerie Charpentier, *Beautés de Provence*, No. 36; 1954, Paris, No. 57; 1958, Paris, No. 11; 1964, Marseilles, No. 46; 1964, New York, Hirsch and Adler Galleries, No. 22; 1966, Paris, No. 82 (repr.); 1967, Edinburgh-London, No. 79 (repr.); 1981, Tbilisi-Leningrad, No. 15 (repr.).

*Literature:*
J. Leymarie, *André Derain ou le retour à l'Ontologie*, Paris, 1949, pl. 8; G. Hilaire, 1959, No. 146; J.-P. Crespelle, "Le Derain des années folles," *Jardin des Arts*, June 1969, p. 82, repr.

# André Derain

## 36
## *Nude on Sofa*
(Nu sur canapé)

Oil on canvas. H. 83 cm.; W. 183 cm.
Signed on lower right: A. Derain
RF 1960-39

In his turn, Derain devoted his attention to the theme of the recumbent woman, to which Manet and Renoir had already provided a fresh approach. This version, whose date doubtless only slightly antedates its reproduction in the July 1931 issue of *Les Arts à Paris*, probably represents Raymonde Knaublich, a young model who posed for Derain and who bore him a son a few years later. G. Papazoff has described her as follows: "A simple woman, endowed with natural intelligence. She was well-built, with a glowing skin, blond hair, a slender shape and agile, delicate hands." (*Loc. cit.*) These were the same qualities that Renoir appreciated in his models.

In this painting, the body is held in an artificial pose, whose very uncomfortableness imparts a twisted movement to the girl's wrist. Brisk, clear, delicate brushstrokes model the parts of the body and the face, which are more vividly lighted. There is no outline limning the nude, but the color values define its consistency; the black drapery throws into relief the luminosity of the pink.

More so than in his *Large Reclining Nude* (No. 29), Derain strives here to emphasize the architecture of forms by sheerly pictorial means, as he personally noted: "The physique of a nude in a painting bears no resemblance to the physique of the same nude in a sculpture." C.G.

*Collections:*
Paul Guillaume (in 1931); Mrs. Jean Walter.

*Exhibitions:*
1955, Paris, No. 24; 1966, Paris, No. 84 (repr.).

*Literature:*
*Les Arts à Paris*, July 1931, No. 18, repr. p. 12; W. George, "L'Art français et l'esprit de suite," *La Renaissance*, March-April 1937, Nos. 3-4, p. 25 (repr.); G. Papazoff, *Derain, mon copain,* Paris 1960, p. 45; A. Derain, "Notes sur la peinture," *Cahiers du Musée national d'Art moderne*, No. 5, p. 355, quoted by G. Salomon.

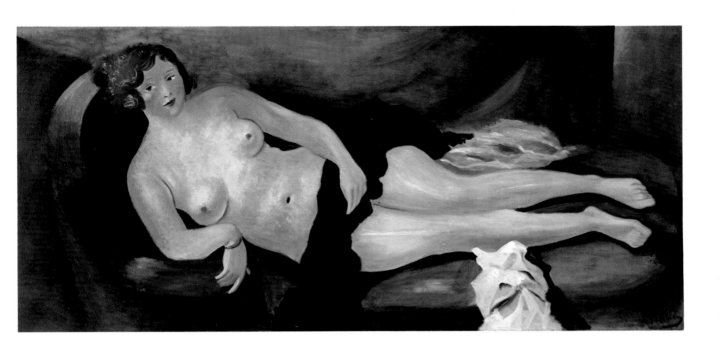

# André Derain

## 37
## *The Painter's Niece*
(La nièce du peintre)

Oil on canvas. H. 171 cm.; W. 77 cm.
Signed on lower right: A. Derain
RF 1963-48

Derain painted several likenesses of his niece Geneviève. The first portrait, done in 1925 (Derain exhibition in Tokyo, 1981, reproduction No. 25), already reveals a face whose seriousness of expression never belied itself down through the model's adult years. The two portraits in the collection, painted in 1931 and 1932, represent an adolescent girl; in later life she became Madame Taillade, and her personal account of the circumstances of the sittings was published in the catalogue of the 1966 exhibition; subsequently, in 1937-1938, Derain did a painting entitled *Geneviève with an Apple* (Paris, Madame Taillade's collection). A less severe expression appeared in the very handsome half-length portrait of 1938 (1974 exhibition in Paris, Galerie Schmit, *Portrait français du XIX^e et XX^e siècle*, reproduction No. 20). Geneviève also appears in the painting entitled *The Painter and his Family* (André Derain collection), behind the artist, holding a dog in her arms.

This portrait offers no perspective to the beholder's gaze. The figure is in the foreground of the composition, and each foot is supported by one side of the picture, so lightly that she seems to be suspended: the foot bearing the body's weight is poised on tiptoe, to describe the same angle with the floor as the one that is poised on the right side. The body has a second point of support on the bent knee resting on the chair: from this there emerges an elaborated position illustrative of Derain's comment concerning perpendicular lines: "If, given the layout of a straight line, I wish to assert that this line represents an absolute vertical, this assertion can be justified only if this vertical is opposed to another line that gives it this quality; this is said in order to affirm that with regard to representation, one takes any element whatsoever which gets its quality only through some other element that is relative thereto. In the present case, this line will be a perpendicular" (*loc. cit.*). This procedure was continued by Balthus, one of Derain's greatest admirers.

The faintly arched body allows the dress to float out behind it. The brushstroke emphasizes the lightness of the dress, in contrast —as frequently occurs in Derain's art, for the purpose of misleading the beholder— with the heavy, incurvated lines of the armchair, the curve of whose feet, which lacks concordance with the forms of the figure, further accentuates its strangeness. A large number of alterations and reworkings on the chair back attest to the difficulty of its insertion.

The curve of the hat and of the chair back, as well as the arabesques of the flowers, are there to relieve the verticality of the figure. The sundry accessories —the hat, the hand-held flowers, the basket— inevitably recall the procedures employed by Corot and Renoir.     C.G.

*Collections:*
Paul Guillaume; Mrs. Jean Walter.

*Exhibitions:*
1938, Pittsburgh, Pennsylvania, Carnegie Institute, No. 181 (repr.); 1954, Paris, No. 78; 1966, Paris, No. 85 (repr.).

*Literature:*
W. George, "André Derain," *Formes*, 1933 (repr.); J.-P. Crespelle, "Le Derain des années folles," *Le jardin des arts*, June 1969, p. 83 (repr.); A. Derain, "Notes sur la peinture," *Cahiers du Musée national d'Art moderne*, No. 5, p. 361, quoted by G. Salomon.

# André Derain

## 38
### *Landscape of Southern France*
(Paysage du Midi)

Oil on canvas. H. 65 cm.; W. 54 cm.
Signed on lower right: A. Derain
RF 1963-39

According to certain photographs shot by Michel Delmas, who occasionally visited Derain in the Provençal village of Eygalières, this is a view of the latter place, clearly showing the old keep and the clock tower, as well as the ancient ramparts on the left overlooked by the façade of the chapel of the Penitents, with, at its feet, the stand of cypress trees that leads to the old cemetery. This landscape was probably done in 1932 or 1933, the years during which Derain stayed in the area.

Amid a setting of calm and quietness, the play of values contributes to outlining the various planes, which are richer and more numerous than in the other landscapes in the collection. The tall trees in the foreground oppose their pale green foliage to the dark growth of the cypresses bordering the cemetery. The rippling and rolling of the terrain is thrown into relief by the low walls, the rocky pathways and the small bridge, as well as by the color values. This village seems to have been a great source of inspiration for Derain, and Paul Guillaume acquired a large number of his views of Eygalières.          C.G.

*Collections:*
Paul Guillaume; Mrs. Jean Walter.

*Exhibitions:*
1936, Pittsburgh, Pennsylvania, Carnegie Institute, No. 190; 1954, Paris, No. 82; 1957, London, No. 60; 1966, Paris, No. 86 (repr.); 1981, Tbilisi-Leningrad, No. 16 (repr.).

*Literature:*
W. George, "André Derain," *Formes*, XXXI, 1933, repr.

# André Derain

## 39
## *The Road*
(La route)

Oil on canvas. H. 65 cm.; W. 50 cm.
Signed on lower right: A. Derain
RF 1963-43

The Provençal village of Eygalières, painted from the local road that runs from Eygalières to the Saint-Rémy road, looms up between the two plane trees on either side. The warm colors mark off the various elements in the composition: trees with leafy branches, earth, rocks. The village in full sunlight is clearly circumscribed.

Nothing disrupts the uniform, violently blue sky, produced by random brushstrokes blended with yellow flecks.

The sky weighs down upon the landscape, which clings steadfastly to its shades of ochre, brown and green, mordantly defining the borderline between the two worlds.

Edmond Jaloux (in "Derain et le paysage français," *Formes*, 1931, pp. 20-21) quotes a remark by Derain concerning this conflict, as follows: "The drama of the landscape," Derain used to say, "is in the meeting between the sky and the earth."                                                    C.G.

*Collections:*
Paul Guillaume; Mrs. Jean Walter.

*Exhibitions:*
1940, Rio de Janeiro, National Museum of Fine Arts, *French Painting*, No. 26; 1941, Los Angeles, The Young Memorial Gallery, *Exhibition of French Art*, No. 53-bis; 1954, Paris, No. 26; 1957, London, Wildenstein Gallery, No. 59 (repr.); 1958, Paris, No. 7; 1966, Paris, No. 87 (repr.); 1977, Paris, No. 44 (repr.).

# André Derain

40

## Trees and Village

(Arbres et village)

Oil on canvas. H. 50 cm.; W. 61 cm.
Signed on lower right: A. Derain
RF 1963-40

This landscape of Eygalières, a tiny village in the Alpilles region, in southern France, characterized by its dramatic sky, is posterior to 1930. In his work devoted to Derain at that period, Elie Faure noted as follows: "The tree in the landscape seems to stand there only for the purpose of summarizing and gathering in solitude."

No human or animal presence enlivens Derain's landscapes. A barrier of trees opens with a narrow pathway that proceeds toward the village. The color masses limit the zones of shadow and light and the relief is obscured by extraordinarily bright luminosity. As in the preceding landscapes, there is a dead tree that fixes the light in a more violent coloring than the others, as if it were concentrating within itself the whole of the artist's solitude.   C.G.

*Collections:*
Paul Guillaume; Mrs. Jean Walter.

*Exhibitions:*
1966, Paris, No. 88 (repr.).

*Literature:*
Elie Faure, *André Derain*, Paris, 1923, p. 32.

# André Derain

## 41

### *The Painter's Niece, Seated*

(La nièce du peintre assise)

Oil on canvas. H. 97 cm.; W. 78 cm.
Signed on lower right: A. Derain
RF 1963-47

This portrait represents Derain's niece, Geneviève. She is depicted in a completely relaxed pose, in which the slight neck movement echoes the graceful position of the hand on her wrist; she is seated against a background on roughly brushed-in foliage. Her wide-brimmed hat is tossed back over her shoulder. Her pose and her dreamy expression are reminiscent of Corot, whom Derain so greatly admired. Her eyes have a far-off look, but the white flecks that Derain so skilfully placed on his models' faces help to bring her closer to the beholder, in keeping with a procedure used by the Dutch school of painting. This is truly an individualized portrait, in accordance with tradition, aimed at performing a psychological analysis over and above the conveying of physical resemblance.

In this portrait, Derain used two very different techniques: the forearm, sharply outlined in black, is painted with long, smooth brushstrokes. In contrast, the blouse and the flesh tones are done with a light, swiftly applied paint. The loosely-fitting dress is rendered by dark but discontinuous outlines, which edge the filmy fabric of the muslin.                                   C.G.

*Collections:*
Paul Guillaume; Mrs. Jean Walter.

*Exhibitions:*
1933, New York, No. 7; 1936, New York, Brummer Gallery, No. 2; 1939, New York, World Fair; 1958, Paris, No. 2; 1966, Paris, No. 89 (repr.); 1976, Rome, No. 43 (repr.); 1977, Paris, No. 45 (repr.); 1984, Melun, *André Derain*, No. 13.

*Literature:*
W. George, "André Derain," *Formes* XXXI, *1933 (repr.)*; *M. Florisoone, "L'Art français contemporain,"* La Renaissance, *May 1939, No. 2, p. 27(repr.); D. Sutton, 1959, p. 155, pl. 66.*

# André Derain

## 42
## *Roses in a Vase*
(Roses dans un vase)

Oil on canvas. H. 55 cm.; W. 46 cm.
Signed on lower right: A. Derain
RF 1963-52

The centered vase is the point of departure for a truly symmetrical composition in which delphinium and broom are arranged in a star-shaped pattern around roses in a median position.

The subdued atmosphere and the dark background are also reminiscent of Fantin-Latour's still lifes, which have always enjoyed popularity in the United States. This painting, which was an entry in a contest exhibition at the Carnegie Institute in Pittsburgh, in 1934, was awarded the Allegheny prize by the Allegheny County Garden Club, given for the "best painting of a garden or flowers... This painting exudes a most extraordinary radiance for observers who realize how hard it is to render the real colors of flowers" (Saint-Gaudens, *loc. cit.*, page 140).

Derain painted another closely similar work, displayed in a later exhibition (Paris, 1955, No. 16), in which he used the same swift, vibrant brushstroke to loosely outline the vase against the background but in which the jug handle, instead of facing forward, is moved to the right.

C.G.

*Collections:*
Paul Guillaume; Mrs. Jean Walter.

*Exhibitions:*
1934, Pittsburgh, Pennsylvania, Carnegie Institute; 1954, Paris, No. 85; 1957, London, Wildenstein Gallery, No. 48; 1958, Paris, No. 8; 1960, Paris, No. 23; 1966, Paris, No. 90 (repr.); 1981, Marcq-en-Barœul, No. 16; 1984, Melun, *André Derain*, No. 11.

*Literature:*
*Art Digest*, 15 October 1934 (repr.); *New York Times*, 21 October 1934 (repr.); *Pittsburgh Post Gazette*, 19 October 1934 (repr.); H. Saint-Gaudens, "Consider the International," *The Carnegie Magazine*, October 1934, p. 138 (repr.), p. 140.

# André Derain

## 43

## *Roses on a Black Background*

(Roses sur fond noir)

Oil on canvas. H. 73 cm.; W. 60 cm.
Signed on lower right: A. Derain
RF 1963-51

In a series of notes on painting (*loc. cit.*), Derain commented as follows: "There is a greater amount of mystery in black than in a triangle or in an organized figure. Nor does the reproduction of shapes along a plane produce a form. But who shall decree the rhythmic meaning of a form if a preliminary material is not designed? A line drawing must therefore engender light more than form."

In a strictly perpendicular composition, Derain details luminous forms; he inundates the flower petals with light; this brilliance is cast back onto the dark-hued vase by enigmatic small white specks that confer an intense luminosity, which is reflected in the bowl by an equally bright splash of pink.

This still life embodies two procedures beloved of the artist: the white flecks, which he locates arbitrarily on an object, thereby highlighting its luminosity and perhaps endowing it with enhanced symbolism, and the application of paint with a brushstroke that barely skims the surface of the canvas, as shown in the bowl done in green with occasional white touches.                                    C.G.

*Collections:*
Paul Guillaume; Mrs. Jean Walter.

*Exhibitions:*
1933, New York, No. 13; 1954, No. 81; 1966, Paris, No. 91 (repr.); 1967, Edinburgh-London, No. 82 (repr.); 1981, Marcq-en-Barœul, No. 17; 1984, Melun, *André Derain*, No. 12 (color repr.).

*Literature:*
A. Derain, "Notes sur la peinture," *Cahiers du Musée national d'Art moderne*, No. 5, 358, quoted by G. Salomon.

# Paul Gauguin (attributed to)

Paris, 1848-Atouana, 1903

## 44
## *Landscape*

(Paysage)

Oil on canvas. H. 76 cm.; W. 65 cm.
Signed and dated on lower right: P. Gauguin, 1901.
RF 1963-107

This painting contains recognizable elements of equatorial flora such as it appears in a number of canvasses painted during Gauguin's later years. The center of the composition is occupied by small figures.

The brushwork is not consistent: in some places it is precise and tight, while in others the paint is much more roughly applied. Laboratory examination has revealed the following disparities: the parallel brushstrokes characteristic of Gauguin are used for the round tress and the meadow, whereas the foreground of plant growth, the sky and, more generally, the periphery of the canvas are handled in a broader, looser manner.

The signature, whose graphism is not the one usually found on Gauguin's later paintings, is worked solidly into the paint, except for the figure "9." For these various reasons, there are grounds for doubting whether this is an authentic painting by Gauguin, and its earlier provenance is unknown. It is rejected by Douglas Cooper. This may possibly be a case of an unknown hand's having completed a work left unfinished by Gauguin.                M.H.

---

*Collections:*
H. Böhler, Vienna; Huinck and Scherjon, Amsterdam; Joseph von Sternberg; Mrs. Jean Walter.

*Exhibitions:*
1943, Los Angeles, Los Angeles Museum, *The Collection of Joseph von Sternberg*, No. 12; 1964, Paris, Galerie Knoedler, *L'Héritage de Delacroix*, No. 13 (repr.); 1966, Paris, No. 52 (repr.); 1981, Tbilisi-Leningrad, No. 17 (repr.).

*Literature:*
R. Rey, *Gauguin*, 1923, pl. 18; Lee Van Dovski, *Gauguin*, 1950, No. 374, p. 353; G. Wildenstein, *Paul Gauguin*, vol. 1, Paris, 1964, No. 600 (repr.).

# Marie Laurencin

Paris, 1883-Paris, 1956

## 45
## *Spanish Dancers*

(Danseuses espagnoles)

Oil on canvas. H. 150 cm.; W. 95 cm.
Signed on lower right in black: Marie Laurencin.
RF 1963-45

When Marie Laurencin returned to France after spending the World War I years in Spain, she abandoned the subdued chromatism of her earlier works and a certain geometrism inherited from analytical Cubism.

The painting entitled *Spanish Dancers* is characteristic of the elaboration of Marie Laurencin's new style, and she produced her best work during the years from 1920 to 1930. The faces, already schematized, had not yet been reduced to lips and burning eyes, although these are the facial features that predominate. Laurencin has depicted herself kneeling in the foreground, in a pathetic self-portrait that is untempered by the bright pink of her brief costume. Moreover, despite the sharp, blithe colors, the considerable amount of space devoted to greys is surprising, and it imbues the composition with an undefinable melancholy. Laurencin and the girl on the right, whose arms are so harmoniously interlinked that Laurencin's left arm could equally well terminate in the right hand of her companion, appear to be borne aloft in a dancing levitation. On the left, the third girl, who is apparently excluded from this complicity, has been handled with a different technique and in different, less interrelated colors. With her long, tapering legs, she is performing a step which was repeated, textually, by Laurencin in some 1926 engravings entitled *Spanish Letters* and *The Dancing Girl or Barbette* (D. Marchesseau, 1981, Nos. 109 and 125). In the strange climate of this ambiguous paradise, animals are neither tamed nor domestic. They are the free companions of a lost Eden, they are man's equals and confidants. The arabesque formed by the young women is intensified by the presence of a dog and by the curve of a horse, punctuated by the unusual almond shape of its eye, the large-sized twin of those of the girl in blue. The irrefragable alliance between woman's world and the animal kingdom was frequently celebrated by Laurencin: in the same year as *The Spanish Dancers*, in 1921, with *The Amazons* (Y. Abé-D. Marchesseau, 1980, pl. 39), and also with *The Does* (No. 47), *Women with Dog* (No. 49), and many other works.

H.G.

*Collections:*
Paul Rosenberg (in 1921); Paul Guillaume (?); Mrs. Jean Walter.

*Exhibition:*
1966, Paris, No. 104 (repr.).

*Literature:*
*L'Amour de l'Art*, August 1921 (repr.); Y. Abé-D. Marchesseau, 1980, No. 43 (color repr.).

# Marie Laurencin

## 46
## *Portrait of Mademoiselle Chanel*
(Portrait de Mademoiselle Chanel)

Oil on canvas. H. 92 cm.; W. 73 cm.
Signed on upper right in black: Marie Laurencin.
RF 1963-54

In the autumn of 1923, like Marie Laurencin, Coco Chanel was working for Diaghilev's Ballets Russes. Laurencin was designing the sets and costumes for *The Does (Les Biches)*, while Chanel was doing the costumes for *Le Train Bleu*, a "one-act operetta" based on a libretto by Jean Cocteau and with music by Darius Milhaud, which had its first performance at the Théâtre des Champs-Elysées on 20 June 1924. Laurencin, who for about a year had been undertaking a career as a painter of society portraits (R. Gimpel, page 218), had been commissioned by Chanel to do her portrait. However, when the latter was finished, the model refused to accept the portrait, which was an allusive evocation of a psychological nature rather than a formal representation of her person. Laurencin reacted vigorously: as she exclaimed to R. Gimpel, "But I pay her for my dresses!" She added: "She wants me to do a new portrait, but she won't get it. I can pretty up the one I've done of her and sell it. Rosenberg is interested." (R. Gimpel, page 253.) However, a second, smaller (81×59.5 cm.) portrait of Chanel does exist, and it is quite similar to the one in the Walter-Guillaume collection except for a few minute details such as the dash of light color which, underneath the poodle, replaces the dark blue appliqué on Chanel's dress, onto which Laurencin affixed her signature (reproduction in Charlotte Gere, *Marie Laurencin*, London, 1977, page 40). Laurencin has given her model a languid, graceful pose and draped her in a long black scarf arranged around the neck and body, enhancing the bareness of the shoulder. This artist was particularly fond of this accessory, which recurs several times in her works (for example, in *The Cage*, 1917; *Woman with Dog and Birds*, 1917; *Girl with Dove*, 1928; Y. Abé-D. Marchesseau, 1980, Nos. 31, 32 and 67, respectively). Its long expanse of color makes it fit perfectly into the picture as a whole, which is done in large flat tints. Although the color range is reduced, its harmonious subtlety felicitously echoes the melancholic sophistication and charm of the composition. Here again, there is animal life. This time it is a pet dog on Chanel's lap, the virtual twin of the one in *Woman with Dog and Bird* (Y. Abé-D. Marchesseau, 1980, No. 49). In that same year, in one of her portraits of baroness Gourgaud, Laurencin also depicted the latter with one of her dogs (Y. Abé-

D. Marchesseau, 1980, No. 52); in 1931, in her portrait of Madame Robert Tritton, she depicted the dog Val with its mistress (auction, Christie's, London, 28 June 1983, No. 353). And we know that her deep sensitivity and her fondness for animals had induced her to paint Pierre Gimpel as a child in the company of his favorite cat, Petit Gris (R. Gimpel, page 218). Other animal portrayals are more synonymous with liberty. It is not without interest to note that during her oppressive stay in Spain, after the departure of her friends (the Gleizes and the Picabias), Laurencin started introducing birds into her paintings, the symbol of the freedom of which she dreamed. They occur in certain of her works mentioned above (Y. Abé-D. Marchesseau, Nos. 31, 32 and 67) and also in the concentrated, elegant form of the bird in flight in the *Portrait of Mademoiselle Chanel*, as well as in certain prints (*The Concert*, 1926, D. Marchesseau, No. 100). Here, the bird is used together with a dog that, like those in *Spanish Dancers* (No. 45), in *Women with Dog*. (No. 49) and also like the animals (even) in *Les Biches* (No. 47), is pointing his muzzle upward, accented by his great oblong eye, in a characteristic depiction.                                             H.G.

Collections:
P. Rosenberg (?); Paul Guillaume (?); Mrs. Jean Walter.

Exhibitions:
1966, Paris, No. 105 (repr.); 1980, Athens, No. 13 (color repr.); 1981, Tbilisi-Leningrad, No. 18 (color repr.).

Literature:
J. Lassaigne, *Cent chefs d'œuvre des peintres de l'Ecole de Paris*, Paris, 1947, p. 164 (repr.); F. Mathey, *Six femmes peintres: Berthe Morisot, Eva Gonzalès, Séraphine Louis, Suzanne Valadon, Maria Blanchard, Marie Laurencin*, Paris, 1951, pl. XIV (color repr.); *Dictionnaire universel de la peinture*, Le Robert, 1975, vol. 4, repr. p. 173; Y. Abé-D. Marchesseau, 1980, No. 53 (color repr.).

# Marie Laurencin

## 47
## *The Does*
(Les Biches)

Oil on canvas. H. 73 cm.; W. 92 cm.
Signed and dated on lower right in black: Marie Laurencin, 1923.
RF 1963-58

René Gimpel noted as follows: "Madame Laurencin has designed handsome sets for *Les Biches*, and the ballet performers are assuming the poses of her figures. In the aisles, I hear people saying, 'Look at the audience, the women all look like Marie Laurencin figures'." (*Journal d'un collectionneur, marchand de tableaux*, page 267.) In 1923, on the recommendation of Francis Poulenc, the composer of the ballet's music, Marie, who had carved out a niche for herself on the Paris scene, was commissioned by Diaghilev to design the sets and costumes for *Les Biches*, a "one-act ballet with songs." With the libretto by Jean Cocteau, who was depicting the elegant, mannered Parisian society of the 1920s, Bronislav Nijinska, the sister of Nijinsky, devised a piquant choreography, intermingling American dances with the bases of classicism. Nijinska herself — costumed in pink and decked out with accessories lifted straight from Victor Margueritte's *La Garçonne* (flowing tie, bead necklace, tapering cigarette holder) — won unanimous acclaim in the ragtime-mazurka, while Nemtchinova, wearing white stockings and gloves, a light-blue velvet costume with long, tight sleeves and bouffant trousers, distinguished herself in the adagietto.

*Les Biches* had its first performance on 6 January 1924 in Monte Carlo, where it was staged with two other ballets, *Les Tentations de la Bergère* — music by Montéclair (1666-1737) revised by Henri Casadesus — and *Les Fâcheux*, by Georges Auric, adapted from Molière. *Les Biches* scored a triumph, and was eagerly awaited in Paris, where it was performed at the Théâtre des Champs-Elysées as part of the events in connection with the Eighth Olympiad. The sets and costumes of the other two ballets were designed by Juan Gris and Georges Braque, respectively. Laurencin had won full recognition from her contemporaries, who hailed her as the equal of the very greatest. Her sets and costumes were copied down to the last detail when the ballet was performed at Covent Garden in 1964.

Geneviève Allemand-Lacambre has described the elaboration of the set, noting the existence of two maquettes (reproduced in *Les Biches, Marie Laurencin, Jean Cocteau, Darius Milhaud, Francis Poulenc*, Paris, 1924, folios 18 and 19): "The first maquette is a drawing with a few patches of color — grey, blue, pink; the second is a watercolor that exactly corresponds to our painting." (Paris, 1966, page 225.) This painting, thus prepared by means of a watercolor, was the model for the backdrop constructed by Prince Schervaschidzé. This backdrop stood behind a sofa in a large white room one façade of which had a balcony. Laurencin worked on it in southern France in the summer of 1923, and continued her work after returning to Paris. René Gimpel carefully noted the date of 26 September: "She is busy with the sets and costumes for *Les Biches*, one of the Ballets Russes productions." In 1921, doubtless attracted by the transparent allusion in the title, Laurencin had already produced an entrancing painting devoted to the correspondences between young women and animals (Y. Abé-D. Marchesseau, 1980, No. 38). For the theatre curtains of the ballet, she did an engraving (D. Marchesseau, 1981, No. 69) in which all the main features of the painting appear. The figure on the left has disappeared, and a girl wearing a striped skirt with a big bow in the back appears on the right, approximately in the place occupied by the guitar. The composition is looser than that of the painting. In the latter, the design proceeds from and is organized around the central figure, a woman or a doe, or, more precisely, a doe-woman. Around her, like the points of a star, gravitate the other elements — imaginary beasts with supple, serpentine bodies, the stringless guitar, and the strange figure on the left, who appears to be undergoing a metamorphosis, with her arm ending in a deer's hoof clasping a species of mermaid's tail emerging from some undefined realm. At the time, Laurencin had made frequent use of the theme of the mermaid, half woman and half animal, neither wholly one or the other and partaking of both. In particular this theme occurs as the principal subject of two prints, from 1922 and 1925, respectively (D. Marchesseau, 1981, Nos. 56 and 85), in which the mermaid, who is more like a serpent woman than a fish woman, an object of desire and seduction, is coiled around the supple curves of her tail. The stage backdrop is also composed like a kaleidoscope in which delicate hues subtly intermingle and echo one another. Laurencin, for whom this participation in *Les Biches* was tantamount to a manifesto, hung in her living room the preliminary oil for the

# Marie Laurencin

backdrop curtain. The painting shown here is clearly visible in the photograph by Marc Vaux illustrating the article entitled *Chez Marie Laurencin*, published in *L'Art vivant* in 1925 (*L'Art vivant*, No. 3, 1 February 1925). It is therefore clear that she probably did not art with it (through her dealers, Paul Rosenberg and Hessel?) until some later date.

After *Les Biches*, Laurencin, who had contributed to designing the sets for *La Maison Cubiste*, in 1912, was once again in demand for the designing of sets and costumes: *Les Roses*, for the Soirées de Paris of count Etienne de Beaumont (1924); *A quoi rêvent les jeunes filles*, at the Comédie-Française, performed by Marie Bell and Madeleine Renaud (1928); *L'Eventail de Jeanne*, for Jeanne Dubost (1929); and, later, *Un Jour d'été*, with music by Durey (1940) and *Dominique et Dominique* (1954). Aside from her work in the theatre world, after the cancellation of the commission from the Mendelssohn-Bartholdy family in Berlin, in 1920, Laurencin designed two maquettes in 1926, representing a seated young woman and an athlete for the luxury restaurant of X.M. Boulestin, on Southampton Street, London; the rest of the decoration was designed by J.E. Laboureur and Allan Walton, while the fabrics were designed by Dufy. Laurencin also had a hand in the decorations for the *Ambassade Française* at the International Exposition of Decorative Arts in 1925, on which occasion she contributed a few paintings to *Le Boudoir de Madame l'Ambassadrice*, designed by André Groult, the husband of her friend Nicole and a brother-in-law of Paul Poiret. This team work, enhanced by a few other items produced by the Société des Artistes Décorateurs, was published as a collection by Charles Moreau.

H.G.

*Collections:*
Paul Guillaume (?); Mrs. Jean Walter.

*Exhibition:*
1966, Paris, No. 106 (repr.).

*Literature:*
G. Day, *Marie Laurencin*, Paris, 1947 (repr.); F. Mathey, *Six femmes peintres: Berthe Morisot, Eva Gonzalès, Séraphine Louis, Suzanne Valadon, Maria Blanchard, Marie Laurencin*, Paris, 1951, No. 79, p. 14 (repr.); Y. Abé-D. Marchesseau, 1980, No. 56 (color repr.).

Laurencin, *The Does* (engraving)

# Marie Laurencin

## 48
## *Portrait of Madame Paul Guillaume*
(Portrait de Madame Paul Guillaume)

Oil on canvas. H. 92 cm.; W. 73 cm.
Signed on upper right in grey: Marie Laurencin.
RF 1963-55

In *La grande peinture contemporaine à la collection Paul Guillaume* (excerpts from which were published in *La Renaissance*, April 1929, pages 172-185), Waldemar George commented on Marie Laurencin's portrait of Mrs. Paul Guillaume, which he reproduced along with the great collector's most representative works, as follows: "This is a portrait of Mrs. Paul Guillaume depicted as an ingenue of the period of the *monarchie censitaire* [period of the Restoration and the July Monarchy]. Blues, pinks and greys. The opaque black mass of smooth hair disrupts the diaphanous array of pastels. The daughters of the old Carlists... carried their heads in the same way as Madame Laurencin's model, and had the same fine hands and unusually shapely waist. Constantin Guys would have loved to sketch her majestic, provocative stature with a few pen strokes..." (*op. cit.*, page 185). The artist organized her painting around the pattern of a somewhat condensed pyramidal composition and a spatial stability that is unusual in her work. However, her favorite accessories accompany the model, who is portrayed in a graceful pose. Once again, here are the flowers, the long scarves and the animal. The latter — mysterious, immense and disproportionate — is performing an act of allegiance to the melancholy model, who is lost in thought. This is a far cry from Derain's portrait of Mrs. Guillaume, which dates from the same period (No. 31). The dark helmet of hair, the mordant line of the arched eyebrows, the modelling of the face in which the nose emerges clearly are, after all, infrequent in Laurencin's paintings. Yet these unwonted features do also appear in another portrait, *Woman with a Rose* (auction, Sotheby's, London, 4 July 1979), which bears a close resemblance to this *Portrait of Madame Paul Guillaume*. The model, handled in the same manner and with an identical technique, wears a pink dress, whose design and neckline make it similar to that of Mrs. Guillaume. Unlike the latter, she has a blue scarf over one shoulder, and she has blond hair. She is posed among pink curtains. The wide oblique swathe to the right of Mrs. Guillaume can be interpreted as a curtain, this being likewise one of Laurencin's favorite accessories; she used it also in decorative compositions such as the painting entitled *Women with Dog* (No. 49). The pink of the curtain echoes the pink in the dress, just as the grey of the dog, on which rests the model's disproportionately long arm, echoes the painting's background color. There is thus achieved a two-toned chromatic harmony that is as subtle as a musical chord.

This *Portrait of Madame Paul Guillaume* is dated 1924 by Daniel Marchesseau (Y. Abé-D. Marchesseau, 1980), whereas it is assigned a somewhat later date, "circa 1928," by Geneviève Allemand-Lacambre, on the basis of a sojourn by the painter and her model at Professor Gosset's home in Normandy. In fact, the January 1929 issue of *Les Arts à Paris*, No. 16, page 29, contains a photograph of Mrs. Guillaume, Marie Laurencin and Professor Gosset taken at the latter's home. But Paul Guillaume and Professor Gosset had known each other for several years. Just for the record, it should be noted that at this same period, Laurencin painted a portrait of Professor Gosset dated 1929.

H.G.

*Collections:*
Paul Guillaume (in 1929); Mrs. Jean Walter.

*Exhibitions:*
1966, Paris, No. 108 (repr.); 1980, Athens, No. 14 (color repr.); 1981, Tbilisi-Leningrad, No. 19 (repr.).

*Literature:*
W. George, undated, p. 166 (repr. p. 167); *La Renaissance*, April 1929, No. 4 (repr. p. 177); F. Mathey, *Six femmes peintres: Berthe Morisot, Eva Gonzalès, Séraphine Louis, Suzanne Valadon, Maria Blanchard, Marie Laurencin*, Paris, 1951, No. 67, p. 13 (repr.); G. Charensol, "Paul Guillaume, curieux homme et homme curieux," *Plaisir de France*, December 1966, repr.; Y. Abé-D. Marchesseau, 1980, No. 57 (color repr.).

# Marie Laurencin

## 49
## *Women with Dog*
(Femmes au Chien)

Oil an canvas. H. 80 cm.; W. 100 cm.
Signed on upper left in black: Marie Laurencin.
RF 1963-57

Marie Laurencin admitted that "Although the character of men intimidates me, I feel quite at ease with everything that is feminine" (*Le Carnet des Nuits*, page 161). In fact, men do not have a place in Laurencin's work, with the exception of a few specific portraits (*Nils von Dardell*, 1913; *Martin Fabiani*, 1939; *André Salmon*, 1942; *Jean Cocteau*, circa 1946; and, of course, *Apollinaire and his Friends*, 1909). This absence of men is not the result of ruthless exclusion; rather, it stems from ontological nonexistence. Laurencin's work, the unconscious mirror of her own desires, emerges as the perpetual celebration of an elusive Golden Age. This painting contains the atmosphere of *Les Biches*. The faintly lunar ambience of the cold tones of the scene is tempered by the pinks and by the broad swathe of yellow, a color that is unwonted in this form in Laurencin's palette.

The delicate colors are amplified by a refined mirror-glass frame, which quite felicitously echoes the subtlety of the painting. Lady Cunard, whose portrait had been done by Laurencin, owned several of the latter's works which had been framed in this way because they otherwise interfered with the harmony of their owner's eighteenth-century drawing room. The idea for the mirror frames was that of Rose Adler, a well-known bookbinder, and of Madame Natanson.

As in the painting of *The Spanish Dancers* (No. 45), the animal intervenes to provide a link between the two women. The same species of beast, represented by an upward-thrust head and a pupil-less eye, is found in another Laurencin painting of the same period, entitled *Woman with Feather*, dated 1925 (Y. Abé-D. Marchesseau, 1980, No. 64). Geneviève Allemand-Lacambre had already established a link between certain features of the *Women with Dog* and works dated 1924-1925 (1966, Paris, page 227); this would tend to indicate that these years are a likely date for the work. The source of inspiration, which comes directly from *Les Biches* (No. 47), can only corroborate this dating.                                    H.G.

*Collections:*
Paul Guillaume (?); Mrs. Jean Walter.

*Exhibitions:*
1946, Paris, No. 43; 1966, Paris, No. 107 (repr.).

*Literature:*
Y. Abé-D. Marchesseau, 1980, No. 58 (color repr.); *Grand Dictionnaire Encyclopédique Larousse*, 1984, vol. 6 (color repr.).

# Henri Matisse

Le Cateau, 1869-Nice, 1954

## 50
## *The Three Sisters*

(Les Trois Sœurs)

1917
Oil on canvas. H. 92 cm.; L. 73 cm.
Signed on lower right: Henri Matisse.
RF 1963-63

*The Three Sisters* is one of the very few paintings that Paul Guillaume purchased at auction, doubtless because it reminded him of the famous triptych in the Barnes collection, the sale of which had probably been transacted by him. This is an outstanding example of Matisse's consummate skill at utilizing a surface area and infusing life into it. In this work, Matisse achieved a miraculous balance of forms and colors, of fullness and voids, of curves and straight lines, to the point where nothing in it could be changed without detracting from a perfect harmony. Several sources have been put forward, including Manet's *The Balcony*, Japanese wood-block prints, and, more convincingly, the detail of a fifteenth-century Italian or Flemish composition. But with Matisse, sources are more a matter of affinities or correspondences than of influences.

This painting is a portrait of Laurette, Matisse's usual model at the time, with her two cousins. (We have retained the traditional title.) There is an obvious comparison between it and the large triptych at the Barnes Foundation, which has been analyzed in detail by Alfred Barr (1951, pages 192-193), and which shows the three sisters three times, in poses and clothing that are different each time; the version that most closely resembles the present painting is the righthand panel. Comparisons can also be made with other works of 1916-1917 portraying Laurette by herself, her eyes downcast, dressed in green and poised on a pink armchair (Gelman collection, Mexico City; *Tout l'œuvre peint*, color plate XXXV); with her gaze looking up, in the same color scheme (private collection, Switzerland; *Matisse* exhibition, Zurich-Düsseldorf, 1982-1983, No. 52, color repr.); and in the same mauve armchair (private collection; *Tout l'œuvre peint*, plate XXXVI; Zurich-Düsseldorf exhibition, No. 48).

The overall spirit of these paintings, the procedural pattern adopted and the problem to be solved recur in all of them, but actually, they are fully autonomous works in each of which Matisse reinvents the choice and harmonies of ostensibly incompatible colors and a precisely plotted organization of surfaces. Here, this concern, which is constant in his work, both in prints and in paintings as well as in mural compositions, yields a picture of relatively modest size and of obviously monumental character: "In easel paintings, one can have principles of mural painting. But what is of primary importance is that the mural painting is a SURFACE to which one seeks to impart LIFE." The preceding statement was made by Matisse to G. Diehl (in February 1942, not included in *Ecrits et propos sur l'art*).

However, there is no stiffness: the dissymmetry of the individual faces, the variety of the poses, the liberties taken with perspective and the sinuousness of the lines point the way toward the more relaxed style of the other Matisse works in the Walter-Guillaume collection, a style to which Matisse remained faithful through 1925, the year in which he painted the *Decorative Nude on Flowered Background* (Paris, Musée National d'Art Moderne).

David (?), *The Ladies of Ghent*,
Paris, Musée du Louvre.

# Henri Matisse

The motif of a seated woman, portrayed full face or in three-quarter view, or occasionally from the back, sitting in a chair or on the floor or ground, is one of the most constant themes in Matisse's work. The question remains as to whether the frequency of its occurrence was accounted for by its affording the possibility of protracted painting sessions with a model who was comfortably posed, or by reminiscences of the Davidian tradition (the painting entitled *The Three Ladies of Ghent* was attributed to David by unanimous opinion when the young Matisse was becoming acquainted with the Louvre), or, again, by the mere satisfaction of representing a lovely, elegant, calm woman in a relaxed pose. These sundry motivations are not mutually exclusive, and all of Matisse's work is made up of the infallible formal arrangements of human beings, flowers and attractive objects.

M.H.

*Collections:*
Auguste Pellerin; Pellerin auction, 7 May 1926, Paris, No. 66 (repr.); Paul Guillaume; Mrs. Jean Walter.

*Exhibitions:*
1929, Paris; 1935, Paris, No. 424; 1936, New York; 1937, Paris, Petit Palais, *Les Maîtres de l'art indépendant*, 1895-1937, No. 21; 1945, Paris, Galerie Charpentier, *Portraits français*, No. 158 (repr.); 1946, Paris, No. 55 (repr.); 1948, Philadelphia, Philadelphia Museum of Art, *Matisse*, No. 29 (repr.); 1966, Paris, No. 53 (repr.); 1978, Rome, Villa Medici, *Henri Matisse*, No. 12 (repr.); 1979, Paris, Centre national d'art et de culture Georges Pompidou, *Paris-Moscow*, 1900-1930, No. 165 (repr.); 1981, Moscow, Pushkin Museum of Fine Arts, *Moscow-Paris*; 1982, Zurich, Kunsthaus - Düsseldorf, Kunsthalle, *Henri Matisse*, No. 53 (repr.); 1983, Paris, Centre Georges Pompidou, *Bonjour, Monsieur Manet* (unnumbered, repr. p. 50).

*Literature:*
M. Sembat, *Henri Matisse*, Paris, 1920, p. 61 (repr.); *Les Arts à Paris*, No. 13, June 1927, p. 23 (repr.); E. Tériade, "Nos enquêtes. Entretien avec Paul Guillaume," *Cahiers d'art*, 1927 (repr. p. 28); Ternovets, "La vie artistique à Paris," *Petchat i Revolioutsia*, No. 1, Moscow, 1928, p. 69 (repr.); W. George, undated, p. 68, p. 70 (repr. p. 61); J. Cassou, "Henri Matisse," *L'Amour de l'art*, No. 5, May 1933, pp. 107-112 (repr. p. 108); M. Morsell, "French Masters of the Twentieth Century in the Valentine Show," *Art News*, 11 January 1936 (repr.); J. Lassaigne, *Cent chefs-d'œuvre des peintres de l'Ecole de Paris*, Paris, 1947, p. 6 (repr.); A.H. Barr, 1951; G. Diehl, *Henri Matisse*, Paris, 1954, p. 69 (repr. No. 80); R. Escholier, *Matisse, ce vivant*, Paris, 1956, p. 181; G. Diehl, *Henri Matisse*, Paris, 1970 (unpaginated); L. Aragon, *Henri Matisse*, Paris, 1972, vol. II (color repr., pl. XVI); *Tout l'œuvre peint*, No. 225 (repr.).

# Henri Matisse

## 51

## *Girl and Vase of Flowers, or The Pink Nude*

(La jeune fille et le vase de fleurs ou Le nu rose)

Oil on canvas. H. 60 cm.; W. 73 cm.
Signed on lower right in purplish red: Henri-Matisse.
RF 1960-32

Matisse was a northerner, and his initial discovery of southern light occurred during a trip to Corsica, followed by a stay in the Toulouse area in 1898. Subsequently, there came his travels in Italy, a stay in Collioure, and visits to Andalusia and Morocco, before he discovered Nice, where he spent the (rainy!) winter of 1916, at the Hotel Beau Rivage. He thereafter returned regularly to Nice where, beginning in 1918, he stayed at the Hotel de la Méditerranée, which, in 1929, was replaced by the Palais de la Méditerranée on the Promenade des Anglais. To quote the artist: "When I realized that every morning I would be seeing that light again, my happiness seemed unbelievable... I come from the north. What decided me to settle here was the wonderful colored reflections of January, the luminous daylight." In Nice, he did a series of works whose invariable features included tall French windows — opened or closed, sometimes shuttered — long, draped curtains looped back to either side, brightly-colored and intricately-patterned wallpaper and hexagonally-tiled floors, whence emanates an atmosphere of calm privacy. This present painting introduces something new into the somewhat academic theme of the female nude: his model is not posed, but is proceeding silently through the stillness of a bedroom, her striped towel trailing beside her. The mordantly marked perspectives of the table and sofa, enhanced by the obliques of the window and by the curtain ties, invite the beholder's gaze to converge toward the figure, set in the center of the composition. The artist rules out any hint of individualization in order to trace a soft outline around the female body, which is displayed like a smooth, modelled sculpture. Already, some ten years earlier, he had described his goal, which was to move beyond the realm of the particular in order to achieve the realm of the general: "I plan to paint the body of a woman... I plan to condense the significance of this body by seeking out its essential lines... The new image achieved thereby... will have a broader, more fully human meaning" ("Notes d'un peintre," *La Grande Revue*, 25 December 1908). Employing these same procedures, he painted the *Nude with Spanish Rug* (private collection; *Tout l'œuvre peint*, No. 302) and *Woman with Parasol* (private collection; *Tout l'œuvre peint*, No. 354).

The bouquet of flowers and the swan-neck oval mirror frequently recur in the works of Matisse's Nice period. They are found in *The Boudoir* (No. 53) and also, for example, in the *Vase of Flowers on a Dressing Table, The Art Lesson* (Edinburgh, National Gallery of Modern Art), *Woman Seated Indoors* (Barnes Foundation, Merion, Pennsylvania), *The Breakfast* (Philadelphia Museum of Art). By the interplay of its reflections, the mirror can be considered as a substitute for the window, or as an additional, different opening which enables a superposed view of the perspective of the work as a whole.          H.G.

*Collections:*
Paul Guillaume (in 1928); Mrs. Jean Walter.

*Exhibitions:*
1929, Paris; 1966, Paris, No. 55 (repr.).

*Literature:*
*Les Arts à Paris*, No. 14, May 1928, p. 8 (repr.); W. George, undated, p. 72 (repr. p. 66); *Jardin des Arts*, May 1972, p. 56 (repr. p. 57); *Tout l'œuvre peint*, No. 340 (repr.).

# Henri Matisse

## 52
### *Women with Sofa, or The Divan*
(Femmes au canapé ou Le divan)

Oil on canvas. H. 92 cm.; W. 73 cm.
Signed on lower right in purplish red: Henri Matisse.
RF 1963-68

"How beautifully you've captured the atmosphere of a hotel room in Nice! But that sea blue should be brought forward... And that black rod from which the white curtains hang. It's in its place. Everything is exactly right... It wasn't easy. It makes me angry." The foregoing was the handsome tribute paid by Renoir during his first visit to Matisse, in front of a painting entitled *The Open Window* (as reported by R. Escholier in *Matisse, ce vivant*, Paris, 1956, pages 115-116). We have already noted the frequency of the theme of the passage from the shut-in world of the dwelling place to the open universe of the outside, which runs like a leitmotiv through Matisse's work; it was perceptible in 1896, in *The Open Door*, painted in Brittany (reproduced in A.H. Barr, 1951, p. 298), reduced to its most exacerbated expression in its extreme limits in the painting entitled *French Window at Collioure* (private collection; *Tout l'œuvre peint*, No. 185), or captured in the extraordinary perception shown in *The Windshield* (or *The Road to Villacoublay*, Cleveland Museum of Fine Arts, MacBride Collection; *Tout l'œuvre peint*, No. 250). The painting entitled *Women with Sofa* concentrates and develops more elaborately the procedures in *Girl and Vase of Flowers* and *The Boudoir*. The vaster perspective, from an overhead angle, juxtaposes two views, one toward the floor, whose tiling suggests surface rather than depth, and the other, more classical, toward the very remote distance of the sea horizon, beyond the half-open window. The first one brings us inside the room and into ourselves, in a kind of introspective movement. But the second one takes its point of departure in the beholder and moves outwardly toward infinity. Through his plastic vocabulary, Matisse succeeds in suggesting two completely contradictory physical and mental attitudes and reconciles them. The place of passage of the two universes is the half-open, transparent window, tangible in its materiality but acceding also to the additional meaning of the symbol. Matisse explained his own pattern of procedure, the experience of which he lets us share through his painting. To Tériade's question, "What about the window?", he answered: "My aim is to render my emotion. This mood is created by the objects by which I am surrounded and which react within me. *Windows have always interested me because they are a passageway between the interior and the exterior*" (Henri Matisse, *Ecrits et propos sur l'art*, Paris, 1972, page 123). For Matisse, "interior" and "exterior" are not two worlds set up against each other: the protected interior — the ego — opens (or halfway opens, as shown here) onto the exterior, the "others," who are a potential danger. It should be noted that, in Matisse's exterior, there are never any identifiable individuals; only cosmic space, the sky, the sea, trees and occasionally a building intercalated between the horizon and the window.

*Women with Sofa* perfectly illustrates this movement from the interior to the exterior, concentrating the emotional and intellectual power of the procedure. The scene, with its two figures, is sublimated beyond its anecdotal representation, to achieve what Matisse called "the essential." With no fear of the apparent contradiction in this affirmation, we can be sure that Matisse succeeds in translating its concept not *into* an image but *by* an image.

Matisse, *The Violin Case*,
New York, Museum of Modern Art.

# Henri Matisse

Nothing permits dispersion. The artist's alterations of the sofa are evidence of his concern with guiding the beholder. To prevent our gaze from straying, the mirror itself reflects nothing. Unlike objects in traditional compositions, the objects here have been thrust back, releasing a central void. Matisse had already experimented with this arrangement in *The Pink Studio* (Pushkin Museum, Moscow; *Tout l'œuvre peint*, No. 145) and *The Red Studio* (New York, Museum of Modern Art; held in custody for the Guggenheim Museum; *Tout l'œuvre peint*, No. 151). It is also found in *The Violin Case* (New York, Museum of Modern Art; *Tout l'œuvre peint*, No. 292), whose atmosphere and composition so closely resemble those of Women and Sofa, as well as in *Large Interior in Nice* (Art Institute of Chicago, Chapman Foundation; *Tout l'œuvre peint*, No. 353), of which the painting in the Walter-Guillaume collection can be considered as the prefiguration.

In this context, color fully plays its role; the choice and intensity of colors are not gratuitous: rather, they help to suggest the emotion. "To say that color has again become expressive amounts to recounting its history. For a long time, color was merely a complement of drawing... All the way from Delacroix to Van Gogh and, principally, to Gauguin, and including the Impressionists... and Cézanne... it is possible to trace this rehabilitation of the role of color, the restitution of its emotive power" (*Propos de l'artiste recueillis par G. Diehl, Problèmes de la Peinture*, Paris, 1945). Going back beyond the artists of the nineteenth century, Matisse takes up the quarrel of the late seventeenth century between the defenders of line drawing and those of color on the basis of the principles of Roger de Piles. However, in Matisse's work there is no theorization; rather, there is the realization of his work by his most intimate resources.

H.G.

*Collections:*
Paul Guillaume (in 1924); Mrs. Jean Walter.

*Exhibitions:*
1923, Paris, Chambre syndicale de la curiosité et des Beaux-Arts, 18, rue de la Ville-l'Evêque, *Exposition d'œuvres d'art des XVIII<sup>e</sup>, XIX<sup>e</sup> et XX<sup>e</sup> siècles*, for the benefit of the National Committee for Assistance to Scientific Research; 1945, London, Victoria and Albert Museum, *Picasso and Matisse*, No. 29; 1946, Glasgow-Birmingham-Brussels-Amsterdam, *Picasso and Matisse*, No. 24; 1960, Paris, No. 74 (repr.); 1966, Paris, No. 56 (repr.); 1978, Rome, Villa Medici, *Henri Matisse*, No. 14 (repr.); 1980, Athens, No. 17 (color repr.); 1981, Tbilisi-Leningrad, No. 23 (color repr.).

*Literature:*
*Les Arts à Paris*, No. 9, April 1924, p. 13 (repr.); W. George, undated, p. 76; A. Frey, *Henri Matisse*, Paris, 1935 (pl. 40); *Tout l'œuvre peint*, No. 344 (repr.).

Matisse,
*Large Interior in Nice*,
Chicago, Art Institute.

# Henri Matisse

## 53
## *The Boudoir*
(Le Boudoir)

Oil on canvas. H. 73 cm.; W. 60 cm.
Signed on lower left in purplish red: Henri-Matisse.
RF 1963-64

This painting displays the characteristic elements of Matisse's Nice period and, more specifically, of the Hôtel de la Méditerranée, whose demolition in 1929 was a source of regret to the artist. "It was a fine old hotel, that's for sure! It had such handsome Italian-style ceilings! Such tiling! It was a mistake to tear it down. I lived there for four years for the pleasure of painting nudes and figures in an old rococo room. Do you remember the daylight that came in through the shutters? It beamed up from below like theatre footlights. Everything was fake, absurd, wonderful, delightful." The design, which leads the eye toward the expanse of light through the window giving out onto the exterior space and the palm tree, is repeated in *Woman with Sofa* (Basel, Kunstmuseum, Doetsch-Benziger bequest; *Tout l'œuvre peint*, No. 359) and is developed in *The Painter and his Model* (New York, Bakwin collection; *Tout l'œuvre peint*, No. 290). To achieve this, Matisse applied the principles defined by him in 1908: "The simplest means are those that best enable the artist to express himself" ("Notes d'un peintre," *La Grande Revue*, 25 December 1908).

The colors in this painting are very light and the technique is suggestive of that of watercolor. Matisse used these subdued tones in works of transition between his Parisian production of dark harmonies and simplification of lines in relation to synthetic Cubism, and the ensuing production, which asserted itself during the 1920s. This painting can be assigned the date of 1921, during which year the presence of his daughter Marguerite led Matisse to paint compositions with two figures, as noted by A. Barr (A.H. Barr, New York, 1951, page 210). Marguerite's presence is corroborated by Georges Charensol, who has left the following recollection: "I saw Matisse's *Boudoir* on his easel, when he was in the process of painting it at the Hôtel de la Méditerranée in Nice, with his daughter Marguerite as a model" (in *Plaisir de France*, December 1966). In any case, the date of 1925 listed by the catalogue of the Basel exhibition, and that of 1929 listed by Bertram, must be dismissed, since Matisse had moved out of the Hôtel de la Méditerranée in 1921 and was living on Place Charles Félix, in the Old Town of Nice. Finally, it should be noted that along with several works belonging to Paul Guillaume, this painting was listed as being for sale at the 1931 Matisse show in Basel.

H.G.

*Collections:*
Paul Guillaume (in 1929); Mrs. Jean Walter.

*Exhibitions:*
1931, Basel, Kunsthalle, *Henri Matisse*, No. 88; 1944, Paris, Galerie Charpentier, *La vie familiale, scènes et portraits*, No. 242 (repr.); 1966, Paris, No. 54 (repr.); 1980, Athens, No. 16 (color repr.); 1981, Tbilisi-Leningrad, No. 22 (repr.).

*Literature:*
W. George, undated, p. 74 (repr. p. 64); A. Bertram, *Henri Matisse*, London, 1930 (pl. XXIV); J. Lassaigne, *Cent chefs-d'œuvre des Peintres de l'Ecole de Paris*, Paris, 1947 (repr. p. 67); G. Charensol, "Paul Guillaume, curieux homme et homme curieux," *Plaisir de France*, December 1966; *Tout l'œuvre peint*, No. 348 (repr.).

# Henri Matisse

## 54
## *Woman with Mandolin*

(Femme à la mandoline)

Oil on canvas. H. 47 cm.; W. 40 cm.
Signed on lower left in purplish red: Henri Matisse.
RF 1963-69

"Ah! Nice is a beautiful part of the world! The daylight is soft and mellow despite its brilliance! For some unknown reason, I often find myself comparing it to the light in Touraine... In Touraine, the light is slightly more golden, while here it's silvery" ("Correspondence between Henri Matisse and Charles Camoin," *La Revue de l'Art*, No. 12, 1971). This silvery light is rendered here with pale colors, resembling those of a watercolor, in the same mood as those in *Girl with Vase of Flowers* and *The Boudoir*. The window theme is still present, but is handled from a new approach. The plastic notations do not make the gaze converge toward the opening, but the geometrical organization enables a direct crossing and the immediate perception of the distance. However, the perspective of the room, reduced to the grey wall below the window sill and the colored partition, is reversed, with the distance line of the righthand wall extending in a contrary direction. Another modification in perspective occurs in the girl's reflected image on the window pane, moved some distance to the right in relation to reality, in order to show a large expanse of dark color. It constitutes a variation on the mirror theme, which is so frequent in the work of Matisse, who is known to have been captivated by Ingres's image of Madame de Senonnes. This motif was fully developed in Matisse's painting entitled *The Reflection (Woman Before a Mirror)*, a later work, dated 1935, in which the mirror is merely a pretext for capturing the model under two different aspects (tenth *Biennale des Antiquaires*, 1980, Paris, Grand Palais, No. 29). The theme of correspondences is likewise present, applied here to colors rather than to the expression of forms. The pinkish grey of the facing wall concentrates the tones of the window frame and of the buildings of Les Ponchettes, and dissolves in the girl's skirt and collar and in the reflection in the glass, while the pale yellow of the wall on the right is echoed in the splay of the window opening and in the blouse, whose motif — a new example of this echoing composition — recalls the design of the wallpaper.

This work, which, like *The Boudoir* (No. 53), was exhibited in Basel in 1931 and was listed for sale, was painted in the apartment on Place Charles Félix, to which Matisse had moved in the fall of 1921. Like the painting entitled *Girl at the Window, Setting Sun* (Baltimore Museum of Art, Cone collection: *Tout l'œuvre peint*, No. 366), which depicts the same view out over Les Ponchettes and the sea, and like other contemporary works in which the model is holding or is playing on a musical instrument (for example, *The Violinist at the Window*, which also belonged to Paul Guillaume, reproduced in A. Bertram, *Henri Matisse*, London, 1930, plate XV), it can be dated at circa 1922; this date is confirmed by the date of its purchase by the Galerie Bernheim-Jeune from the artist, on 15 January 1923.                H.G.

*Collections:*
Bernheim-Jeune (purchased from Matisse on 15 January 1923; Druet (sold on the same day, 15 January 1923); Paul Guillaume (in 1930); Mrs. Jean Walter.

*Exhibitions:*
1931, Basel, Kunsthalle, Henri-Matisse, No. 38; 1966, Paris, No. 57 (repr.); 1980, Athens, No. 18 (color repr.); 1981, Tbilisi-Leningrad, No. 24 (repr.).

*Literature:*
*Les Arts à Paris*, No. 17, May 1930, p. 11 (repr.); G. Diehl, *Henri Matisse*, Paris 1954, No. 86 (repr.); *Goya*, No. 7, July-August 1955, p. 30 (repr.); *Tout l'œuvre peint*, No. 352 (repr.).

# Henri Matisse

## 55
## *Blue Odalisque or The White Slave*
(Odalisque bleue ou L'esclave blanche)

Oil on canvas. H. 82 cm.; L. 54 cm.
Signed on lower right in brown: Henri-Matisse.
RF 1960-31

In the early part of the century, Matisse was enabled to discover the Eastern world that had fascinated his teacher, Gustave Moreau, first, at the Islamic art exhibition at the Musée des Arts Décoratifs in 1903, and later in Munich, in 1910. These initial contacts were confirmed by his travels in North Africa over the ensuing years, which resulted in several paintings. However, Matisse did not begin his odalisque series until later on.

For Matisse, the painting of odalisques was a new way of perceiving the nude. As he commented to his friend Tériade: "I paint odalisques in order to paint nudes. But the problem is how to paint nudes without their looking artificial" (*L'Intransigeant*, 14 and 22 January 1929, reprinted in Henri Matisse, *Propos sur l'art*, page 93). Thus, the odalisque theme, which had been so frequently used by artists since the successes of Orientalism and was so often compromised by the excesses of fake exoticism, was given a new lease on life here. The orientalizing inspiration is suggested rather than imposed. In fact, the painting is unencumbered by any accessory, and the beholder's gaze is immediately captured by the female figure, covered only by a transparent veil, standing in the angle formed by two walls with ceramic-pattern reflections. The pose with arms raised behind the back of the neck or over the head was a favorite with Matisse, who used it in several of his odalisque paintings, thereby enhancing the shapeliness of his models (*Tout l'œuvre peint*, Nos. 377, 383, 407, 408). As noted by I. Fontaine (*Matisse* exhibition, Musée National d'Art Moderne, 1979, No. 37), "the raised arm pose was frequently that of the odalisques of that year, 1923," in connection with a charcoal and stump drawing reminiscent of the *Blue Odalisque*, the name under which the work in the Paul Guillaume collection is listed in all the early publications. The date of its purchase by Bernheim-Jeune, on 22 March 1922 (registration No. 29960), is reason for assuming that the painting had been done somewhat earlier.

In other odalisques that are contemporary with this one, the color range can be quite intense; in the present case, it is extremely restrained and the paint is applied lightly, reminiscent of watercolor and of the manner of *The Boudoir* (No. 53).　　　　　　　　　　　　H.G.

*Collections:*
Bernheim-Jeune (purchased from Matisse on 22 March 1922); J. Quinn (?) (sold on 26 September 1922); Paul Guillaume (in 1929); Mrs. Jean Walter.

*Exhibitions:*
1929, Paris; 1938, Paris, Galerie Max Kaganovitch, *Œuvres choisies*, No. 24; 1939, Geneva, Galerie Moos, *Exposition d'art français*, No. 44 (repr.); 1966, Paris, No. 58 (repr.); 1980, Athens, No. 19 (color repr.); 1981, Tbilisi-Leningrad, No. 25 (repr.).

*Bibliography:*
W. George, undated, p. 74 (repr. p. 71); A. Basler, *L'Amour de l'art*, No. 7, July 1929 (repr. p. 256); A. Bertram, *Henri Matisse*, London, 1930 (pl. XVI); P. Courthion, *Henri Matisse*, Paris, 1934 (pl. XLI); G. Diehl, *Henri Matisse*, Paris, 1954, p. 78; *Tout l'œuvre peint*, No. 382 (repr.).

# Henri Matisse

## 56
### *Woman with Violin*
(Femme au violon)

Oil on canvas. H. 55 cm.; W. 46 cm.
Signed on lower left in purplish red: Henri-Matisse.
RF 1960-30

Matisse was a musician himself (he played the violin; he had purchased an instrument that had belonged to the first violinist of the Parent string quartet and began each day with a few musical exercises, as described by George Besson in "Arrivée de Matisse à Nice. Matisse et quelques personnages," *Le Point*, No. 21, July 1939). Early in his career, Matisse introduced musicians or, occasionally, instruments alone, into his works (*The Piano Lesson*, New York, Museum of Modern Art, which once belonged to Paul Guillaume; *The Music Lesson*, Barnes Foundation, Merion, Pennsylvania; *Interior with Violin*, Copenhagen, Statens Museum for Kunst, Rump collection; *Violinist at a Window*, Paris, Musée National d'Art Moderne). In his paintings done in Nice during the years 1921-1923, around the instrumentalists there are scenes of domestic life in which the backgrounds frequently show the screen of *The Moorish Screen* (*The Piano Lesson*, Dundee, Scotland, *Tout*

*l'œuvre peint*, No. 401; *The Checker Game, Tout l'œuvre peint*, No. 402) or motifs of its decorative richness (*The Two Musicians*, Mrs. Leigh B. Block collection, reproduced in *Henri Matisse*, 2 November-1 December 1973, Acquavella Galleries, New York, No. 28). There thus appear the circular motifs of the blue background, whose shape contrasts with the stripes on the violinist's blouse and the various solid-color areas.

Matisse also did a very similar painting, slightly smaller than the one in the Walter-Guillaume collection, of which it can be considered to be a variation (Baltimore Museum of Art, Cone collection, *Tout l'œuvre peint*, No. 374). The girl's left arm is resting on the table, on which lies her instrument, in the place of the violin case, thereby making space for the solid-color expanse of the table, as in the painting in the Walter-Guillaume collection.

H.G.

Matisse, *Woman with Violin*,
Baltimore, Museum of Art.

*Collections:*
Bernheim-Jeune (purchased from the artist on 13 February 1922); Voyet (sold on 15 May 1923); Paul Guillaume (in 1929); Mrs. Jean Walter.

*Exhibitions:*
1929, Paris; 1937, Paris, No. 38; 1966, Paris, No. 59: 1969, Bordeaux, Galerie des Beaux-Arts, *L'art et la musique*, No. 129.

*Literature:*
W. George, undated, p. 78 (repr. p. 62); *Kunst und Dekoration*, August 1931 (repr.); *Tout l'œuvre peint*, No. 400 (repr.).

Henri-Matisse

133

# Henri Matisse

## 57
## *Reclining Nude with Drapery*
(Nu drapé étendu)

Oil on canvas. H. 38 cm.; W. 61 cm.
Signed on lower right in purplish red: Henri-Matisse.
RF 1963-65

According to Waldemar George, in Paul Guillaume's dining room in the apartment on Avenue de Messine, there hung two paintings of nudes that formed a pair (W. George, undated, page 76). Actually, although these two works were of similar size, they did not, strictly speaking, form a pair; rather, they were a variation on the same theme, in the musical sense of the term. They are now separated: one of them belongs to a private collection (*Tout l'œuvre peint*, No. 338), while the other, the *Reclining Nude with Drapery*, which remained in Paul Guillaume's collection, is part of the French national collections. The odalisque's pose — arms raised, legs drawn up — is that of the *Odalisque in Red Trousers* (Musée National d'Art Moderne), but it even more strikingly calls to mind the painting entitled *Odalisque with Magnolias* (New York, private collection; *Tout l'œuvre peint*, No. 423). The model's trousers, held in with a green sash, which appear in both these works, likewise appear in *The Hindu Pose* (New York, Stralem collection; *Tout l'œuvre peint*, No. 408), and the date of 1923-1924 also applies to the *Reclining Nude with Drapery*. However, the plastic and pictorial intention is quite different. To the same extent that the *Odalisque with Magnolias* resorts to richness and contrast of motifs, the emphasis in the *Reclining Nude with Drapery* is on the understatement, not to say the starkness of procedures;

these two works thereby illustrate the two extreme poles of Matisse's sensibility. The model's sharp-angled facial features evoke the objects that Matisse was fond of collecting — African masks, "the sculptures into which the Negroes of Guinea, Senegal and Gabon infused with stunning purity their most panic passions," as described by Apollinaire in his account of the painter's collection, in *Médaillon: Un Fauve*, a text from 1909, not published until 1950 by M. Adéma (*Arts et Spectacles*, No. 285, 17 November 1950, reprinted in *Chroniques d'art*, Paris, 1981, page 82).

Matisse seems to have been concerned at an early date with the distorted pose of the model, which prefigures that of the extremely linear *Pink Nude*, painted much later, in 1936 (Baltimore Museum of Art, Cone collection; *Tout l'œuvre peint*, 471); he applied it to his sculpture in 1907, with his *Recumbent Nude I* (*Tout l'œuvre peint*, S3). In parallel with his odalisque investigations, he elaborated his *Recumbent Nude II* in 1927 and *Recumbent Nude III* in 1929; these can be compared with his graphic works, as can also the *Large Seated Nude with Raised Arms*, 1923-1925 (*Tout l'œuvre peint*, S20, S23 and S19). At the same time, the *Reclining Nude with Drapery* is evidence of the painter's concern with rendering volumes, which gradually disappeared from the later *Odalisques*.     H.G.

---

*Collections:*
Paul Guillaume (in 1929); Mrs. Jean Walter.

*Exhibitions:*
1929, Paris; 1931, Paris, Galerie Georges Petit, *Henri Matisse*, No. 130; 1966, Paris, No. 60 (repr.).

*Literature:*
W. George, undated, p. 76 (repr. p. 73); *La Renaissance*, April 1929, No. 4 (repr. p. 174); A. Basler, *L'Amour de l'Art*, No. 7, July 1929 (repr. p. 253); A. Bertram, *Henri Matisse*, London, 1930 (pl. XX); A. Barnes-V. de Mazia, *The Art of Henri-Matisse*, New York-London, 1933, No. 163; *Tout l'œuvre peint*, No. 422 (repr.).

Matisse, *Odalisque with Magnolias*,
New York, private collection.

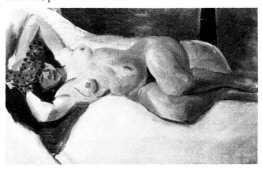

Matisse, *Reclining Nude*,
Brussels, private collection.

135

# Henri Matisse

## 58
### *Odalisque in Red Trousers*
(Odalisque à la culotte rouge)

Oil on canvas. H. 50 cm.; W. 61 cm.
Signed in black on lower left: Henri-Matisse.
RF 1963-66

Even though the geometric motifs on the background panels are different, the *Odalisque in Red Trousers* of the Walter-Guillaume collection invites comparison with the one in the Musée National d'Art Moderne, painted in Nice, in Matisse's apartment on Place Charles-Félix and dated 1921 by Isabelle Fontaine. Although in both paintings, the odalisque figure reclines on the same green-and-yellow-striped fabric-covered couch, and although in both, she wears trousers trimmed with a golden-glinting print motif caught by wide, gaudily-designed bracelets at mid-calf, it is impossible to propose such an early date for the *Odalisque in Red Trousers*; rather, the date would seem to be closer to that of the *Odalisque with Magnolias*, with which it has certain analogies, of which the distribution of space is by no means the least important.

Matisse was making increasingly lavish use of intricate decorative motifs, in which the background still lifes (here, the round table, ewer and bouquet) mingled with the profusion of flowered backdrops. Under this heading, there were *The Moroccan Tray* (New York, private collection; *Tout l'œuvre peint*, No. 415) and *Jewish Stories* (Philadelphia Museum of Art, White collection; *Tout l'œuvre peint*, No. 411), which show the aiguière that is in the *Odalisque with Red Trousers*. This accessory is also included in the group of everyday objects used by Matisse (reproduction page 32, catalogue of the *Matisse* exhibition, Galerie Dina Vierny, Paris, 1980). Subsequently, without relinquishing his use of strident colorings, Matisse employed a different approach to decorative elements, handling them in a manner that was both more vigorous and more rigorous, as in the *Odalisque in Grey Trousers* (No. 59).                                        H.G.

*Collections:*
Paul Guillaume (in 1929); Mrs. Jean Walter.

*Exhibitions:*
1929, Paris; 1931, Paris, Galerie Georges Petit, *Henri Matisse*, No. 129; 1946, Paris, No. 56; 1966, Paris, No. 61 (repr.); 1978, Rome, Villa Medici, *Henri Matisse*, No. 15 (repr.).

*Literature:*
W. George, undated, p. 9 (repr.); A. Barnes-V. de Mazia, *The Art of Henri-Matisse*, New York-London, 1933, No. 164; J. Lassaigne, *Cent chefs-d'œuvre des Peintres de l'Ecole de Paris*, Paris, 1947, p. 65 (color repr.); *Tout l'œuvre peint*, No. 437 (repr.).

# Henri Matisse

## 59
## *Odalisque in Grey Trousers*
(Odalisque à la culotte grise)

Oil on canvas. H. 54 cm.; W. 65 cm.
Signed on lower left in black: Henri-Matisse.
RF 1963-67

In his article devoted to the 1927 Salon d'Automne, the art critic Jacques Guenne showed himself to be keenly attuned to the chromatic force of Matisse's painting, commenting as follows: "With all those blue, red, violet and yellow stripes, with that great grey-patterned red wallpaper, I don't know how this small Matisse painting fails to become like the most awful display of a wallpaper dealer in a lower-class neighborhood. Or, rather, what I do know is that this artist is blessed with the grace of color. Believe me, he reconciles two violently warring colors in the twinkling of an eye!

"Just try to lay that green fabric on a red couch without causing an outcry from your friends. And I dare you to think of any painter who has ever cast on a canvas a more exquisite patch of color than Matisse did when he made that bouquet of yellow flowers bloom forth from his brush!" (*L'Art vivant*, 5 November 1927, No. 69, page 869). In that same year, issue No. 7/8 of *Les Cahiers d'Art* reproduced, along with the *Odalisque in Grey Trousers*, the series of similarly inspired odalisques in which there systematically recur the same brazier and the small green Louis XV table. Certain of these works are visible in a photograph of Matisse's studio in Nice, taken in 1928-1929 and reproduced in the catalogue of the Matisse exhibition held in Zurich and Düsseldorf in 1982-1983 (illustration No. 38). In this same catalogue, there is an unexpected photograph of "Bonnard imitating the pose of an odalisque in Matisse's apartment," likewise taken in 1928-1929 (illustration No. 37), showing the small Louis XV table and the lampas wall-hanging that is the basis for the gaudy background of the *Odalisque in Grey Trousers*, and that depicts the surroundings amid which Matisse worked. In the foreground is a sofa; behind it is the Louis XV table, on which stands a vase; and stretched between two beams hangs the expanse of lampas fabric, which also recurs, with the brazier, in a pencil drawing of a still life entitled *Interior with Brazier*, in which divers objects replace the customary odalisque on the striped sofa (*Henri Matisse* exhibition, Galerie Dina Vierny, Paris, 1980, reproduction page 52). In the background, reflected in the mirror over a vaguely Louis XV mantelpiece, characteristic of the late nineteenth century, there is another wall-hanging patterned with

arches and plant motifs, visible in a number of Matisse's works, including the famous *Moorish Screen*. Using these fairly ordinary accessories as a basis, the artist wrests from them a vigorousness that, in the *Odalisque in Grey Trousers*, is reminiscent of Matisse's Fauve period. Here, decorative power is carried to its extreme, with enormous vigor underlain with the exigency of the forceful chromatism. The vertical stripes in the background, interpreted in diverse fashions, are tied in with the horizontality of the sofa, while the odalisque, carried beyond anecdotal picturesqueness, disrupts, with the aid of the accessories, what would surely have been the barrenness of this arrangement if it had been depicted all by itself. At this point, the female figure dissolves into the space of the picture and into its sundry decorative elements, with which she becomes incorporated. H.G.

*Collections:*
Paul Guillaume (in 1929); Mrs. Jean Walter.

*Exhibitions:*
1927, Paris, *Salon d'Automne*, No. 1055; 1929, Paris; 1931, Paris, Galerie Georges Petit, Henri-Matisse, No. 139 (repr.); 1966, Paris, No. 62 (repr.); 1978, Rome, Villa Medici, *Henri Matisse*, No. 17 (repr.); 1981, Moscow, Pushkin Museum of Fine Arts, *Moscow-Paris*.

*Literature:*
L'Art Vivant, No. 69, 5 November 1927, p. 869 (repr. pp. 884-885); Les Cahiers d'Art, Nos. 7/8, 1927, p. 270 (repr.); Les Arts à Paris, No. 16, January 1929, p. 18 (repr.); W. George, undated, p. 80 (repr.); A. Bertram, Henri Matisse, London, 1930 (pl. XXI); A. Barnes-V. de Mazia, The Art of Henri-Matisse, New York-London, 1933, No. 174; G. Diehl, Henri-Matisse, Paris, 1954, p. 78, No. 100, p. 144 (repr.); R. Escholier, "Matisse et le Maroc," Le Jardin des Arts, No. 24, October 1956, p. 712 (repr.); Tout l'œuvre peint, No. 450 (repr.).

# Amedeo Modigliani

Livorno, 1884-Paris, 1920

## 60
### *The Red-haired Girl*

(Fille rousse)

Oil on canvas. H. 40.5 cm.; W. 36.5 cm.
Signed and dated on lower right: Modigliani 1915.
RF 1960-46

If Modigliani the painter is impregnated with the work of Modigliani the sculptor, which he performed with Brancusi, his inspiration was, so to speak, never marked by the experiences of his private life, which was frequently unhappy, and the anonymous faces that succeed one another in his work are those of models who served as landmarks blazing the trail of his aesthetic progress.

Without having belonged to the Cubist movement, Modigliani comes close to it here, through the geometrization of volumes. The neck, reduced to a kind of cylinder, participates in this simplification. Against the rigid, mineral background, the face opposes its budding embonpoint, and the eyebrows oppose their round arches, the auburn hair its wavy lines, the chin, mouth and nose their arabesques. The eyes contain a deep gaze, but this gaze eludes that of the artist, conferring a free, fully complete appearance upon the face. The reduction of color to a blend of grey and reddish browns is disrupted only by a small light green patch in the upper left.

The stiffness and hieraticism of the painting's design are attenuated by the slight dissymmetry of the lighting and of the facial features as well as by the slight incline of the head. The close-up presentation of the face and the somewhat foreshortened framing recur in several portraits from the years 1914 and 1915. It was this series of paintings that Francis Carco had in mind —he was one of the rare first-hand witnesses of Modigliani's work— when he noted that Modigliani "wrested the tortured relief of a face from bituminous depths that formed a mass" (*L'Eventail*, 15 July 1919).                C.G.

---

*Collections:*
Paul Guillaume; Mrs. Jean Walter.

*Exhibitions:*
1958, Paris, No. 28; 1966, Paris, No. 119 (repr.); 1968, Tokyo, Seibu-Kyoto Department Store, National Museum of Modern Art, *Modigliani*, No. 14 (color repr.); 1981, Moscow, Pushkin Museum, *Moscow-Paris*, 1900-1930, p. 309; 1983, Paris, Grand Palais, Salon des Indépendants, *Montmartre, les Ateliers du génie*, p. 29, color reproduction.

*Literature:*
J. Lanthemann, 1970, No. 62 (repr. p. 175); *Tout l'œuvre peint*, No. 71 (repr.); "Notes d'André Derain", *Manuscrit 6887, published by G. Salomon*, Cahiers du Musée National d'Art Moderne, *No. 5, 1980, p. 351; J. Lassaigne, 1982, p. 24, fig. 71.*

## 61

# *Paul Guillaume, Novo Pilota*
(Paul Guillaume, Novo Pilota)

Oil on cardboard bonded onto sheathed plywood. H. 105 cm.; W. 75 cm.
Signed and dated on lower right in black paint: MODIGLIANI; 1915 (below).
On upper left on two lines: PAUL GUILLAUME; upper right, drawing of the Star of David, and below, *Stella* MARIS;
on lower left, emphasized by two intersecting curved lines, on two lines, in green paint blended with a tinge of white:
NOVO PILOTA; on lower right, between the signature and the date, a drawing of a swastika.
RF 1960-44

Modigliani and Paul Guillaume became acquainted in 1914 through Max Jacob (*Les Arts à Paris*, June 1927, No. 13, page 24). Modigliani's biographers all agree that this was an important year for the artist: he had just met Beatrice Hastings, an English poetess who, under the name of Alice Morning, wrote a column entitled "Impressions of Paris" for *The New Age* (a London periodical), and who was thus a privileged witness to this period. Theirs was a stormy love affair that corresponded to a highly creative phase in Modigliani's career. Paul Guillaume installed the painter in a Montmartre studio, not far from the Bateau Lavoir. The painting shown here was done at Beatrice Hasting's place, on Rue Norvins, in a house in which Emile Zola had once lived (*Les Arts à Paris*, No. 11, October 1925, page 13). Its style and intent make it reminiscent of another portrait, dated 1916, in which Paul Guillaume was in a seated pose, portrayed half-length and full face, one arm leaning on a chair; the same self-assurance is evident in the face and bust (Milan, Civica Galleria d'Arte Moderna). Two oil portraits done in 1915 show similar Cubist deformations in the face: one is a half-length portrayal against a neutral background (Ghent, former Roland Leten collection), in which the model is bareheaded; the other depicts the art dealer, again bareheaded, wearing a suit, in his library, before an upright piano that delimits the background (Toledo Museum of Art, Toledo, Ohio). A large number of drawings are included in this series.

On a background made up of broad colored sections, the artist has sung the praises of the great collector of African art, aged barely twenty-three, represented as the youthful guide of contemporary painting. His last name, written in capital letters, moves out of the frame in the upper left; in the lower left are the words "Nova Pilota;" on the right, "Stella Maris." These formal inscriptions are integrated with the portrait. The signature, in small letters, carefully affixed fairly high up on the right side, provides a basis for imagining the beginning of a list of artists who might be taken in charge by the young dealer. His eyes are barely open toward the outside world, but the gaze within them betrays self-assurance. The nose, handled in the Cubist manner, the half-open mouth, the well-groomed mustache and the forward-jutting chin are meticulous touches that form a contrast with the polyhedric shape of the head, the forehead partially concealed by a hat that is pulled way down. The sloping shoulders blur out the presence of the bust in favor of the faintly effeminate gesture of the crooked left arm and of the right hand that is in a guiding gesture.

This portrait is revelatory of the artist's Cubist procedure, and also of a species of overly emphatic depiction of both the dealer and the artist. By its aesthetic development, it expresses the meeting between two contrasting personalities who nevertheless worship in the same cult of living art.

C.G.

*Collections:*
Paul Guillaume (in 1925); Mrs. Jean Walter.

*Exhibitions:*
1926, Paris, No. 3102; 1929, Paris; 1935, Paris, No. 59; 1937, Paris, No. 70; 1945, Paris, Galerie de France, No. 2; 1946, Paris, No. 61; 1958, Marseille, No. 8; 1958, Paris, No. 25; 1962, Paris, Galerie Charpentier, *Chefs-d'œuvre des collections françaises*, No. 51 (repr.); 1966, Paris, No. 122 (repr.); 1978, Ghent, Musée des Beaux-Arts, *Bateau Lavoir*, No. 52 (repr.); 1981, Paris, No. 93 (repr.).

*Literature:*
*Les Arts à Paris*, No. 11, October 1925, p. 13 (repr.); W. George, 1926, p. 94; W. George, 1929, p. 137 (repr. p. 139), p. 142, p. 152; W. George, 1929, *La Renaissance*, No. 4 (repr. p. 184); M. Georges-Michel, *Les Montparnos*, Paris, 1929, p. 53; A. Pfannstiel, 1929, presentation of catalogue, p. 7; M. Dale, 1929, pl. 28; *Les Cahiers de Belgique*, April-May 1931 (repr. p. 170); *Kunst und Dekoration*, August 1931 (repr.); A. Basler, pl. 6; J. Lassaigne, 1947, p. 123; G. di San Lazzaro, 1947, color pl. No. 1; A. Pfannstiel, 1956, p. 67, No. 40; A. Ceroni, *Amedeo Modigliani, peintre, suivi des "Souvenirs" de Lunia Czechowska*, Milan, 1958, No. 55; M. Hoog, *Peinture moderne*, Paris, 1959, p. 225; *Les lettres françaises*, 20 January 1966, Max Jacob, "Apologie de Paul Guillaume," reproduction of a detail; J.-P. Crespelle, *La folle époque*, Paris, 1968, repr. p. 265; J.-P. Crespelle, *Modigliani. Les femmes, les amis, l'œuvre*, Paris, 1969, pp. 198-202, insert figure; J. Lanthemann, 1970, No. 110; *Tout l'œuvre peint*, No. 100; R.V. Gindertael, 1976, p. 38, pl. 12; C. Mann, 1981, pp. 117, 120, fig. 80; J. Lassaigne, 1982, p. 30, fig. 100.

# Amedeo Modigliani

## 62
## *Antonia*
(Antonia)

Oil on canvas. H. 82 cm.; W. 46 cm.
Signed on lower right in black paint: Modigliani.
Inscription on upper left: in a beige impasto rectangle, inscribed in black in the thickness of the paint, the name "Antonia," followed by a double-cruciform sign.
RF 1963-70

This portrait, whose model we know only her first name, is traditionally dated 1915, and displays certain analogies (elongated, cylindrically-shaped neck, geometric background lines, rounded facial outline) with the female figures of this period, including the portraits entitled *Madame Pompadour* (Chicago, Art Institute, Joseph Winterbotham, collection), *The Red-haired Girl* (No. 60), and *Portrait of an Auburn-haired Woman* (Turin, Galleria d'Arte Moderna).

The portrait of Antonia reveals a freely-interpreted approach to Cubist procedures, although Modigliani never really belonged to the movement: the double line of the nose, the patterns of the ear and hair suggest a rendering of the model's profile. The eyes are reduced to two oval shapes, yet the woman is very present, revealing a certain complicity with the artist. Her dark dress is echoed in the background wall-hanging. In this harmony of brown and dark blue, the window does not admit daylight, but the axis of its cross-piece is on the axis of the face and echoes the double-cruciform sign that follows Antonia's name; the graphism of the name, in letters that emerge against a background similar by its brushstroke to the handling of the face, adds an additional correspondence to the evocation of the young woman.

If Modigliani does not use the customary means —gaze, expressive facial features— to express his feelings vis-à-vis his model, he possesses his own specific pictorial language, which abounds in suggestive signs.                C.G.

*Collections:*
Paul Guillaume (in 1923); Mrs. Jean Walter.

*Exhibitions:*
1923, Prague, *Vystava francouzskeho unémi XIX a XX stoleti*, No. 275; 1958, Paris, Galerie Charpentier, *Cent tableaux de Modigliani*, No. 27; 1966, Paris, No. 120 (repr.); 1978, Paris, No. 93; 1980, Athens, No. 20 (color repr.); 1981, Paris, Musée National d'Art Moderne, No. 91 (repr.).

*Literature:*
A. Pfannstiel, 1929, catalogue presentation, p. 8; A. Pfannstiel, 1956, No. 45, p. 69; J. Lanthemann, 1970, No. 75; *Tout l'œuvre peint*, No. 59 (repr.); R.V. Gindertael, 1976, p. 33, color pl. 7; D. Hall, *Modigliani*, Edinburgh, 1979 (color pl. 19); J. Lassaigne, 1982, p. 22, fig. 59.

Modigliani, *Madame Pompadour*, Chicago, Art Institute.

# Amedeo Modigliani

## 63
### *Woman with Velvet Neckband*
(Femme au ruban de velours)

Oil on paper bonded to cardboard. H. 54 cm.; W. 45.5 cm.
Signed on lower left: Modigliani.
RF 1960-45

This portrait is evidence of the artist's questing spirit in all its variety. By its dark color range, it bears similarities with his early portraits. The dominance of sinuous lines foreshadows the style that Modigliani would be using toward the end of his life.

The *Woman with Velvet Neckband* is not an isolated work. The same model is depicted elsewhere, in a sketch dashed off with a few pencil strokes (1981 exhibition in Paris, *Woman's Head*, 42 × 25 cm., reproduction page 194, No. 150, private collection, Paris). A drawing that more closely resembles the painting shows the background lines emerging as a forest setting, wholly unexpected on the part of this artist, and the thickness of the brushstrokes underlines the shadows that set the face apart, enhancing the pureness of its curves (*Woman's Head*, 48 × 36 cm., New York, Parke-Bernet auction,

12 May 1965, No. 43). S. Delbourgo and L. Faillant-Dumas (1981 exhibition in Paris, pages 41 and 44) have used the findings of x-ray investigations to point out the similarities between the brushwork on the face of this model and that of the *Seated Nude* (1981 exhibition in Paris, fig. 24, private collection, Paris).

The painter employs subdued means to trace the outline of the face with a single, fluid line. He mordantly emphasizes the hairstyle, painted in a dark hue, and, similarly, the linear austerity of the velvet ribbon disrupts the sinuousness of the lines of the face, shoulders and dress. This purity of line, linked to the hieratic expression of the face, set with expressionless eyes, evokes the Negro masks, certain elements of which were assimilated by Modigliani to enhance his aesthetic pattern of procedure.

C.G.

*Collections:*
Paul Guillaume (in 1929); Mrs. Jean Walter.

*Exhibitions:*
1929, Paris; 1958, Paris, No. 26; 1966, Paris, No. 121 (repr.); 1968, Tokyo, Seibu-Kyoto Department Store, National Museum of Modern Art, *Modigliani*, No. 13 (color repr.); 1981, Tbilisi-Leningrad, No. 26 (color repr.).

*Literature:*
W. George, undated, p. 145 (repr.); A. Ceroni, *Amedeo Modigliani, peintre, suivi des Souvenirs de Lunia Czechowska*, Milan, 1958, No. 41 (repr. p. 47); *Tout l'œuvre peint*, No. 63 (repr.); J. Lanthemann and C. Parisot, 1978, p. 114, No. 103; J. Lassaigne, 1982, p. 24, fig. 63.

# Amedeo Modigliani

## 64

## *The Young Apprentice*
(Le jeune apprenti)

Oil on canvas. H. 100 cm.; W. 65 cm.
Signed on upper left in black paint: Modigliani.
RF 1963-71

Modigliani's admiration for Cézanne emerges in a series of portraits in which the artist devotes himself to a quest for deep-lying relationships between the figure and its setting. Here, the chair and table seem to participate in the model's pose by freeing the tensions of the head and body through their supporting role. There is a similar relationship in the portrait entitled *Elvire, Seated, Elbows on a Table* (St. Louis, Missouri, City Art Museum, gift of Joseph Pulitzer, Jr.), as well as in a series of pictures of boys painted from 1917 to 1919: *Little Red-headed Boy* (Villeneuve d'Ascq, Musée d'Art Moderne du Nord, Masurel bequest), *Boy in Blue Jacket* (Indianapolis Museum of Art, gift of Mrs. Julian Bobbs in memory of William Ray Adams), *Seated Man* (Paris, private collection), and, especially, *The Peasant* (London, Tate Gallery). These can be compared for resemblances with Cézanne's portraits depicting people drinking and smoking (Venturi, No. 679 and ff.), particularly the one entitled *The Smoker*, in the Pushkin Museum (Moscow) —same pose, same quest for meditative expression, same unification of the pictorial surface. Is this a specific borrowing or merely a meeting of minds? This work remains inserted in the method of stylization peculiar to Modigliani, in which the sharpness of outlines and the flattening of forms hint rather of a lesson gleaned from Gauguin.

The facial contours are softened by sinuous lines, lightened by colors that are paler than those in the preceding works. The face and hands are handled with surprising restraint, reminiscent of the artist's background as a sculptor: blurred brushstrokes on sparingly detailed hands, which betray more strength than skill.                    C.G.

Cézanne, *The Smoker*
Moscow, Pushkin Museum.

*Collections:*
L. Zborowski, Paris; Paul Guillaume (in 1928); Mrs. Jean Walter.

*Exhibitions:*
1929, Paris; 1935, Paris, No. 427; 1945, Paris, Galerie de France, *Modigliani 1884-1920, Peintures*, No. 24; 1958, Paris, No. 54 (repr.); 1966, Paris, No. 123 (repr.); 1980, Athens, No. 21 (color repr.); 1981, Paris, No. 96 (repr.).

*Literature:*
*Les Arts à Paris*, May 1928 (repr. p. 27); W. George, undated (repr. p. 141), p. 152; W. George, *La Renaissance*, No. 4, April 1929, p. 182; A. Pfannstiel, 1929, preface to catalogue, p. 38, pl. p. 11; F. Neugass, "Modigliani," *L'Amour de l'Art*, May 1931, p. 196 (fig. 32, 33), p. 197; A. Basler, 1931, pl. 21; F. Neugass, "Les sources de l'art d'Amedeo Modigliani," *L'Art et les Artistes*, 1934, No. 149, p. 333 (repr.); (Apollonio), 1950, p. 170; G. Jelidka, *Modigliani*, 1884-1920, Erlenbach-Zurich, 1952, pl. 35; A. Pfannstiel, 1956, p. 134, No. 241; A. Ceroni, *Amedeo Modigliani, peintre, suivi des "Souvenirs" de Lunia Czechowska*, Milan, 1958, No. 103; J. Lanthemann, 1970, No. 372; *Tout l'œuvre peint*, 1972, No. 258; R.V. Gindertael, 1976, p. 55, color pl. 29; J. Lanthemann and C. Parisot, 1978, No. 372 (repr. p. 133); D. Hall, *Modigliani*, Edinburgh, 1979, pl. 40; B. Zurcher, *Modigliani*, Paris, 1980, pl. 48; J. Lassaigne, 1982, fig. 258, p. 74.

# Claude Monet

Paris, 1840-Giverny, 1926

## 65
## *Argenteuil*

(Argenteuil)

Oil on canvas. H. 56 cm. ; W. 67 cm.
Signed on lower left: Claude Monet.
RF 1963-106

In and around the year 1875, river banks, more especially the banks of the Seine near Argenteuil, supplied Monet with subjects for many paintings. The one shown here is part of a series dated 1875 (Wildenstein, Nos. 368 to 372) depicting the same site, with a few variations in the framing and arrangement of the boats. If to this are added the canvasses painted at the same scene the previous year, including the famous *Bridge of Argenteuil* (Musée d'Orsay, Paris, Personnaz bequest), this repetition can be viewed as the foreshadowing of the *series* pattern developed by Monet, particularly after 1891.

A broad expanse of sky punctuated with a few scattered clouds and, more importantly, the surface of the water itself, enabled Monet to investigate the effects of light, whose most fleeting nuances he rendered thanks to intensely fractured brushstrokes. The shadows are light and colored. All these were elements that, coupled with the absence of anecdote, scandalized his contemporaries, who were used to dark, overly finished painting, and who long remained insensitive to Impressionist poetics. As for the composition, although it does not wholly abide by conventional rules, it is nonetheless accurately structured, through the lines of the masts.

Recent cleaning has restored the initial delicately shimmering glow of this painting, which once belonged to the painter Romaine Brooks, the friend of Natalie Clifford Barney, who was Rémy de Gourmont's "Amazon"; both women were linked to the between-war Paris literary and artistic scene.                                    M.H.

Monet, *Pleasure Boats at Argenteuil*,
France, private collection.

Monet, *Red Boats at Argenteuil*
Cambridge, Massachusetts, Fogg Art Museum.

*Collections:*
Romaine Brooks, Nice (circa 1921); Mrs. Jean Walter (circa 1955).

*Exhibitions:*
1921, Wiesbaden, Germany, Biebrich Palace, *Exhibition of French Art in the Rhineland*, No. 377; 1931, Paris, Orangerie des Tuileries, *Monet*, No. 69; 1966, Paris, No. 18 (repr.); 1980, Athens, No. 22 (color repr.); 1981, Tbilisi-Leningrad, No. 27 (color repr.).

*Literature:*
J. Bouret, "L'éblouissante collection Walter-Guillaume," *Réalités*, No. 239, December 1965 (color repr.); Bortolatto, *Claude Monet*, Milan, 1972, No. 129, pp. 96-97 (repr.); D. Wildenstein, *Claude Monet, biographie et catalogue raisonné*, vol. 1, Paris, 1974, No. 370 (repr.); J. House, *Monet*, Oxford, 1977, p. 33, No. 17 (color repr.); M. Hoog, *Monet*, Paris, 1978, No. 35 (color repr.); J. Isaacson, *Claude Monet, Observation et réflexion*, Neuchâtel, 1978, p. 109, No. 48 (erroneous reference) (color repr.); H. Keller, *Miroir de l'Impressionnisme*, Amsterdam, 1980, plate 84.

# Pablo Picasso

Malaga, 1881-Mougins, 1973

## 66
## *The Embrace*

(L'étreinte)

1903
Pastel. H. 100 cm.; W. 60 cm.
Signed on upper right in blue pencil: Picasso
RF 1960-34

Most of Picasso's early works describe a world fraught with gravity and even with sadness. Here, descriptive, sentimental and lachrymose details are eliminated in favor of a presentation in which stark nudity, the simplicity of the loving gesture and the reduction of the bed and alcove to quasi abstract surfaces make anecdotic or literary commentary problematical. The concealment of the faces (which is very rare with Picasso, all of whose work betrays an obsession with physiognomic expression) further precludes the possibility of assigning any simplistic significance to this important, elaborated work. For the defining of this significance, we cannot use the frequently made comparison with the couple in the painting entitled *Life* (Museum of Art, Cleveland, Ohio), in which the man is drawing away from the woman, and the interpretation of which is not clear.

Contrary to what was customary in Picasso's work of this period, the colors are not reduced to an arbitrary muted blend; admittedly, these are simplified colors, but they are plausible, and curiously, they reproduce the three colors of the French flag.

This theme attracted other artists around 1900, but what became the verism of poverty in Steinlen's hands, intense dramatization in those of Munch and decorative sumptuousness in Klimt's work takes on monumental, timeless grandeur in Picasso's work. Palau emphasizes what he calls "Romanism," which, according to him, "has here replaced Gothicism, not only because the upper parts of the bodies of the embracing couple form a semicircular arch, but also because of the weight of the volumes that seem to echo sculpture" (*loc. cit.*).

Palau relates a number of drawings (Nos. 849-855) to this pastel. Three of them (Nos. 849-851, Paris, Musée Picasso) are quick sketches depicting a couple in which the woman is visibly pregnant, as she is here, but in which the two individuals are confronting each other and gesticulating. Two other drawings (854, Musée Picasso Nos. 474 and 855, private collection) are more closely similar to this pastel.

The pastel technique, although not exceptional in Picasso's work, was however infrequently used by him in such large-sized works.                                    M.H.

*Collections:*
A. Vollard, Paris; Paul Guillaume (in 1930); Mrs. Jean Walter.

*Exhibitions:*
1918, Paris, Galerie Paul Guillaume, *Œuvres de Matisse et de Picasso*, No. 25; 1931, New York, Demotte Gallery, *Picasso*; 1932, Paris, Galerie Georges Petit, no catalogue listing; 1946, Paris, No. 66; 1950, Paris, Galerie Charpentier, *Autour de 1900*, No. 135; 1960, Paris, Musée National d'Art Moderne, *Les sources du XXᵉ siècle*, No. 551; 1966, Paris, No. 92 (repr.); 1966, Paris, Grand Palais, *Picasso, Peinture*, No. 16 (repr.); 1967, Amsterdam, Stedelijk Museum, *Picasso*, No. 5.

*Literature:*
C. Zervos, "Picasso, œuvres inédites anciennes," *Les Cahiers d'Art*, Nos. 5/6, 1928, p. 216 (repr.); *Les Arts à Paris*, No. 17, May 1930, p. 6 (repr.); A. Jakovski, "Midis avec Picasso," *Art de France*, No. 6, 1946, p. 10 (repr.); J. Lassaigne, 1947 (pl. p. 147); J. Lassaigne, *Picasso*, Paris, 1949, No. 10 (repr.); A. Cirici-Pellicer, *Picasso avant Picasso*, Geneva, 1950, No. 170 (repr.); F. Elgar, R. Maillard, *Picasso*, Paris, 1955 (repr.); D. Sutton, *Picasso Peintures/époques bleue et rose*, Paris, 1955, pl. VI; C. Zervos, third edition, 1957, vol. 1, No. 161, p. 76; A. Blunt, P. Pool, *Picasso, the Formative Years. A Study of his Sources*, London, 1962, Nos. 85-90 (analogies); P. Cabanne, "Picasso," *La Galerie des Arts*, May 1966, No. 34 (repr. p. 16); P. Daix, G. Boudaille, 1966, IX, 12 (repr.); A. Fermigier, Paris, 1969, p. 36 (repr. p. 37); D. Porzio, M. Valsecchi, 1973, *Connaître Picasso*, p. 109 (color repr.); F. Elgar, *Picasso*, Paris, 1974, No. 12 (repr.); J. Palau i Fabre, "Les années de formation," *Pablo Picasso*, Paris, 1975 (introduction by J. Cassou), repr. p. 71; T. Reff, "Temas de amor y muerte de las obras juveniles de Picasso," *Picasso, 1881-1973*, Barcelona, 1974, pp. 21-24 (English text in *Picasso in Retrospect*, New York, 1980, p. 24); P. Cabanne, *Le siècle de Picasso*, vol. 1, Paris, 1975 (repr. p. 124), p. 127; T. Hilton, *Picasso*, New York, 1975, p. 40, No. 23 (repr.); *Tout l'œuvre peint*, No. 88 (repr.); J. Palau i Fabre, 1981, No. 856 (repr.).

# Pablo Picasso

## 67
## *The Adolescents*

(Les adolescents)

Oil on canvas. H. 157 cm.; W. 117 cm.
Signed on upper right, in matching color, with brush: Picasso.
RF 1960-35

This painting is little known, and has seldom been exhibited (it was not included in any of the major American or European retrospectives during the twenty years leading up to 1984), doubtless because of its fragility; it is one of the most grandiose creations of Picasso's Gosol period, in the Spanish village in which he stayed in 1906 (the date of 1905 listed by Zervos is obviously wrong, a mistake that has since been corrected in all the literature). The critics have frequently emphasized the sculptural, antique character of Picasso's canvasses imbued with "pink classicism" and depicting nudes, in which the sobriety, the rigidity and the absence of modern accessories contrast with the works of his preceding expressionist period, in which the figures were generally *situated*. Jean Cassou is wont to point out the Mediterranean character of this passing phase in Picasso's work and its resemblance with the art of Maillol.

Unlike the painting entitled *The Two Brothers*, showing one brother carrying the other, which is closely similar in both style and technique (two versions: Basel, Kunstmuseum, and Paris, Musée Picasso), here there is no anecdotal element to elicit a commentary.

A third, different version of *The Two Brothers* —one standing and the other seated (Washington, D.C., National Gallery, Chester Dale collection)— is more closely similar; the two apparently isolated figures emerge as if linked by subtle plastic bonds. But in the present painting, the starkness is even greater.

The figure on the left was prepared by means of two sketches (Palau 1237, Galerie Berggruen, Paris, and Palau 1240, Worcester, Massachusetts, Art Museum), in each of which the figure is situated in space by summary indications of arcades and ground, whereas the painted version shown here achieves monumentality through its absence of accessories. There was no direct study for the righthand figure, that of the androgynous body of an adolescent. Quite possibly Picasso had the same model pose twice, slightly modifying his build. The pose of the righthand figure could well have been inspired by that of the amphora bearer in Raphael's *The Burning of the Borgo* (Vatican chambers), reproductions of which were readily available. In this case, following a dissociation process that is frequent with Picasso, another group in the same fresco (man carrying an old man) could have inspired him to paint *The Two Brothers*, noted above, which was done during the same period. Undulating lines show through faintly beneath the legs of the two figures. These lines are those of the sketch of another widthwise composition that was erased by the artist.

M.H.

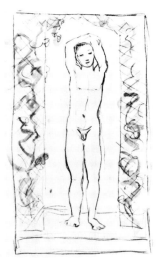

Picasso,
*Boy with Arms Raised*
Paris, Berggruen collection.

---

*Collections:*
A. Vollard, Paris; Paul Guillaume (in 1930); Mrs. Jean Walter.

*Exhibitions:*
1932, Paris, Georges Petit, No. 42; 1932, Zurich, Kunsthaus, *Picasso*, No. 33; 1936, New York, Jacques Seligmann, *Picasso, "Blue" and "Rose" Periods*, 1901-1906, No. 30 (repr.); 1961, Vallauris, *Hommage à Pablo Picasso*, No. 1; 1966, Paris, No. 93 (repr.); 1980, Paris, Palais de Tokyo, Musée d'Art et d'Essai, *La grisaille*, unnumbered.

*Literature:*
*Les Arts à Paris*, No. 17, May 1930, p. 19 (repr.); W. George, *Formes IV*, April 1930 (repr. fig. 1); *Formes*, XII, February 1931, p. 1 (publicity); J. Merli, *Picasso, el artista y la obra de nuestro tiempo*, Buenos Aires, 1948, No. 137; D. Sutton, *Picasso, peintures/époques bleue et rose*, Paris, 1955, pl. XIV; C. Zervos, third edition, 1957, vol. 1, No. 324, p. 150; P. Daix, G. Boudaille, 1966, XV, No. 11 (repr.); J. Palau i Fabre, 1981, No. 1239 (repr.).

# Pablo Picasso

## 68
## *Composition: Peasants*
(Composition: Paysans)

Gouache on paper. H. 70 cm.; W. 50 cm.
Signed on lower left in red pencil: Picasso.
RF 1963-76

This large gouache is a study for one of Picasso's largest works (2.18 m. × 1.30 m., Barnes Foundation, Merion, Pennsylvania; Zervos I, 384) and one of his most complex prior to *Les Demoiselles d'Avignon*. On 17 August 1906, Picasso wrote to his friend Leo Stein as follows: "I'm busy doing a painting of a man with a little girl. They are carrying flowers in a basket, and alongside them are oxen and wheat, or something like that." A sketch was enclosed (Palau, page 466).

The final composition is more vividly colored than this sketch; the flowers, roughly suggested here, are a blend of red, yellow, pink and green. The canvas is crowded; the disproportion of the figures, the somewhat chaotic and unbalanced design, the absence of depth led Alfred Barr to detect the influence of El Greco. What is involved here is doubtless not so much a specific source (*Saint Joseph and the Infant Jesus*), as suggested by several scholars, as it is common procedures: elongation and stylization of figures, disproportion of the persons depicted, refusal of perspective... all these being features that also make it possible to point to the influence of Gauguin.

Actually, for Picasso, the year 1906 was a period of intense but unhomogeneous investigation, during which, taking advantage of his already extensive visual culture, he gradually renounced the naturalism of the preceding periods in favor of a stylization that, a few months later, culminated in *Les Demoiselles d'Avignon*. However, this investigation, which was coherent in its general line of direction, did not exclude divergent attempts at other

Picasso, *Peasants*, Merion, Penn., Barnes Foundation (oil on canvas, H. 2.18 m, L. 1.30 m).

Picasso, *Study of Figures*, private collection (watercolor and red chalk); H. 0.28 m, L. 0.20 m.

Picasso, letter to Leo Stein, 17 August 1906.

*Collections:*
New York, Valentine Dudensing Gallery; Paul Guillaume; Mrs. Jean Walter.

*Exhibitions:*
1948, Paris, Galerie Charpentier, *Danse et Divertissements*, No. 167 (repr. with the title of "Dancers"); 1966, Paris, No. 94 (repr.).

*Literature:*
C. Zervos, 1957, 1, No. 312, p. 140; P. Daix and G. Boudaille, 1966, XV, No. 61 (repr.); *Tout l'œuvre peint*, No. 288 (repr.); J. Palau i Fabre, 1981, No. 1323 (repr.).

# Pablo Picasso

## 69
## *Woman with Comb*
(Femme au peigne)

Gouache on paper. H. 139 cm.; W. 57 cm.
Signed on lower right in red pencil: Picasso.
RF 1963-75

things; *The Peasants*, painted in Gosol, is an example of this.

The peasant theme, situated at the limit of the genre scene, might find its reference in the literature and poetry of the period. There is a hint of the street-song album cover here. These are fairly marginal, disconcerting works in Picasso's production, and this preliminary study, as well as the final version (whose presence at the Barnes Foundation has clearly done nothing to bring it renown), have seldom been exhibited or reproduced. Daix and Boudaille (XV, 50 to 61) and Palau (Nos. 1323 to 1330) group together an array of preliminary studies that show the development of the definitive composition; in Palau's opinion, the one in the Walter-Guillaume collection was also done in Gosol, prior to the return to Paris, and is hence earlier. Actually, these studies differ in the degrees of their incompleteness and by the details of their designs, but already, in the sketch enclosed with the letter noted above, the composition is basically complete. The only outstanding variation, in Palau's No. 1324 (private collection), is the appearance on the left of an additional figure, which may be only an "idea" for a different position of the female figure.　　　　　　　　　　　　　　　　　　　　M.H.

In 1906, Picasso produced a number of depictions of a woman arranging her hair. The versions most closely similar to the one shown here are a bronze (Spies, 7, Museum of Art, Baltimore, Maryland), a drawing that features several sketches in slightly different poses (private collection, Zervos, VI, 751), and another, more carefully done drawing (University of East Anglia, Norwich, England), dated by W. Rubin as being, respectively, from the spring, summer and fall of 1906 (1980 catalogue, New York, pp. 74-75). All of them portray the woman in a crouching position, with her right arm bent up toward the left shoulder.

The disequilibrium of the body, the foreshortening of the sketch, and the disproportionate size of the head infuse a strangeness into this somewhat atypical work; according to Daix-Boudaille, it was painted in Paris, while according to Rubin, it was done in Gosol (hence prior to mid-August 1906, cf. No. 68), and it contrasts with the calmer, more static nature of the other figures from the summer of 1906 (cf. No. 67).

There is reason to wonder whether the apparent disagreement between the two parts of the body might not be caused by the method of execution. This gouache was doubtless painted flat on an expanse of cardboard whose central part bears the mark of a deep fold. A shift in the position of the cardboard on the table may have brought about a discontinuity of the *"cadavre exquis"* type, which Picasso voluntarily incorporated into the picture.　　M.H.

*Collections:*
Paul Guillaume (in 1929); Mrs. Jean Walter.

*Exhibitions:*
1929, Paris; 1966, Paris, No. 96 (repr.); 1980, New York, Museum of Modern Art, *Pablo Picasso, a Retrospective* (color repr. p. 71); 1981, Madrid, Museo Español de Arte Contemporáneo; 1982, Barcelona, Museo Picasso, *Picasso, 1881-1973*, No. 42 (repr.).

*Literature:*
W. George, undated (repr. p. 118); H. Mahaut, *Picasso*, Paris, 1930, pl. 10; C. Zervos, third edition, 1957, vol. I, No. 337, pl. 158; P. Daix and C. Boudaille, 1966, No. XVI, 5 (repr.); J. Palau i Fabre, 1980, I, 368; *Tout l'œuvre peint*, No. 338 (repr.); J. Palau i Fabre, 1981, No. 1368 (repr.); P. Cabanne, "Picasso," *La Galerie des Arts*, No. 34, May 1966, p. 18.

# Pablo Picasso

## 70
## *Nude on Red Background*

(Nu sur fond rouge)

Oil on canvas. H. 81 cm.; W. 54 cm.
Signed on upper right: Picasso.
RF 1963-74

This simple figure is one of the most significant in Picasso's work in late 1906, an essential moment in the extremely swift maturing of his artistry (the date of 1905 listed by Zervos is clearly erroneous). The year 1906 marked the period of the end of his naturalism and of the expressive investigation of the blue and rose periods. The colors were becoming simplified, the relief was hardening and becoming sculptural. It was the time of the intervention of the primitive arts, and specifically of Negro masks; the importance and role of these in Picasso's development have been a highly controversial matter (cf. J. Laude, *La peinture française et "l'art nègre" [1905-1914],* Paris, 1962, and A. Fermigier, *op. cit.*). This female face, with its severely deformed features, its accentuated lines that build up the face and its empty stare, clearly invites comparison with the African sculptures with which Picasso was familiar. *Les Demoiselles d'Avignon* was painted only a few months later. However, the gesture of the left hand, the curves of the shoulders and hips, the gracefully dissymmetrical sweep of the hair —a feature that Picasso frequently called into play— are elements that maintain a feeling of peaceful life, devoid of any relationship to the harshness of the works of the ensuing period.

The theme of a woman combing or holding her hair is of frequent occurrence in Picasso's 1905-1906 works, either as an isolated figure or inserted into a complex composition (*The Harem*, Museum of Fine Art, Cleveland, Ohio). None of these works bears any close resemblance to this one.                                                         M.H.

*Collections:*
A. Vollard, Paris; Paul Guillaume (in 1929); Mrs. Jean Walter.

*Exhibitions:*
1920, Paris; 1932, Paris, Galerie Georges Petit, *Picasso*, No. 30; 1932, Zurich, Kunsthaus, *Picasso*, No. 32; 1935, Springfield, Massachusetts; 1950, Paris, Galerie Charpentier, *Autour de 1900*, No. 136 (repr.); 1966, Paris, No. 95 (repr.); 1966, Paris, Grand Palais, *Picasso, Peinture*, No. 37 (repr.); 1980, Athens, No. 23 (color repr.); 1981, Tbilisi-Leningrad, No. 29 (repr.); 1982, Rome, Villa Medici, *Picasso e il Mediterraneo*, No. 3 (repr.); 1983, Paris, Grand Palais, Salon des Indépendants, *Montmartre, les ateliers du génie*, p. 25 (repr.).

*Literature:*
W. George, undated p. 119 (repr.), p. 122; W. George, *La Renaissance*, 1929, No. 4 (repr. p. 183); H. Mahaut, *Picasso*, Paris, 1930, pl. 11; W. George, "L'exposition Picasso chez Georges Petit," *Formes*, No. 25, May 1932 (repr.); *Les Cahiers d'Art*, Nos. 3/5, 1932, p. 15 (repr.); P. Éluard, *A Pablo Picasso*, Geneva-Paris, 1944, p. 71 (repr.); J. Sabartès, *Picasso*, Paris, 1946, pl. 2 (repr.); C. Zervos, third edition, 1957, No. 328, p. 152; P. Daix, *Picasso*, Paris, 1964, p. 54 (repr.); J. Bouret, "L'éblouissante collection Walter-Guillaume," *Réalités*, No. 239, December 1965 (color repr.); P. Daix and C. Boudaille, 1966, p. 321, pl. XVI, 8 (color repr. p. 317); A. Fermigier, Paris, 1969 (repr. p. 74); F. Elgar, *Picasso*, Paris, 1974, No. 23 (repr.); J. Palau i Fabre, "Les années de formation," *Pablo Picasso*, Paris, 1975 (introduction by J. Cassou), color repr. p. 81); *Tout l'œuvre peint*, No. 341 (repr.); J. Palau i Fabre, 1981, No. 1359 (repr.); Y. Le Pichon, *Les peintres du bonheur*, Paris, 1983, repr. fig. 3, p. 232.

# Pablo Picasso

## 71
## *Large Still Life*
(Grande nature morte)

Oil on canvas. H. 87 cm.; W. 116 cm.
Signature painted on lower right: Picasso.
RF 1963-80

In the wake of the strict Cubist period, Picasso returned to a more relaxed art, in which objects retrieved a more recognizable appearance. However, a number of the procedures and/or practices from the period 1911-1913 are still present in this still life painted in 1917: thus, in accordance with an arrangement inherited from Cézanne, the table is depicted simultaneously from the side and from top to bottom. The same applies to certain of the objects arranged in an apparent disorder, including the fruit dish, the bottle and the stemmed glass, which are usual accessories in Cubist still lifes. There are few colors: the blend of brown tones, set off by the black rectangle, is the same as that of the Cubist period. The outlines are traced with a dark line.

All these objects float in the center of the picture, amid a preserved space, with the surrounding edges left blank by Picasso; but the location of his signature clearly proves that this painting was deliberately left unfinished.

The general design, the multiplicity of points of view, and the choice and distribution of objects obviously come from Cézanne. But they reflect more than a scattered lesson: Picasso here took over and submitted to the same formal imperatives the elements of two of Cézanne's best-known still lifes —the one (private collection) that belonged to Gauguin and is reproduced in the center of Maurice Denis's *Homage to Cézanne* (Musée d'Orsay), and the *Still Life with Bottle, Glass and Onions* (Musée d'Orsay). M.H.

*Collections:*
Paul Guillaume; Mrs. Jean Walter

*Exhibitions:*
1966, Paris, No. 97 (repr.); 1980, Athens, No. 24 (color repr.); 1981, Tbilisi-Leningrad, No. 30 (repr.).

*Literature:*
C. Zervos, 1949, vol. 3, No. 211, pl. 76.

# Pablo Picasso

## 72
### *Women at the Fountain*
(Femmes à la fontaine)

Oil on canvas. H. 50 cm.; W. 52 cm.
Signed on lower right in blue pencil: Picasso.
RF 1963-78

## 73
### *Women at the Fountain*
(Femmes à la fontaine)

Oil on canvas. H. 19 cm.; W. 24 cm.
Signed and dated in black ink on lower right: Picasso 21
RF 1963-79

In 1921, Picasso and his family spent the summer in Fontainebleau. During this period, influenced perhaps by the name of the town, and perhaps also by the decorations painted in the chateau by Il Rosso, commissioned by François I, Picasso worked on a large composition devoted to the subject of *Three Women at a Fountain*; its definitive version is in New York's Museum of Modern Art.

These two small paintings are part of the series of preparatory sketches. W. Rubin lists at least nine drawings and paintings devoted to this subject, plus seven studies of details, including heads and hands. "As the sketches progressed, both the woman on the right (whose hands are clasped around her crossed legs in the initial version) and the one on the left were increasingly inclined toward the center of the composition" (W. Rubin, *Picasso in the Collection of the Museum of Modern Art*, New York, 1972).

The two sketches in the Walter-Guillaume collection therefore are situated at the earliest stages of the development of the definitive work. If the central figure and the righthand figure underwent no major changes from one version to the next, the lefthand figure did, however, have one clearly defined variation. In No. 72, bearing her water jug on her head, she is stiff and hieratic, like a canephora, whereas in No. 73, leaning against a rock in a suppler pose, she holds the jug in her outstretched right hand. The origins of the two poses lie perhaps in Poussin's painting entitled *Eliezer and Rebecca* (Musée du Louvre). But her tunic already displays the stiff, vertical folds of the final version, clearly inspired by ancient Greek statuary.     M.H.

Picasso, *Three Women at the Fountain*, New York, Museum of Modern Art.

*Collections:*
Paul Guillaume; Mrs. Jean Walter

*Exhibition:*
1966, Paris, Nos. 98 and 99 (repr.).

*Literature:*
Not listed by Zervos.

72

73

# Pablo Picasso

## 74
## *Large Bather*
(Grande baigneuse)

Oil on canvas. H. 182 cm.; W. 101.5 cm.
Signed and dated on lower right: Picasso 21.
RF 1963-77

This canvas belongs to the so-called neoclassical period of Picasso's work, which developed during the years 1919 to 1924 in parallel with other paintings whose inspiration remained indebted to Cubism. "...Picasso carried on simultaneously and with the same incontestable mastery the art that, for him, prolonged the early tradition and the art that might be the foundation of a new tradition" (P. Reverdy, *Pablo Picasso*, 1924).

Reminiscences of ancient Greek and Roman art recur throughout the years of Picasso's formative period. But during the period 1919-1924, "only the spirit... antique, because in fact, his compositions from that period largely depict young, amply-built women, nude or partially clothed, with their extremities so amplified as to be in some cases even enormous, with cow-eyed gazes, and devoid of all grace... They are natural forms divinized in a pagan spirit" (H. Mahaut, *Picasso*, 1930).

The *Large Bather* in the Walter-Guillaume collection can be compared with the head of a woman in the Musée de Rennes (on loan from the Musée National d'Art Moderne) and also with a pastel (Zervos, IV, No. 330), but the woman, who is drying her feet, is situated more precisely in space, seated on a cube, with in the background a line evoking the horizon, whereas in the present picture, the sharply delineated and accentuated folds of drapery serve only to set off the massive nude, and her indistinct outlines. It is actually closer to a small nude (Zervos IV, No. 309, New York, Museum of Modern Art) whose monumental forms and dreamy-eyed gaze are similar.　　　　M.H.

*Collections:*
Paul Guillaume; Mrs. Jean Walter.

*Exhibitions:*
1946, Paris, No. 68 (repr.); 1966, Paris, No. 100 (repr.); 1979, Paris, Centre Georges Pompidou, Paris-Moscow, 1900-1930 (repr. p. 169); 1980, New York, Museum of Modern Art, *Pablo Picasso, a Retrospective* (color repr. p. 235); 1980, Paris, Centre Georges Pompidou, *Les réalismes*, 1919-1939 (color repr., p. 203); 1982, Rome, Villa Medici, *Picasso e il Mediterraneo*, No. 10 (repr.); 1983, Athens, No. 5 (color pl.).

*Literature:*
F. Carco, *Le nu dans la peinture moderne*, 1863-1920, Paris, 1924, pl. XIV; P. Reverdy, *Pablo Picasso*, Paris, 1924, p. 61 (repr.); L. Deshairs, "Pablo Picasso," *Art et Décoration*, March 1925 (repr. 79); E. d Ors, *Pablo Picasso*, Paris, 1930, pl. 34 (Rombey collection); J. Lassaigne, *Picasso*, Paris, 1949 (repr. No. 67); C. Zervos, 1949, IV, No. 329; V. Goldberg, "Monument to Tempestuousness," *Saturday Review of Literature*, May 1980, repr. p. 49; B. Rose, "Picasso, Artist of the Century," *Vogue*, April 1980, repr. p. 281.

# Pablo Picasso

## 75
## *Woman in White Hat*
(Femme au chapeau blanc)

1921
Oil on canvas. H. 118 cm.; W. 91 cm.
Signed on lower right: Picasso.
RF 1963-72

Picasso, who was perpetually evolving, simultaneously painted schematized figures captured in motion and other figures that contrast with the latter by their static quality and by their stocky physical appearance. The choice of certain accessories —here, a voluminous hat— seems to be designed to complement the fullness of the model's body, whereas her facial features are fairly delicate.

Picasso depicted this woman (whose face vaguely evokes that of his wife Olga) a number of times with this same hat, either alone or with another woman, likewise hatted. The most closely similar version is a large drawing (Marina Picasso collection, Zervos XXX, 260, *Picasso* exhibition, Munich, 1981, No. 130), in which the woman holds a book in her left hand. This accessory earned this painting the title of *Woman with Missal*; it is not known whether the title was bestowed by Picasso, but it clearly modifies the picture's meaning. G. Metken (*Picasso*, catalogue, Munich, 1981, No. 130) discerns a resemblance with the meditative faces in Millet's paintings. The grave expression and the forms, which are free from actual caricatural deformation (except for the left hand) explain this resemblance, which can also be extended to include Corot, whose work influenced Picasso more than once, and who painted several female figures shown leaning on their elbows. Picasso owned a Corot painting entitled *Seated Italian Girl* (*Donation Picasso* exhibition, Paris, 1978, No. 8).

The blue blouse and the red chair-back, together with the white of the skirt and hat, create the same tricolor effect as in *The Embrace* (No. 66), but in pastel shades.    M.H.

Picasso, *Woman with Missal*
Marina Picasso collection.

# Pablo Picasso

## 76
## *Large Nude with Drapery*
(Grand nu à la draperie)

1923
Oil on canvas. H. 160 cm.; W. 95 cm.
Signed on upper left: Picasso.
RF 1960-33

Despite the opinion of certain scholars, this *Large Nude* is not a companion piece to No. 74, whose date, size and spirit are different.

However, both these paintings are part of the large nudes of Picasso's neoclassical period, during which time he "constructed several Colossus-like women, 'cow-eyed Junos,' whose big, fractured hands are clasping stone-like clusters of fabric" (Jean Cocteau, *Picasso*, Paris, 1923).

Oddly enough, this painting contains reminiscences of the 1906-1907 period, specifically in the schematization of the facial features, in the heaviness of the female forms and even in the choice of the pose, which is the reverse of the pose in *The Coiffure*, from 1906 (New York, private collection, Daix-Boudaille, XVI, 7). The heavy shoulders and the twisting movement of the body also evoke Michelangelo's Sibyls and Prophets in the Sistine Chapel.

"The forms are handled and analyzed independently one from the other; they appear as geometrical solids tending to assemble along the plane of the canvas. The articulations are concealed by the mass of the flesh; these figurative breaks make it possible to express volume without departing from the two-dimensional plane. The grey and pink flesh tones are characteristic of the 'antique' period (and also of the Gosol period), and in this work they attain exceptional softness and luminescence" (M.L. Bernadac, catalogue for *Picasso et la Méditerranée*, Rome-Athens, 1982-1983).

"Expressionless, frozen to the point of stupor, the giantesses of 1920 are still idols and mother goddesses whose archaism and architectural simplicity show us that the 'return to antiquity' played the same role in Picasso's work as medieval music in that of Stravinsky" (A. Fermigier, *Picasso*, Paris, 1969, p. 160).

Picasso owned an oil painting by Renoir entitled *Seated Bather* and a Renoir sanguine entitled *Bather at her Toilet*, whose connection with the Picasso works of 1921-1923 emerges clearly. *Donation Picasso* exhibition, Paris, 1978, No. 28, No. 51.)
                                                            M.H.

*Collections:*
Paul Guillaume (in 1927); Mrs. Jean Walter.

*Exhibitions:*
1929, Paris; 1936, New York; 1960, Paris, No. 83 (repr.); 1961, Vallauris, *Hommage à Pablo Picasso*, No. 6; 1962, Paris, Galerie Charpentier, *Chefs-d'œuvre de collections françaises (XIXᵉ-XXᵉ siècles)*, No. 62; 1966, Paris, No. 101 (repr.); 1981, Moscow, *Moscou-Paris, 1900-1930* (color repr.).

*Literature:*
*Les Arts à Paris*, No. 13, June 1927 (repr.); W. George, undated, p. 127 (repr.), pp. 128-130; W. George, *La Renaissance*, April 1929, No. 4, p. 182; W. George, *Formes*, April 1930 (repr. fig. 2); H. Mahaut, *Picasso*, Paris, 1930 (cover repr.); A. Basler and C. Kunstler, *La peinture indépendante en France*, 1930 (repr. p. 251) *Les Cahiers de Belgique*, April-May 1931 (repr. p. 117); *Kunst und Dekoration*, August 1931 (repr.); *Art News*, 11 January 1936 (repr.); D. Joseph, *Dictionnaire biographique des Artistes contemporains*, Paris, 1934, vol. III, p. 134 (repr.); C. Zervos, 1951, vol. IV, No. 308, pl. 13.

# Pablo Picasso

## 77
## *Woman with Tambourine*

(Femme au tambourin)

Oil on canvas. H. 97 cm.; W. 130 cm.
Signed and dated on lower right: Picasso 25.
RF 1963-73

Among the eminently varied array of works by Picasso, this painting is a splendid demonstration of the artist's virtuosity as a colorist. In it, he combines colors that are theoretically the least harmonious, such as the turquoise blue of the bed, the violet of the cushion, the garnet red of the headgear and the tricolor of the skirt. The black ground on the left and the pale or faded colors in the foreground harmonize this fanfare. Most of the colored areas are applied in patches whose borders do not coincide with the outlines of the objects. The forms and colors are also dissociated, for example, in the face, in which the profile of the nose appears twice. The outlines are often delineated in recessed form, with the tip of the brush handle.

This work belongs to a series of paintings with flat, broken forms, the best known of which is the large *Dance*, in the Tate Gallery, London, which contrasts with the static figures and accentuated volumes with which it is contemporary.                                                                M.H.

*Collections:*
Paul Guillaume (in 1927); Mrs. Jean Walter.

*Exhibitions:*
1929, Paris; 1932, Paris, Galerie Georges Petit, No. 167; 1946, Paris, No. 69 (repr.); 1957, Paris, Galerie Charpentier *Cent chefs-d'œuvre de l'art français, 1750-1950*, No. 67; 1960, Paris, No. 84; 1966, Paris, No. 103 (repr.); 1966, Paris, Grand Palais, *Picasso, Peintures*, No. 138; 1980, Athens, No. 25 (color repr.); 1981, Tbilisi-Leningrad, No. 31 (color repr.).

*Literature:*
C. Zervos, "Picasso," *Les Cahiers d'Art*, 1926, pl. 27; *Les Arts à Paris*, No. 13, June 1927 (repr. p. 15); W. George, undated, p. 180 (repr.); E. Joseph, *Dictionnaire biographique des artistes contemporains*, Paris, 1934, vol. III, p. 135 (repr.); M. Gieure, *Picasso*, Paris, 1951, No. 68 (repr.); C. Zervos, 1952, vol. V, No. 415, pl. 167; F. Elgar, R. Maillard, *Picasso*, Paris, 1955 (repr.); W. George, *Arts*, 1959.

# Pierre-Auguste Renoir

Limoges, 1841-Cagnes-sur-Mer, 1919

## 78

## *Snow-covered Landscape*

(Paysage de neige)

Oil on canvas. H. 51 cm.; W. 66 cm.
Signed on lower right: Renoir
RF 1960-21

Unlike the other Impressionist artists, Renoir seldom painted snow scenes. The large canvas entitled *Skaters in the Bois de Boulogne*, dated 1868 (formerly in the von Hirsch collection, sold at Sotheby auction on 26-27 June 1978, No. 717), constitutes a noteworthy exception to the artist's feeling of repulsion toward snow, which he described as "Mother Nature's leprosy," and which was a source of inspiration to his Impressionist friends. "I have never been able to stand the cold; so, in the way of winter landscapes, this is the only picture... I also recall two or three small studies," Renoir confided to Ambroise Vollard (A. Vollard, *En écoutant Cézanne, Degas, Renoir*, Paris, 1938, page 166). Among the latter can be included a small *Snow-covered Landscape* (18 × 64 cm.) that was exhibited at the Musée de l'Orangerie in 1933 (No. 3, Count Doria collection, "painted circa 1868") and the *Snow-covered Landscape* in the Walter-Guillaume collection. Although undated, the latter compares with Renoir's works that were influenced by Impressionism and the plein air work sessions devoted to painting from the motif in the company of his friends Bazille, Monet and Sisley, whose *Snowy Landscape*, painted with small, taut, vigorous brushstrokes, is reminiscent of the highly legible brushwork in the present painting. For that matter, in this scene the snow is not overly present: it reflects the bluish sky and absorbs the shadow of the greenish-rust-colored stand of trees that occupies a large portion of the scene, in the background of which emerge the buildings of the nearby town.

In addition to painting these rare landscapes, Renoir used snow effects in one still life, entitled *Pheasant on the Snow* (Sotheby auction, 1 July 1959; private collection, Geneva, exhibition of *Chefs-d'œuvre des collections suisses de Monet à Picasso*, Paris, 1967, No. 58), painted in 1879 when he was staying with his friend Bérard at Wargemont, who has described its elaboration (reprinted in catalogue of the Centennial Loan Exhibition, 1941, New York, No. 28). Renoir, aware of the impression conveyed by a snowy background, added this element artificially to his still life, which had originally depicted a pheasant resting on a tablecloth, like Monet's *Pheasant*, painted ten years earlier (private collection, Neuchâtel, Wildenstein, No. 141).

H.G.

*Collections:*
A. Vollard (?); Paul Guillaume (?); Mrs. Jean Walter.

*Exhibitions:*
1943, Paris, Galerie Charpentier, *Jardins de France*, No. 114 (repr.); 1966, Paris, No. 19 (repr.); 1980, Athens, No. 28 (color repr.); 1985, London, No. 33 (repr.); Paris, No. 32, (color repr.); Boston, No. 33 (repr.).

*Literature:*
A. Vollard, 1918, vol. II, p. 104 (repr.); M. Drucker, 1955, quoted p. 148.

# Pierre-Auguste Renoir

## 79

## *Portrait of a Young Man with a Girl*
(Portrait d'un jeune homme et d'une jeune fille)

Oil on canvas. H. 32 cm.; W. 46 cm.
Signed on lower left in grey with monogram: A.R.
RF 1963-24

In this couple, François Daulte (*op. cit.*, No. 198) recognizes the pair of models who posed for *Le Moulin de la Galette*. It is generally agreed that Georges Rivière, a friend and defender of Renoir, is represented here, whereas the girl has not been identified. However, she does bear a clear resemblance to the one in the portrait entitled *Young Woman* (private collection, F. Daulte, No. 204), whom Daulte has compared with one of the women seated in the foreground of *Le Moulin de la Galette*, and an even more striking resemblance to the girl in the painting entitled *Alphonsine Fournaise at the Grenouillère* (Musée d'Orsay). It is certain that this double portrait, in which the background green instantly conveys an impression of outdoors, was painted during Renoir's Impressionist period, whose concerns it reflects. In particular, there is the obses-sive study of daylight, which led the artist to paint the unaesthetic deformation affecting the *Female Torso in the Sun* (1876, Musée d'Orsay). Stylistically, however, it bears a greater resemblance to the picture entitled *At the Cafe* (Otterlo, Kroller-Müller Museum) and also the one entitled *In the Atelier on Rue Saint-Georges* (private collection, F. Daulte, No. 188), in which Georges Rivière is again recognizable, than it does to *Le Moulin de la Galette*. It displays the same long, vigorous brushstrokes, a certain indifference with regard to the precise figuration of the background, nor is it free from a certain feeling of coldness vis-à-vis the models. The beholder feels that in these works, Renoir was not seeking to "prettify," but was intent on capturing a precise instant, whatever might be the aesthe-tic consequences.                        H.G.

*Collections:*
Ambroise Vollard (?); Paul Guillaume (?); Mrs. Jean Walter.

*Exhibitions:*
1945, Paris, Galerie Charpentier, *Portraits français*, No. 86; 1966, Paris, No. 20 (repr.).

*Literature:*
A. Vollard, 1918, vol. II, p. 56 (repr.); Le legs fabuleux de Mme Walter," *Match*, 29 January 1966, p. 40 (repr.); F. Daulte, No. 198 (repr.); E. Fezzi, *L'Opera Completa di Renoir nel periodo impressionista 1869-1883,* Milan, 1972, new edition in 1981, No. 24 (repr.).

# Pierre-Auguste Renoir

## 80
## *Bouquet in a Loge*
(Bouquet dans une loge)

Oil on canvas. H. 40 cm.; W. 51 cm.
Signed on lower right in black: A. Renoir
RF 1960-20

Unlike certain artists such as Degas and Toulouse-Lautrec, who frequently drew their inspiration from the theatre and its performers, Renoir was not particularly attracted by these subjects. Indeed, he averted his gaze from the stage and let it dwell on the audience, especially on the spectator whose privacy is protected by a box seat which at the same time draws other people's attention to him (*The Loge*, 1874, London, Courtauld collection). The round bouquet, wrapped in white paper, an accessory of the elegant theatre-goer, is frequently depicted with a theatre loge as a setting (*The First Outing*, London, Tate Gallery). Eva Gonzalès also chose to include such a bouquet in her picture entitled *Loge at the Théâtre des Italiens* (Musée d'Orsay), painted in the same year as Renoir's *The Loge*. In *Two Women in a Loge* (1880, Sterling and Francine Clark Art Institute, Williamstown; F. Daulte, No. 329), Renoir introduced a bouquet whose perspective is quite similar to that of the *Bouquet in a Loge*. Here, the artist abolishes all context save that of the sinuous dark line of the wall, which, with the opposition of the two backgrounds —light and dark— delimited by it, situates the place. He destroys the effect of background depth —which although admittedly a Cézannian concern, was also a concern experienced by Manet during the period in which he was influenced by Japonism, but one that is infrequent in Renoir's works—

while the foreground is fully occupied by the conical volume of the bouquet. The mass of the flowers, handled with small, vigorous brushstrokes, contrasts with the long, sleek strokes used on the wrapping paper and with the looser strokes of the rest of the painting. Another contrast is supplied by the artificial lighting modelling the bouquet with bands of light, the only concession made to the effect of volume, more suggested than actually represented. This *Bouquet in a Loge* can be compared with a *Still Life with Flowers*, dated 1871 (Museum of Fine Arts, Houston, Texas, Robert Lee Blaffer Memorial Collection), in which Renoir combines sundry elements —including a similar bouquet as well as a print based on *The Little Horsemen* (Musée du Louvre), which at the time was attributed to Velázquez and had been copied by Manet— in accordance with an arrangement and choice of objects directly derived from Manet's *Portrait of Zola*, which dates from 1867-1868. Manet's influence on Renoir at that time is a matter of record. Whether by coincidence or by a meeting of two minds, Manet, in his *Olympia* (1863, Salon of 1865), had placed in the black servant's hands a bouquet of the same type, the fold of whose wrapping paper on its left side is identical with the one used by Renoir for his *Bouquet in a Loge*. H.G.

*Collections:*
A. Vollard (?); Paul Guillaume (?); Mrs. Jean Walter.

*Exhibitions:*
1942, Paris, Galerie Charpentier, *Les fleurs et les fruits depuis le romantisme*, No. 156; 1966, Paris, No. 21 (repr.); 1981, Tbilisi-Leningrad, No. 36 (repr.); 1983, Paris, unnumbered.

*Literature:*
A. Vollard, 1918, vol. I, p. 499 (repr. p. 125); E. Fezzi, *L'Opera Completa di Renoir nel periodo impressionista 1869-1883*, Milan, 1972, new edition in 1981, No. 402 (repr.).

# Pierre-Auguste Renoir

## 81
## *Peaches*
(Pêches)

Oil on canvas. H. 38 cm. ; W. 47 cm.
Signed on lower right in blue: Renoir
RF 1963-16

Renoir used peaches and apples as the inspiration for many of his still lifes. Under the guise of apparent simplicity, he frequently displays concern with composition, as evidenced in a carefully studied arrangement of elements. In the painting shown here, the smooth sphere of the fruit on the left emerges as a counterpoint to the mass of the fluted earthenware fruit dish, which recurs in several other Renoir works (*Strawberries*, No. 93). It can also be seen in a composition that, while similar to this one, is of slightly smaller size (approximately 23.5 cm.×38.5 cm.), and is more narrowly framed (1958, Lefevre Gallery, London, reproduced in *The Connoisseur*, January 1958), in which a single fruit set apart on the cloth, but on the right side, counterbalances the compote dish. With the whiteness of the tablecloth and of the bluish compote dish, Renoir contrasts the brightness of the natural daylight with the vivid colorings of the peaches set off by the green of their leaves and the multicolored shimmer of the background, whose plastic and chromatic rendering curiously foreshadows the investigations of lyric Abstract Expressionism of the 1950s. H.G.

*Collections:*
A. Vollard (?); Paul Guillaume (?); Mrs. Jean Walter.

*Exhibitions:*
1942, Paris, Galerie Charpentier, *Les fleurs et les fruits depuis le romantisme*, No. 155; 1946, Paris, Galerie Charpentier, *La vie silencieuse*, No. 53 (repr.); 1966, Paris, No. 22 (repr.); 1980, Athens, No. 29 (repr.); 1981, Tbilisi-Leningrad, No. 34 (repr.); 1983, Paris, unnumbered.

# Pierre-Auguste Renoir

## 82
## *Nude amid Landscape*
(Femme nue dans un paysage)

Oil on canvas. H. 65 cm.; W. 54 cm.
Signed and dated in lower left: Renoir 83
RF 1963-13

Near the end of his life, Renoir admitted that "Boucher's *Diana at her Toilet* was the first painting that cast me under its spell, and ever since I have continued to be enamoured of it the way one remains faithful to one's first loves." In this *Nude amid Landscape*, he renews his ties with Boucher's and Watteau's *Nymphs After the Bath*, to which he had devoted many hours of contemplation in the Louvre at the outset of his career. This *Nude*, dated 1883, was painted after Renoir's return from travels in Italy, where his discovery of the great classic masters had confirmed him in his questioning doubts concerning Impressionism; it shows the persistence of the trends of this movement from which Renoir was seeking to detach himself. Actually, the landscape reflects an Impressionist approach, whereas the more linear nude figure is handled differently, and foreshadows Renoir's evolution after the pattern of Ingres, which achieved its culmination in the painting entitled *Large Bathers*, in Philadelphia.

According to Marie-Thérèse Lemoyne de Forges (Paris, 1966, No. 23), the model here was Suzanne Valadon, whom Renoir painted frequently at the time. The same model posed for the *Bust of Woman Arranging her Hair* (reproduced by Georges Rivière, 1921, page 73) and for the *Seated Bather with Linen* (F. Daulte, No. 445), which is closely akin to this present *Nude* by its theme and pictorial analogies.                                      H.G.

*Collections:*
Bernheim-Jeune; Guillou; Paul Guillaume; Mrs. Jean Walter.

*Exhibitions:*
1954, Paris, Galerie des Beaux-Arts, No. 29 (repr.); 1966 Paris, No. 23 (repr.); 1982, Prague-1893 Berlin, No. 74 (color repr.)

*Literature:*
*L'Art moderne*, vol. II, Paris, 1919 (pl. 122); H. de Régnier, *Renoir, peintre du Nu*, Paris, 1923 (pl. 11); G. Grappe, "Renoir, sa Vie et son Œuvre," *L'Art vivant*, Paris, 1933, p. 282 (repr.); "Le legs fabuleux de Mme Walter," *Match*, 29 January 1966, p. 39 (repr.); H. Dauberville, *La bataille de l'Impressionnisme*, Paris, 1967, p. 572 (repr.); F. Daulte, No. 434 (repr.); F. Daulte, *Auguste Renoir*, Milan, 1972, p. 78 (repr.); M.P. Fouchet, *Les nus de Renoir*, Lausanne, 1974 (repr. p. 127); A. Martini, *Renoir*, "Chefs-d'œuvre de l'art" collection, No. 7, Milan, 1966, 1977 revised edition (color repr plate XVI); J. Leymarie, 1978 (color repr. fig. 47); D. Wildenstein, *Renoir*, Paris, 1980 (color repr. p. 30); E. Fezzi, *L'Opera Completa di Renoir nel periodo impressionista 1869-1883*, Milan 1972, 1981 new edition, No. 590 (color repr.).

# Pierre-Auguste Renoir

## 83
## *Woman with Letter*

(Femme à la lettre)

Oil on canvas. H. 65 cm.; W. 54 cm.
Signed on lower right in dark grey: Renoir
RF 1960-24

This type of figure, portrayed in a rather artificial pose, is fairly unusual in the paintings of Renoir who, with the exception of commissioned portraits, preferred to capture his models in more natural attitudes. In this portrait, the letter is merely a pretext. Michel Hoog views this work as a revival of the "traditional type of fanciful figure encountered in the eighteenth century as well as in Corot's works" (M. Hoog, 1980, No. 30). Indeed, it is hard not to associate this pensive girl with the series of fanciful figures by Fragonard, whose influence on Renoir, outside of the nudes, has perhaps been underestimated.

Holding a basket of oranges, the same girl, dressed in identical fashion, posed for a full-length portrait. This composition, which forms a pair with the painting of a girl holding a basket of fish, was done in 1889 for Durand-Ruel. Renoir painted both of these pictures twice. The two pairs hang, respectively, in the National Gallery in Washington, D.C., and in the Barnes Foundation, Merion, Pennsylvania. The same *Orange Vendor*, seated and in profile view, her right hand holding a fruit and her left hand resting on the handle of her basket set on the ground, is found in a sanguine recently sold at auction (Sotheby's, 1978, No. 828), which has been studied by John Rewald (*Renoir Drawings*, 1946), who dates it at circa 1885-1890. On the back of this drawing there is a watercolor entitled *Girl Reading*, probably posed for by the same model. She closely resembles the person shown in *Girl Reading*

and *The Reading* (F. Daulte, Nos. 529-530, dated 1888 by the author), whose features resemble those of the model in *Woman with Letter*. Vollard dates the latter at 1895 (A. Vollard, 1918, vol. I, No. 48), while the date of 1896 was proposed at the Durand-Ruel show in 1920.

Last but not least, the same model also posed for another painting, entitled *Breton Girl* (private collection, Berne, reproduction in M. Robida, page 33), for which the author suggests the date of 1890-1895. Shown in a three-quarter view half-length portrait, and wearing the same costume, the girl looks lost in thought. Both the handling of the portrait and the model suggest a close kinship with *Woman with Letter*. In particular, there is the dominant blue color, chosen also for the background of the painting, a very unusual choice in Renoir's works.　　　　H.G.

*Collections:*
A. Vollard (?); Paul Guillaume (in 1924); Mrs. Jean Walter.

*Exhibitions:*
1920, Paris, Galerie Durand-Ruel, *Renoir*, No. 63; 1929, Paris; 1939, Geneva, Galerie Moos, *Exposition d'Art français*, No. 55; 1945, Paris, Galerie Charpentier, *Portraits français*, No. 87; 1966, Paris, No. 27 (repr.); 1980, Athens, No. 30 (color repr.); 1981 Tbilisi-Leningrad, No. 40 (repr.).

*Literature:*
A. Vollard, 1918, vol. I, No. 48 (repr. p. 12); *Les Arts à Paris*, No. 10, November 1924 (repr. p. 5); W. George, undated, p. 37 (repr. p. 42); J. Meier-Graefe, 1929 (repr. No. 215, p. 223); W. George, *Arts*, 1959, repr.

Renoir,
*Orange Vendor*
National Gallery,
Washington, D.C.

Renoir, *Breton Girl*
Switzerland, private collection.

# Pierre-Auguste Renoir

## 84

## *Portrait of Two Young Girls*
(Portrait de deux fillettes)

Oil on canvas. H. 46.5 cm.; W. 55 cm.
Signed on upper left in dark red: Renoir
RF 1963-25

In the 1890s, Renoir very much enjoyed depicting two girls shown engaged in the same occupation. In certain cases, he even repeated the subject. This was the case for *The Reading* (F. Daulte, Nos. 599, and 601, *The Two Sisters* (F. Daulte, 600 and 602), and, of course *Young Girls at the Piano* (No. 85). These girls are clearly recognizable as the models whom he so frequently portrayed either singly (F. Daulte, Nos. 603 to 608) or together (F. Daulte, Nos. 599 to 602). And they would seem also to be the persons painted by Renoir in *The Sleeper* (F. Daulte, No. 611), *Young Girl with Braid* (F. Daulte, No. 612) and in two *Nudes*, half-length representations shown from the back (F. Daulte, Nos. 613-614). They are also shown in *Young Girls Gathering Flowers* (F. Daulte, No. 609) and in

*The Meadow* (F. Daulte, No. 610), in which the artist —as in *Young Girls at the Piano*— takes pleasure in contrasting the colors of the dresses and the colors of the hair. The girl on the left, whom Renoir frequently painted in profile views, is in a similar pose, her chin slightly lifted, in both these works, which also depict the same background curtain. The girl on the right —almond-eyed, short nose, full cheeks— is characteristic of a certain feminine type admired by Renoir, i.e. young girls still showing the rounded features of their childhood. The present work, which was contemporary with *Young Girls at the Piano*, and which can be dated circa 1890-1892, shows that Renoir was still in his Ingres period, through certain of its aspects, such as the sharpness of the facial volumes.　　　H.G.

*Collections:*
Abbé Gauguin; auction of M.G., Hôtel Drouot, Paris, 6 May 1901, No. 12; M. Léclanché; Henri Canonne; Henri Canonne auction, Galerie Charpentier, Paris, 18 February 1939, No. 43, sold to Mrs. Paul Guillaume; Mrs. Paul Guillaume.

*Exhibitions:*
1949, Paris, Galerie Charpentier, *L'Enfance*, No. 167; 1966, Paris, No. 25, (repr.); 1980, Helsinki, Ateneumin Taidemuseo, *Impressionnisme* (color repr.).

*Literature:*
A. Alexandre, *La Collection Canonne*, Paris, 1930 (inset plate facing p. 60); "Le legs fabuleux de Mme Walter," *Match*, 29 January 1966, p. 40 (repr.); F. Daulte, 1971, No. 637 (repr.); F. Daulte, *Auguste Renoir*, Milan, 1972 (repr. p. 84); J. Leymarie, *Renoir*, Paris, 1978 (color repr. No. 41 and No. 43); catalogue of exhibition entitled *Renoir: un quadro per un movimento*, Trent, 1982.

# Pierre-Auguste Renoir

## 85

## *Young Girls at the Piano*

(Jeunes filles au piano)

Oil on canvas. H. 116 cm.; W. 81 cm.
Signed on lower right in dark red: Renoir
RF 1960-16

Like most of the Impressionist artists, Renoir was a music lover, and he frequently depicted two girls at a piano. In some cases, the girls were daughters of friends, such as the poet Catulle Mendès or the painter Henry Lerolle (cf. No. 90), while in other cases they were professional models about whom nothing more is known; this would seem to be the case in the present painting. Quite possibly, Renoir was entertaining memories of seventeenth- and eighteenth-century gatherings of musicians or, closer to him in time, Cézanne's *Tannhauser Overture* (Leningrad, Hermitage Museum, circa 1868); or, again, reminiscences of portraits of Madame Manet painted by her husband or by Degas. However, it is not possible for him to have seen Van Gogh's *Portrait of Mlle Gachet at the Piano* (Basel, Kunstmuseum).

In this painting, Renoir used a traditional theme that made it possible to combine the rigid lines of the instrument with the graceful gestures of the performers, and, like Cézanne, avoided anecdotal details that could have changed the picture into a genre scene. One of the girls seems to be reading the music, her left hand holding the score, while the other girl is looking on, following the music with her gaze. The setting is barely suggested; this picture may have been painted in Renoir's home —at the time of his marriage (1890), he had given a piano to his wife, who was an accomplished musician.

Renoir must have been satisfied with the balance between the masses and the lines, which describe a St. Andrew's cross, and with the color harmony that he achieved. Of this composition, there are at least six versions, all of them closely similar; one of them is the picture he painted for his first official commission from the French government. It is extremely difficult to pinpoint the anteriority (or the superiority) of any single version. An attempt in this direction, however, has been made by Meier-Graefe, who, after half a century, remains one of the best analysts of Renoir's work; he gives preference to the present version, considered as a roughed-in study (*Renoir*,

Renoir, *Young Girls at the piano*,
Paris, private collection.

Renoir, *Young Girls at the piano*,
Paris, Musée d'Orsay.

# Pierre-Auguste Renoir

Leipzig, 1929, page 250). In connection with this composition, there are also a few isolated studies of heads in similar poses, like the one in the Barnes Foundation, which probably also belonged to Paul Guillaume (A. Barnes and V. de Mazia, page 306). As for the drawings, it is hard to say whether they are preliminary studies, like the one reproduced by J. Leymarie, *Renoir* (Paris, undated, no page numbers), in which the two girls are depicted in a three-quarters back view, or whether they are reminiscences, such as the extremely linear one in a private collection (Sotheby auction, London, 2 February 1970, No. 28).

At present writing, six versions are known, as follows:

1. The painting shown here, which displays the freshness and swiftness of execution of a rough sketch, but which is signed, meaning that Renoir considered it as finished.

2. The version in the former Durand-Ruel collection, dated 1892, sized 118 cm. × 78 cm. (reproduced by J. Meier-Graefe, 1929, fig. 226).

3. The version in the Musée d'Orsay, executed in 1892 for a French government commission, sized 116 cm. × 90 cm.

At the show at the Musée d'Art et d'Essai in 1982, in the exhibit entitled *Figures et Portraits de Manet à Matisse*, the displaying of this painting side by side with the Walter-Guillaume version brought out the deep differences between these two works; the version shown here is done in acid tones, generally considered as being characteristic of Renoir's preceding period.

4. Metropolitan Museum of New York, Lehman collection, version dated 1892, sized 112 cm × 86 cm. This is the most "finished" picture in the series, but its color range is closer to that in the Walter-Guillaume version than to that in the other highly finished version, in the Musée d'Orsay.

5. Paris, private collection, version sized 115 cm × 90 cm. Exhibition entitled *Renoir dans les collections particulières françaises*, Paris, *Galerie des Beaux-Arts*, 1954, No. 37, repr.

6. Version in the former Cynthia Foy Rupp collection, New York (temporarily in the custody of the Metropolitan Museum), the erstwhile Mendelssohn-Bartholdy collection, Berlin, and the Lewisohn collection, Chicago.

The existence of such a large number of versions, all of them fairly large-sized, differing from one another only by the extent to which they are finished, and primarily by their color ranges, is wholly exceptional in Renoir's work. This should perhaps be viewed as the equivalent of the series paintings done by his friend Monet. Renoir's series is contemporary with that of the *Rouen Cathedral* paintings, and slightly posterior to the *Haystack* series. Although this is an indistinctly lighted indoor scene, Renoir remained faithful here to his work habits (choice of light colors, colored shadows) that were characteristic of the Impressionists' plein air painting, and it is possible that he was endeavouring to pursue his investigations in the same direction as Monet, while remaining loyal to his original thematics, reserving a considerable place for the human figure.                                                                    M.H.

Renoir, *Young Girls at the Piano*, ▶
New York, Metropolitan Museum,
Lehman collection.

# Pierre-Auguste Renoir

## 86
## *Apples and Pears*
(Pommes et poires)

Oil on canvas. H. 32 cm.; W. 41 cm.
Signed on upper left in red: Renoir
RF 1963-19

By its arrangement on a cloth whose artfully wrinkled creases enable effects of volume, and by the elimination of depth suggested by the abstract background, this still life recalls Cézanne. However, this reference is corrected by the handling of the fruit and the contrasty color range. Although Renoir, a lover of nature and of its products, deliberately devoted much effort to representing many still lifes, seldom did he paint any in which the design seems to reflect such a conscious concern with arrangement.

The vigorous volumes and the precision of the outlines of the fruit, as well as the accentuation of the creases in the cloth continue to reflect Renoir's Ingres-influenced period.

Closely akin to this one, there is another still life, of similar size (35 × 46 cm.), doubtless contemporary with it, which also proposes, on a cloth with mordantly marked creases, three apples in equilibrium on a plate accompanied by a lemon (J. Meier-Graefe, 1929, fig. 206). This can also be compared with No. 72 in the M. Gangnat sale, 1925, and with a *Still Life* auctioned by Christie's in November 1963.                                      H.G.

*Collections:*
In Renoir's studio at the time of his death; A. Vollard (?); Paul Guillaume (?); Mrs. Jean Walter.

*Exhibition:*
1966, Paris, No. 28 (repr.).

*Literature:*
*Atelier de Renoir*, vol. I, No. 54 (repr. pl. 21).

# Pierre-Auguste Renoir

## 87
## *Bather with Long Hair*

(Baigneuse aux cheveux longs)

Oil on canvas. H. 82 cm.; W. 65 cm.
Signed on lower right in dark red: Renoir
RF 1963-23

"... peint Monsieur Renoir
Qui devant une épaule nue
Broie autre chose que du noir."*
(Stéphane Mallarmé, Occasional Verse,
*Les Loisirs de la poste*, Thirty-ninth Quatrain,
La Pléiade, publishers, Paris, 1979, page 88).

The above bit of word play by Mallarmé is particularly suitable for describing this *Bather*, a painting that so accurately expresses Renoir's primary naturalism, his simple sensuality, that of a paradisiac golden age and the luminous iridescences that simultaneously bathe the body and the enveloping hazy landscape. Michel Hoog has noted this particularity which is specific to Renoir, who was "the only member of the Impressionist group who had a fancy for depicting female nudes out of doors amid indeterminate settings." (M. Hoog, 1980, No. 32.)

This bathing woman is doubtless contemporary with the one in the Barnes Foundation, from which it differs in minute details only (drapery folds on the far right, long hair falling down the back only) and in a clearer transcription of the landscape: for example, a tree trunk is visible in the background. This work is dated 1895 (reproduction in A. Barnes and V. de Mazia, 1944, page 310). Perhaps even more closely similar, in its handling of the background and the dissolution of the landscape, is the *Bathing woman, Standing*, dated 1896 (auction at Christie's, J. Meier-Graefe suggests what would seem to be a very late date 30 March 1981, No. 40). By proposing a date "circa 1900," (J. Meier-Graefe, 1929, page 322). In the catalogue of the exhibition entitled *Renoir, un quadro per un movimento*, Trent, 1982, Michelangelo Lupo noted fourteen Renoir nudes that are contemporary with the *Bather with Long Hair*.

The painting shown here is characteristic of Renoir's mature years, of his "nacreous" period, when, with the experience of Impressionism, which he had not repudiated, but which he had outgrown, he combined the teachings of the Italian museums and Cennini's theoritical treatises, with which he associated the lesson learned from Ingres, which had been assimilated and transcended.

In *The Coiffure*, also known as *Woman Bathing*, a large sanguine- and white chalk work on canvas (1.45 m. × 1.035 m., Picasso bequest, RF 35.793), which was a preliminary drawing for a painting reproduced in A. Barnes and V. de Mazia, 1944, No. 218, the model seems to be the same girl, with the identical gesture of holding the drapery against her bosom. A few years later Renoir took up sculpture, and for one of his principal works he used this same gesture of a woman holding the drapery in front of her. H.G.

---

*Collections:*
Durand-Ruel (purchased from Renoir on 18 November 1896); O. Schmitz (purchased on 17 November 1911); Paul Guillaume (?); Mrs. Jean Walter.

*Exhibitions:*
1926, Dresden, *International Kunstausstellung*; 1932, Zurich, Kunsthaus, *La collection d'O. Schmitz*, No. 49; 1966, Paris, No. 26 (repr.); 1980, Athens, No. 32 (color repr.); 1980, Marc-en-Barœul, Galerie Septentrion, *Impressionnisme*, No. 34 (color repr.); 1981, Tbilisi-Leningrad, No. 39 (color repr.); 1982, Trent, Palazzo delle Albere, *Renoir, un quadro per un movimento* (color repr., in unpaginated catalogue, and on catalogue cover); 1985, London, No. 94 (color repr.); Paris, No. 92 (color repr.); Boston, No. 94 (color repr.).

*Literature:*
P. Fechter, *Kunst und Künstler*, 1910, p. 21; K. Scheffler, *Kunst und Künstler*, 1920-1921, p. 186 (repr. p. 181); W. Grohmann, "Die Kunst der Gegenwart auf der Internationalen Kunstausstellung," *Der Cicerone*, 1926, (repr. No. 17); M. Dormoy, *L'Amour de l'Art*, 1926, p. 342 (repr. p. 341); E. Waldmann, *Die Kunst des Realismus und des Impressionismus in 19. Jahrhundert*, Berlin, 1927, p. 94 (inset repr. facing p. 450); J. Meier-Graefe, 1929, p. 322 (repr. No. 276); *The Oscar Schmitz Collection*, Wildenstein, 1936, No. 54; J. Leymarie, 1978 (color pl. No. 69).

Renoir
*Bather with Long Hair*,
Barnes Foundation,
Merion, Pennsylvania.

194

# Pierre-Auguste Renoir

## 88
## *Gabrielle and Jean*
(Gabrielle et Jean)

Oil on canvas. H. 65 cm.; W. 54 cm.
Signed on lower left in brown: Renoir
RF 1960-18

Jean Renoir has recorded the following recollections: "When I was still very little, three, four or five years old, my father did not choose my pose himself but took advantage of some occupation that seemed to make me hold still. The paintings of Jean playing with toy soldiers, eating his soup, moving his building blocks or looking at picture books were thus captured on canvas" (Jean Renoir, *Pierre-Auguste Renoir, mon père*, Paris, 1981, page 433). Renoir was an attentive father, and he joyfully compiled what amounts to a veritable family album recording the childhood of his sons, alone or with their mother, or, again, with one of the servants, usually the faithful Gabrielle. Gabrielle Renard (1879-1959) was related to the Charigot family, Renoir's in-laws; she joined the Renoir household staff when Madame Renoir was expecting her second child, who turned out to be Jean, the future cinematographer. In 1914, she left the Renoir's employ to marry an American painter, Conrad Hersler Slade, and died in San Francisco in 1959.

The painting entitled *Gabrielle and Jean* belongs to a vast array of contemporary works in which Renoir depicted Gabrielle and Jean, reflecting a broad range of techniques. The picture shown here doubtless dates from 1895-1896, considering the age of the child, who had been born in September 1894. There are also several directly related drawings. The most closely similar preparatory drawing is the one done in black chalk and sanguine, reproduced by Jean Leymarie (1978, No. 60, private collection; previously reproduced in *The Burlington Magazine*, March 1920). It differs in a few small details from the one in Ottawa's National Gallery of Canada, handled in black chalk (No. 63 of the Forty-third Exhibition of the Drawing Collection, Musée du Louvre, *De Raphaël à Picasso — Dessins de la Galerie Nationale du Canada (Ottawa)*, Paris, 1969-1970, reproduction; A. Vollard, 1918, No. 594). In her *Great Drawings of All Time*, New York, 1962, vol. III, No. 806, Agnes Mongan rightly sees a likeness between this drawing and the works reproduced by Vollard (*op. cit.*, Nos. 154 and 159) as well as a drawing in the collection of Mrs. Murray S. Danforth, Providence, Rhode Island (Agnes Mongan, *One Hundred Master Drawings*, Harvard University Press, Cambridge, Mass-

achusetts, 1949, reproduced on page 194). In this drawing, Renoir sketched two studies for the child's head, plus another showing him playing with Gabrielle and holding a rooster in his hand. This is hence a preliminary study for the slightly different version of *Gabrielle and Jean* in the Walter-Guillaume collection, in which, using a width-geared layout, more tightly designed around the models, Renoir represented an identical scene into which a few different details were introduced: the figurines are clearer and more numerous, a rooster replaces the cow in Gabrielle's right hand, and the lock of hair over her eye, in the painting in the Musée de l'Orangerie, has been swept to one side (former Durand-Ruel collection, reproduction No. 111 in M. Drucker, 1944, in which it is erroneously stated that Jean was born in 1893).

We find the same protagonists seated at a table, amid the same setting, in a painting in the collection of Mrs. H. Harris Jonas, New York (W. Pach, *Renoir, Leben und Werk*, Cologne, 1980, reproduction No. 61). Gabrielle is shown bending over the little boy, whose right arm is

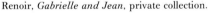

Renoir, *Gabrielle and Jean*, private collection.

# Pierre-Auguste Renoir

reaching out toward the fruit that is being offered him by a small girl seated on the left. She was a neighbor girl who lived in the same building as the Renoirs, and she called Jean "le beau petit Dan" whenever he smiled at her and stretched out his arm, as Gabrielle later reminded Jean.

This latter work, of which a sanguine drawing, devoted to the identical subject, was recently listed in an auction catalogue under the erroneous title of *Child Playing with Claude Renoir seated on Gabrielle's Lap* (Enghien, *Tableaux Modernes*, 13 December 1981, No. 128), is itself quite similar to certain prints (Delteil, L., *Le peintre graveur illustré*, vol. XVII, Paris, 1923, Nos. 50 and 54, and J. Leymarie and M. Melot, *Gravures impressionnistes*, Paris, 1971, reproduction 54), and particularly resembles an etching from 1896 (Delteil, No. 10; Leymarie and Melot, No. 10).

Comparable to this are a large pastel (56 × 76 cm.), in which the little girl is portrayed in a different pose (1970 *Renoir* exhibition, Aux Collettes, Domaine Renoir, Cagnes-sur-Mer, reproduction No. 8) and another, more roughly sketched pastel depicting Gabrielle and Jean alone, in half-length portraits (Sotheby auction, 31 March 1982, No. 62, under the title of *Suzanne and Jean*); in this work, which is similar to the print (Delteil, No. 10; Leymarie and Melot, No. 10), Jean, in the same white dress with a pink bow on the shoulder, has longer hair. The pastel

entitled *Portrait of Jean Renoir*, auctioned at Sotheby's on 1 December 1982, No. 14 (53.5 × 40.5 cm.), should be added to this series.

Another portrait on canvas showing Gabrielle and Jean, sometimes mistakenly listed as *Gabrielle and Coco* (private collection, Bührle, Zurich), is also part of this extensive series to which the picture in the Musée de l'Orangerie belongs.

The matt-complexioned brunette maidservant in dark blue contrasts with the Venetian-blond baby, whose white dress forms a vast, luminous expanse. Their left arms are touching closely in an affectionate pose, while the child's right hand attempts to imitate Gabrielle's, by grasping one of the figurines. The latter are sparsely brushed in and unobtrusive, and cause no break in continuity with the table in the foreground, which is handled not as a hard, inert object but as a soft, undulating material. The variegated surface area and the horizontal plane delimited thereby, somewhat indistinctly, echo the two large vertical bars in the background, which have been given a blurred treatment. These two wall sections, by their contrasts —material, appearance, size, neutral color on the left and multicolor on the right— breathe air into this painting, while at the same time, with the triangular surface of the table, providing geometrical planes that circumscribe the plastic reality of the two figures.                    H.G.

*Collections:*
A. Vollard (?); Paul Guillaume (?); Mrs. Jean Walter.

*Exhibitions:*
1944, Paris, Galerie Charpentier, *La vie familiale, Scènes et portraits*, No. 116 (repr.); 1966, Paris, No. 29 (repr.); 1967, Paris, Orangerie, *Vingt ans d'acquisitions du Musée du Louvre (1947-1967)*, No. 425 (repr.); 1980, Marcq-en-Barœul, Fondation Septentrion, *Impressionnisme*, No. 33; 1981, Paris, unnumbered.

*Literature:*
A. Vollard, 1918, vol. I, No. 104 (repr. p. 26); A. Vollard, *La vie et l'œuvre de Pierre-Auguste Renoir*, Paris, 1919, p. 184 (pl. 37); J. Leymarie, 1978 (color repr. No. 61).

Renoir, *Gabrielle and Jean*, Ottawa, National Gallery of Canada.

# Pierre-Auguste Renoir

## 89
### *Flowers in a Vase*
(Fleurs dans un vase)

Oil on canvas. H. 55 cm.; W. 46 cm.
Signed on lower right in red: Renoir
RF 1963-14

For this bouquet, Renoir assembled different plant species whose variety, appearance and color enable an artfully contrived arrangement, one that verges upon preciousness. The round table supporting the vase is suggested by a colored arc of a circle handled flat, which eliminates the effect of depth and proves that the artist was not indifferent to the investigations devoted to perspective by certain of his contemporaries. This boldness is tempered by the colored halo that envelops the flowers and that does restore the effect of depth. This still life, dated 1898 in *L'Atelier de Renoir* (volume 1, No. 194), has undertones of another painting of a bouquet of substantially the same size (40 × 35 cm.), arranged in the same vase set on a round table, represented, as it is here, by a colored band, with the same overall design and the same distribution of colored masses (reproduction in *La Renaissance de l'Art français et des Industries de luxe*, 1930, No. 1, Josse Hessel collection). The latter work, which displays a choice of flowers that, although less elaborate, is nevertheless closely similar to the one in the Walter-Guillaume collection, doubtless preceded it, or at least was painted at around the same time.

H.G.

*Collections:*
In Renoir's studio at the time of his death; Paul Guillaume (?); Mrs. Jean Walter.

*Exhibitions:*
1966, Paris, No. 30 (repr.); 1983, Paris, unnumbered.

*Literature:*
*L'Atelier de Renoir*, vol. 1, No. 194 (repr. pl.63); J. Bouret, "L'éblouissante collection Walter-Guillaume," *Réalités*, No. 239, December 1965.

# Pierre-Auguste Renoir

## 90

## *Yvonne and Christine Lerolle at the Piano*

(Yvonne et Christine Lerolle au piano)

Oil on canvas. H. 73 cm.; W. 92 cm.
Signed on lower right in red: Renoir
RF 1960-19

This picture, which was preceded by an extensive series of preparatory drawings employing sundry techniques —charcoal, sanguine, pencil— depicts the elder daughters of the painter Henry Lerolle (1848-1929). By their number and diversity, the various drawings testify to the care devoted by Renoir to the composition of this painting (one of them was reproduced by J. Rewald in *Renoir Drawings*, New York, 1946, No. 66, and over the last twenty years certain of them have been sold at auction, including a sale at Sotheby's on 14 April 1962; Galliéra, 10 and 11 December 1962; Sotheby's, 23 June 1965; Parke Bernet, 21 October 1971). In these drawings and sketches, the girls' heads are depicted at varying degrees of nearness to each other and bent down at different angles. One of the drawings is closely similar to the final version (Christie's auction, 30 June 1970, No. 51, previously auctioned at Sotheby's in 1962). It was exhibited at the Musée de l'Orangerie in 1958-1959 at the show entitled *De Clouet à Matisse, dessins français des collections américaines*, No. 182, at which time it was dated circa 1890. However, it is not possible to accept either this date or the one proposed by Meier-Graefe —1886— considering the ages of the two sisters; the elder, Yvonne, was born in 1877, while Christine, two years younger, was born in 1879. The two sisters married two brothers, Eugene and Louis Rouart.

The piano theme was frequent in paintings of the latter half of the nineteenth century, when pianos were everywhere in bourgeois drawing-rooms, and it was depicted several times by Renoir; it was particularly justified in the case of the Lerolle girls. Over and above the fashionableness of the subject, it evokes, as do the two Degas works shown on the background wall, the artistic environment by which the girls were surrounded. Their father, the painter Henry Lerolle, was a founding member of the Société Nationale des Beaux-Arts, and their mother's portrait had been painted in particular by Fantin-Latour (her portrait hangs in the Cleveland Museum of Art). The couple frequently entertained at social gatherings attended by painters, poets and musicians, including Maurice Denis, Mallarmé, Octave Maus, Debussy, and Ernest Chausson, who was married to Mrs. Lerolle's sister.

A photograph reproduced in the *Bulletin of the Cleveland Museum of Art*, December, 1977, page 341, shows the two of them with Degas. Henry Lerolle was also a collector, and had acquired the two Degas pastels represented here by Renoir —*The Dancers* and *Before the Race (Jockeys)* (P.A. Lemoine, *Degas et son œuvre*, 1946-1949, Nos. 486 and 702; Lemoine lists *The Dancers* as being represented in Renoir's painting but does not mention *Before the Race*). In a letter to Madame Bartholomé, Degas recounted the acquisition of this work, which was purchased by Lerolle from Durand-Ruel in 1884: "In agreement with his wife, who has the reputation of leading him, he has just bought a small painting of horses done by me from Durand-Ruel. And he has written admiringly about it to me (Saint-Simon style), is eager to entertain me with his friends... Allow me to become intoxicated with the elixirs of glory, on the other side of the water, behind Les Invalides, on Avenue Duquesne" (M. Guérin, *Lettres de Degas*, 1931, XXXVIII, and footnote page 61). The Lerolles lived at 20, Avenue Duquesne. Renoir likewise chose to evoke this aspect of Lerolle's personality when, in the background of a painting entitled *Christine Lerolle Embroidering* (Switzerland, private collection), more or less contemporary with *Yvonne and Christine Lerolle at the Piano*, he depicted their father examining his art collection in the company of the sculptor Louis-Henry Devillez, who was a fellow collector and to whom the Louvre is indebted for the bulk of its collection of Eugene Carrière's works.

In addition to these two paintings, Renoir did still others of these two girls, although he apparently never painted Guillaume and Jacques, the younger brothers. There are a *Portrait of Christine Lerolle* (reproduced in *Apollo*, November 1965, plate 1), a drawing entitled *Christine Lerolle in Profile, Sewing* (Renoir exhibition, Durand-Ruel, April 1921, No. 119) and also another portrait of Christine (Christie's auction, 28 June 1968, No. 95), prepared by a black pencil drawing (former Bernheim collection, Galerie Charpentier auction, 7 June 1935, No. 22). This portrait, dated 1897, allows a similar date to be assigned to the other works, which are clearly contemporary with one another, give or take a few months.

# Pierre-Auguste Renoir

This date is confirmed by cross-checking. Jeanne Baudot states that Renoir had contemplated the idea of depicting in a single painting the Gobillard children, their cousin Julie Manet —who would later marry Ernest, the brother of Eugene and Louis— and Yvonne and Christine Lerolle; he eventually abandoned this project and "limited himself to doing a few small pictures" (J. Baudot, *Renoir et ses amis, ses modèles*, Paris, 1949, page 48). A few pages later, she writes of "Renoir, who is busy at the Lerolles' house painting a portrait of Yvonne and Christine at the piano" while the Renoirs were living on rue de La Rochefoucauld (*ibid.*, page 67). The Renoirs had moved to this latter address in 1897.

Others of the artists who attended the Lerolles' social gatherings also painted "these two delightfully attractive girls," according to Maurice Denis. The latter, in 1897, revived the formula he had used in 1892 for his *Triple Portrait of Marthe as a Fiancée* (Museum in Saint-Germain-en-Laye) and painted his superb portrait of *Mademoiselle Yvonne Lerolle in Three Aspects* (former O. Rouart collection).

Renoir's approach, which evokes the cultivated atmosphere of the Lerolle home, is quite different. By the presence of the two sisters, he resumes his approach of the 1890s, when he was interested in depicting two girls engaged in the same occupation. He repeated this process a short time later, in *The Letter* (Sterling and Francine Clark Art Institute, Williamstown, Massachusetts), in which the models' poses, the contrast between the light and the dark dresses and the broader-than-high format recall *Yvonne and Christine Lerolle at the Piano*. H.G.

*Yvonne and Christine Lerolle*, photograph, private collection.

*Collections:*
Deposited with Durand-Ruel by the artist from 1 September 1914 to 27 July 1917; in Renoir's studio at the time of his death; with Knoedler - Bernheim-Jeune on a half-ownership basis; Knoedler share sold to Bernheim-Jeune on 18 May 1926; Switzerland, Galerie de l'Art Moderne, 22 October 1928; Rochecouste collection; anonymous [Rochecouste] auction, Hôtel Drouot, 10 June 1937, No. 53 (repr.); purchased at this auction on a half-ownership basis by Mrs. Paul Guillaume and Durand-Ruel, Paris, and later New York; Durand-Ruel share sold to Knoedler on 11 July 1947, and subsequently to Mrs. Jean Walter.

*Exhibitions:*
1944, San Francisco, California Palace of the Legion of Honor; 1966, Paris, No. 31 (repr.); 1981, Paris, unnumbered; 1985, London, No. 97 (color repr.); Paris, No. 95 (color repr.); Boston, No. 97 (color repr.)

*Literature:*
Meier-Graefe, 1929, No. 188, p. 253 (repr.); *L'atelier de Renoir*, vol. 1 (color repr. on cover), No. 201 (repr. pl. 65); *Cahiers d'Art*, 1936, Nos. VIII-X, p. 276 (repr.); S. Alexandrian, *La peinture impressionniste de A à Z*, No. 5, January-February 1974, p. 59 (color repr.).

Renoir, *Yvonne and Christine Lerolle at the Piano,*
private collection.

# Pierre-Auguste Renoir

## 91
### *Gabrielle in the Garden*
(Gabrielle au jardin)

Oil on canvas. H. 55 cm.; W. 46 cm.
Signed on lower left in brown: Renoir
RF 1963-18

Even after detaching himself from Impressionism, Renoir continued to be sharply aware of the play of light, and he enjoyed painting subjects in the open air, as witness his *Bathers*, depicted in a state of osmosis with nature. The full-length portrait shown here, of a figure standing amid trees, is more a pretext for expressing the play of light on vegetation and on a model than it is a truly individualized description. The pose of the model —is it really Gabrielle?— is closely similar to the pose in *The Woman with Basket* (A. Vollard, *La vie et l'œuvre de Pierre-Auguste Renoir*, Paris, 1919, repr. page 176) and, by the relationship between the figure and the landscape background, is reminiscent both of the latter work and of the painting entitled *Woman Walking on Grass* (M. Gangnat auction, 1925, No. 13). The technique —a light, misty scumble applied with a light brushstroke, the rendering of the plant life, frothy foliage and gently curving tree trunk, and the softness of the rounded female figure— foreshadows certain of the works produced in the 1910 decade, particularly the one entitled *Idyll in Cagnes* (J. Meier-Graefe, 1929, No. 356).                                        H.G.

*Collections:*
A. Vollard (?); Paul Guillaume (?); Mrs. Jean Walter.

*Exhibition:*
1966, Paris, No. 33 (repr.).

# Pierre-Auguste Renoir

## 92
## *Bouquet*
(Bouquet)

Oil on canvas. H. 40 cm.; W. 33 cm.
Signed on lower left in dark red: Renoir
RF 1963-15

Renoir was always interested in capturing the light that causes flower colors to vibrate. In Cagnes, he took a genuine delight in transcribing onto canvas evidence of nature's vitality. According to Vollard, "Madame Renoir always kept flowers in the house, arranged in those inexpensive, pretty green vases that caught Renoir's fancy in the shop windows" (A. Vollard, *En écoutant Cézanne, Degas, Renoir*, Paris, 1938, page 234). From this same period, there is a series of works in which is frequently seen the varnished vase cherished by Renoir, shown here filled with red poppies, roses and assorted other flowers. It is particularly recognizable in another painting that is almost the same in its size (41 × 33 cm.), technique, design layout and identical solid blue background, entitled *Anemones in a Vase on a Blue Ground* (private collection, New York, color reproduction in the catalogue of the Renoir exhibition, Japan, October 1971-February 1972, No. 36). It differs only in the choice of the flowers, the mixed bouquet having been replaced by anemones. H.G.

*Collections:*
A. Vollard (?); Paul Guillaume; Mrs. Jean Walter.

*Exhibitions:*
1929, Paris; 1966, Paris, No. 32 (repr.); 1981, Tbilisi-Leningrad, No. 37 (repr.).

*Literature:*
W. George, undated, p. 47 (repr. p. 41); *La Renaissance*, April 1929, No. 4 (repr. p. 180).

# Pierre-Auguste Renoir

## 93
## *Strawberries*

(Fraises)

Oil on canvas. H. 28 cm. ; W. 46 cm.
Signed on upper right in brown: Renoir
RF 1963-17

In Cagnes, Renoir painted several still lifes, most of them in the breadthwise format. The one shown here is constructed by distributing objects and fruits of different textures and shades, while he increasingly tended to disregard composition in favor of a simple arrangement of elements spread on a cloth. This work, dated circa 1905 by J. Meier-Graefe (*Auguste Renoir*, 1912, page 187), depicts accessories that were also used in other paintings. Thus, the fluted compote dish appears in another still life of the Walter-Guillaume collection, entitled *Peaches* No. 81, (see also *The Connoisseur*, January 1958); the same tea canister recurs in a small still life with apples, also in breadthwise format, reproduced in *L'Œil*, September 1978. However, the knife, which, together with the spoon shank emerging from the tea canister, is the only rigid element in the composition, is not a commonly recurring accessory in Renoir's works. (In a painting in the former Maurice Gangnat collection, M. Gangnat auction, June 1925, No. 24, a knife also offsets the straightness of a spoon shank.) Unlike Cézanne, Renoir seldom introduced inert objects into his still lifes.                                    H.G.

*Collections:*
A. Vollard (?); Paul Guillaume (?); Mrs. Jean Walter.

*Exhibitions:*
1942, Paris, Galerie Charpentier, *Les fleurs et les fruits depuis le romantisme*, No. 159; 1966, Paris, No. 34 (repr.); 1985, London, No. 104 (color repr.); Paris, No. 102 (color repr.); Boston, No. 104 (color repr.).

*Literature:*
J. Meier-Graefe, *Auguste Renoir*, Paris, 1912, p. 187 (repr.); J. Meier-Graefe, 1929, p. 381 (repr. No. 304).

# Pierre-Auguste Renoir

## 94
## *Recumbent Nude (Gabrielle)*
(Femme nue couchée [Gabrielle])

Oil on canvas. H. 67 cm.; W. 160 cm.
Unsigned
RF 1960-22

Although Renoir, expressing the full harmony between the female body and nature, painted many pictures of bathers, he seldom depicted his nudes in interior settings. Looking beyond Manet and his *Olympia*, beyond Ingres and his *Odalisques*, beyond Goya and his *Maja desnuda*, it is impossible not to establish the relationship between this *Recumbent Nude* and the nudes of Rubens and Titian —whose *Venus and the Organist* was so greatly admired by Renoir— which are as sensual as those of Renoir.

In 1912, Meier-Graefe did a comparison of three "large, breadthwise paintings that depict female nudes" (page 176). One of them, dated 1903, belonged to Durand-Ruel. The second, dated 1907, was the property of Mlle Dieterle. The third was in Renoir's home. Today, two of them are in the national collections: the *Recumbent Nude* of the Walter-Guillaume collection (which was in Renoir's studio at the time of his death) and the *Large Nude*, a 1975 bequest from Mr. and Mrs. Robert Kahn-Sriber (former Dièterle collection, RF 1975-18). The one dated 1903 (former Durand-Ruel collection), after passing through several ownerships, was included in an auction sale not long ago

(Christie's, 16 May 1977). Although there is a four-year difference between the painting in the former Durand-Ruel collection and the one received in 1975 by the French national museum authority, there is an unquestionable kinship between them, even if doubt is cast on the identity of the model (did Gabrielle pose for the 1907 paintings?). Of the three large nudes listed by Meier-Graefe, only the one in the Walter-Guillaume collection is neither dated nor signed. Comparison between it and the *Nude* in the former Durand-Ruel collection, of almost identical size (65.5 cm. × 155 cm.), shows a striking analogy between the two works. The upholstery of the sofa in our painting is handled less carefully, a curtain appears on the right (this work is of slightly greater width), Gabrielle's drapery is less extensively spread out, and her left leg is drawn under the right one. However, a detailed examination is necessary in order to distinguish between the two paintings.

In the absence of objective elements, it is hence difficult to pinpoint the date of the painting in the Walter-Guillaume collection. According to *L'Atelier de Renoir*, it is dated 1906 (volume 1, No. 339), while Vollard puts it at 1908 (vol. 1, No. 363). Certain scholars have put forward this date on the basis of the 1906 etching (Delteil, L., *Le peintre graveur illustré*, vol. XVII, Paris, 1923, Nos. 13 to 15). But the etching, which is based on the Durand-Ruel version and not on the Walter-Guillaume version, cannot constitute a reference element. In any case, it is impossible to consider any date posterior to 1907, the year in which Renoir delivered the painting into Durand-Ruel's custody (an operation that he repeated in 1914, as is shown by the gallery's records). In addition, it is fully as impossible to specify the sequence in which the pictures were painted, and it is equally conceivable that the Durand-Ruel *Nude* preceded the *Recumbent Nude* of the Walter-Guillaume collection, and vice versa. Lastly, let us note a large drawing remounted on canvas, and highlighted in sanguine, which appeared in 1958 and was auctioned a few years ago (Galliéra, 5 June 1970). This extremely linear work gives the impression of being a kind of tracing done from the Durand-Ruel *Nude*, which is of the same size, and it cannot shed light on the elaboration of the work with which we are concerned here, unless it is actually a transfer drawing.

*Collections:*
Deposited by the artist with Durand-Ruel from 18 July 1907 to 14 November 1907 and from 1 September 1914 to 27 July 1917; in Renoir's studio at the time of his death; A. Vollard (?); Paul Guillaume (?); Mrs. Jean Walter.

*Exhibitions:*
1927, Paris, Galerie Bernheim-Jeune, *Renoir*; 1939, Belgrade, Prince Paul Museum, *French Painting in the Nineteenth Century*, No. 100 (repr.); 1940, Montevideo, *Pintura francesa de los siglos XIX y XX, de David a nuestros dias*, No. 5; 1940, Rio de Janeiro, National Museum of Fine Arts, *Pintura francesa*, No. 88: 1941, Los Angeles, Los Angeles County Museum, *The Painting of France since the French Revolution*, No. 112; 1950, Paris, Galerie Charpentier, *Autour de 1900*, No. 147; 1966, Paris, No. 37, (repr.).

*Literature:*
J. Meier-Graefe, *Auguste Renoir*, Paris, 1912, footnote, p. 176; A. Vollard, 1918, vol. I, No. 363 (repr. p. 91); *L'Atelier de Renoir*, vol. I, No. 339 (repr. pl. 106); A. Vollard, "Renoir intime, ses modèles et ses bonnes," *La Renaissance de l'Art Français*, No. 3, March 1920 (repr. p. 109); M.P. Fouchet, *Les nus de Renoir*, Lausanne, 1974, p. 71 (repr.).

Other uncertainties surround this painting, i.e. in connection with the manner of its purchase. If we give credence to the catalogue of the Centennial Loan Exhibition, Duveen Galleries, New York, 1941, which displayed the Durand-Ruel version as No. 72, a second version had been in Pierre Renoir's possession. But it is attested that in 1939, this work belonged to Mrs. Paul Guillaume. If we concede that Duveen Galleries' information was not up-to-date in 1941, the plausible conclusion is that this was a relatively late purchase made by Paul Guillaume from Renoir's heirs, since the work was in the artist's studio at the time of his death (*L'Atelier de Renoir*, volume I, No. 339).                                         H.G.

Renoir, *Recumbent Nude*, former Durand-Ruel collection.

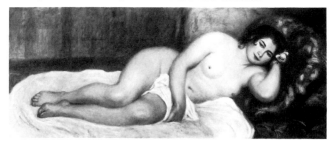

Renoir, *Large Nude*, Paris, Musée d'Orsay.

# Pierre-Auguste Renoir

## 95
### *Claude Renoir at Play*

(Claude Renoir jouant)

Oil on canvas. H. 46 cm.; W. 55 cm.
Signed on lower right in brown: Renoir
RF 1963-22

Of is three sons, Claude, born in 1901, was the one most frequently represented by Renoir. As Jean Renoir described matters in his own case, Renoir captured his children while they were engaged in some activity. So it was with Claude, absorbed in his game of tin soldiers, described by Ambroise Vollard as scattered over the floor in Renoir's studio, with the maid what's-her-name kept busy on hands and knees picking them up. (A. Vollard, *En écoutant Cézanne, Degas, Renoir*, Paris, 1938.)

Concurrently with *Claude Renoir at Play*, Renoir did an entire series of paintings portraying Claude busy with everyday activities. The paintings that most closely resemble the portrait in the Walter-Guillaume collection are unquestionably *The Small Head of Coco* (M. Gangnat auction, No. 157), and *Coco Writing* (private collection, Paris, reproduced in J. Leymarie, 1978, No. 74), in which Claude, dressed in a red outfit like the one in the Walter-Guillaume painting, emerges against an indeterminate background. Even more closely similar, despite the introduction of a second figure, is the painting entitled *Woman and Child (Coco) playing Dominoes* (given in memory of Governor Alvan T. Fuller by the Fuller Foundation). The neutral background, the slightly-from-above angle from which the table and the child are viewed, as if by a standing adult, are identical in every respect.

The date of 1905 supplied by *Coco Writing* can be used for *Claude Renoir at Play*. It was probably by mistake that this work was reproduced in *L'Atelier de Renoir* under the title of *Claude Renoir in Blue, Playing*. The child is obviously dressed in red. In addition, the date of 1910 that is listed is clearly wrong, since Claude, whom Renoir painted in 1909 (*Claude Renoir in Clown Costume*, No. 97), was not nine years old when this portrait was done.                                                                H.G.

*Collections:*
In Renoir's studio at the time of his death; Paul Guillaume (?); Mrs. Jean Walter.

*Exhibitions:*
1927, Berlin, A. Flechtheim Gallery, *Renoir*, No. 19; 1928, Berlin, A. Flechtheim Gallery, *Renoir*, No. 53; 1966, Paris, No. 35 (repr.).

*Literature:*
*L'Atelier de Renoir*, vol. I, No. 334 (repr. pl. 104); F. Daulte, *Auguste Renoir*, Milan, 1972, p. 64 (color repr. No. 1).

# Pierre-Auguste Renoir

## 96
## *Bouquet of Tulips*
(Bouquet de tulipes)

Oil on canvas. H. 44 cm.; W. 37 cm.
Signed on lower right in black: Renoir
RF 1963-20

As Renoir confided to his friend Georges Rivière, "Painting flowers is restful to my mind. I don't feel the same mental tension as when I am facing a model. When I paint flowers, I pose colors, I experiment with values dauntlessly" (Georges Rivière, *Renoir et ses amis*, Paris, 1921).

That is precisely what Renoir did in this work that is bursting with color, dated 1905 in *L'Atelier de Renoir*, in which, against the red background, there emerge the green of the hazily depicted half-length vase and the curving lines of the many-hued blooms.                    H.G.

*Collections:*
In Renoir's studio at the time of his death; A. Vollard (?); Paul Guillaume (in 1929); Mrs. Jean Walter.

*Exhibitions:*
1929, Paris; 1942, Galerie Charpentier, *Les fleurs et les fruits depuis le romantisme*, No. 154; 1966, Paris, No. 36 (repr.); 1981, Tbilisi-Leningrad, No. 38 (repr.).

*Literature:*
W. George, undated (repr. p. 40); *L'Atelier de Renoir*, vol. I, No. 312 (repr. pl. 96).

# Pierre-Auguste Renoir

## 97
### *Claude Renoir in Clown Costume*
(Claude Renoir en clown)

Oil on canvas. H. 120 cm.; W. 77 cm.
Signed and dated on lower right in grey: Renoir
RF 1960-17

For their father, Renoir's children, whom he frequently depicted when they were busy playing and unaware of his presence, were involuntary models portrayed with immense tenderness. Very seldom did he actually have them pose, as his youngest boy, Claude, did here, and as did also his son Jean, in 1910, for the painting entitled *Jean in Hunting Outfit*. Years later, Claude described these modelling sessions, in which he was dressed in the red silk costume for a morning's "duty," with woollen hose which made his legs itch, and which he exchanged for silk stockings after a break in the session (M. Robida, page 44). However, Claude, born in 1901 and aged about eight, was by no means impatient, because this way he could skip school!

This full-length portrait of the child, shown against a subdued setting of what are doubtlessly imaginary columns and in a timeless costume, is reminiscent of the portraits of the young princes and aristocrats painted by Velázquez and Goya. The beholder is reminded of the portrait of Don Manuel Osorio Manrique de Zuñiga (New York, Metropolitan Museum of Art), he of the absent-minded gaze, whose red costume and great white collar stand out against a neutral ground. This full-length por-

trait of Claude dressed as a clown, dated 1909, whom Renoir also depicted in a half-length portrait from the collar up (*The Collarette*, Galliéra auction, 10 December 1964, No. 156), is distinctly different from the many children's portraits that Renoir painted as commissions during the period 1875-1890. The child emerges more as a "red Pierrot" than as a clown, and his sumptuousness consists in the shimmering red harmonies of his timeless costume, suffused with warm tones that reflect and are amalgamated with the painting's neutral background; these glowing reds were of frequent occurrence in Renoir's works of his so-called "Venetian" period, and they are found, for example, in the painting entitled *Gabrielle in a Red Blouse* (New York, Maurice Wertheim collection).

Probably from the same period, there is a *Portrait of Claude* (Museum of Sao Paulo) showing him seated, in a left-side three-quarter view, recognizable by the fullness of his face, the mass of hair and the heavy fringe on his forehead.

A few years earlier, Jean Renoir had also posed for his father in a fancy-dress costume, for a painting entitled *The White Pierrot* (circa 1902, Detroit Institute of Arts, Detroit, Michigan, the Robert Hudson Tonnehil Bequest). This work, of smaller size (81 × 61 cm.) than *Claude Renoir in Clown Costume*, and displaying with equal magnificence the model's costume against a neutral background, was also the property of Paul Guillaume, after having remained in Renoir's studio and being part of Claude Renoir's collection. Does the same apply to the present *Claude Renoir in Clown Costume*, which also seems to be one of the works that had remained in Renoir's studio?

H.G.

*Collections:*
Deposited by the artist with Durand-Ruel from 1 September 1914 to 27 July 1917; in Renoir's studio at the time of his death; Claude Renoir (?); A. Vollard (?); Paul Guillaume (?); Mrs. Jean Walter.

*Exhibitions:*
1928, Berlin, Flechtheim Gallery, *Renoir*, No. 56 (?); 1938, Paris, Galerie Bernheim-Jeune, *Renoir*, No. 32; 1966, Paris, No. 38 (repr.); 1985, London, No. 110 (color repr.); Paris, No. 108 (color repr.); Boston, No. 110 (color repr.).

*Literature:*
A. Vollard, 1918, vol. I, No. 584 (repr. 147); *L'Atelier de Renoir*, vol. II, No. 374 (repr. pl. 120); A. Vollard, *Renoir intime, ses modèles et ses bonnes,"* La Renaissance de l'Art français, No. 3, March 1920 (repr. p. 111); G. Rivière, *Renoir et ses amis*, Paris, 1921, p. 241 (repr.); M. Robida, *Renoir, Portraits d'enfants*, Paris, 1959, p. 44; F. Daulte, "Renoir, son œuvre regardé sous l'angle d'un album de famille," *Connaissance des Arts*, No. 153 (repr. pl. 27); *La peinture impressionniste de A à Z*, "Le monde des grands musées" collection, No. 5, January-February 1974, p. 61 (color repr.); H. Leppien, *Der zerbrochene Kopf*, Hamburg, Kunsthalle, 1981 (repr.).

Renoir, *The Collarette*,
private collection.

# Pierre-Auguste Renoir

## 98
## *Seated Bather Drying Her Leg*
(Baigneuse assise s'essuyant une jambe)

Oil on canvas. H. 51 cm.; W. 41 cm.
Signed on lower right in red: Renoir
RF 1963-26

By her pose, this *Seated Bather*, which is the last in date of the Renoir nudes in the Walter-Guillaume collection, bears a resemblance to the earliest one, dated 1883. However, aside from the common gesture, there is no similarity. The approach to the nude, to her volumes, to the shimmering of the light on her skin is markedly different. The long, juxtaposed brushstrokes have replaced the sleekness of the matter, and the background dissolves into an artistic disarray of multicolored strokes echoed by the white and red draperies.

This work, assigned the date of 1914 by J. Meier-Graefe (1929, p. 413), is closely similar to the *Bathers* in the Barnes Foundation (reproduction in M. Drucker, 1955, No. 138).

There are three other works, of slightly smaller sizes, reproduced in *L'Atelier de Renoir* (vol. II, plate 171, Nos. 542, 543 and 544), which are comparable from the standpoints of both subject and handling to this *Seated Bather Drying Her Leg*. In *L'Atelier de Renoir*, these works are dated, respectively, 1916-1918, 1915-1919, and 1918.

H.G.

*Collections:*
Paul Rosenberg; A. Barnes; Paul Rosenberg; Paul Guillaume (in 1924); Mrs. Jean Walter.

*Exhibitions:*
1929, Paris; 1966, Paris, No. 40 (repr.).

*Literature:*
*Les Arts à Paris*, No. 9, April 1924, p. 9 (repr.); W. George, undated, pp. 44-45 (repr. p. 39); J. Meier-Graefe, 1929, p. 413 (repr. No. 383).

# Pierre-Auguste Renoir

## 99
## *Blonde Girl with Rose*
(Blonde à la rose)

Oil on canvas. H. 64 cm.; W. 54 cm.
Signed on lower right in black: Renoir
RF 1963-27

This portrait is typical of Renoir's last manner by its tonalities, in which dominates the violence of a red untempered by the touches of the other colors, by the general blurredness that affects the figure, and by heavy application of the paint which, although thick, reveals the texture of the canvas in places.

The young woman has been identified as Andrée-Madeleine Heuschling (1900-1979), nicknamed Dédée, Renoir's last model, concerning whom he commented as follows: "She is so lovely! I have worn out my ageing eyes on her youthful skin, and I realized that I am not a master, but a child." An actress, performing under the stage name of Catherine Hessling, she married Jean Renoir in 1920 and acted in several of his films, including *Nana*, his adaptation of Zola's novel in 1927. This portrait bears a haunting resemblance to the one in the Petit Palais (J. Laffon, *Catalogue sommaire illustré des peintures*, Paris, 1982, No. 708), in which Dédée, portrayed half-length in a three-quarters left-side view, is wearing the same low-necked gown and is also holding a rose. Even more closely similar is the portrait entitled *Andrée Full-face in Pink on a Blue Ground*, reproduced in *L'Atelier de Renoir* and dated, in that publication, at 1915 (vol. II, plate 154,

No. 482). The young woman portrayed half-length is in exactly the same pose as in the painting in the Walter-Guillaume collection, and the impression conveyed is that this latter painting was a later development of this portrait.

Although dated 1918 in *L'Atelier de Renoir*, Meier-Graefe lists it at 1915; this latter date is also accepted by Marie-Thérèse Lemoyne de Forges (Paris, 1966), through comparison with the portrait of *Tilla Durieux* (New York, Metropolitan Museum of Art dated 1914). The similitude of the poses is indeed astonishing; however, in *Tilla Durieux*, the color red dominates without being aggressive, and the form is more clearly delineated. If the pose of the *Blonde Girl with Rose* is reminiscent of *Tilla Durieux*, the manner in which it is handled is closer to that of *Woman with Bouquet* (M. Gangnat sale, 1925, No. 149), of *Woman with Mandolin* (New York, Hillman collection) or of *The Concert* (New York, P. Rosenberg collection), which the scholars agree date from the very last years of Renoir's life. However, this work, which is clearly visible in a photograph of Renoir's studio shot by George Besson in 1917, cannot be posterior to that date. It was in the artist's studio at the time of his death and eventually became the property of his son Claude.                                                    H.G.

*Collections:*
In Renoir's studio at the time of his death; Claude Renoir; Paul Guillaume (in 1929); Mrs. Jean Walter.

*Exhibitions:*
1928, Berlin, Flechtheim Gallery, *Renoir*, No. 58 (repr. p. 7); 1929, Paris; 1963, Marseilles, Musée Cantini, *Renoir*, No. 48; 1966, Paris, No. 41 (repr.); 1980, Athens, No. 33 (color repr.); 1980, Paris, Conservatoire National des Arts et Métiers, *Image et magie du cinéma français*, No. F 2 (repr.); 1981, Tblisi-Leningrad, No. 41 (repr.).

*Literature:*
G. Rivière, *Renoir et ses amis*, 1921, Paris (inset color reproduction, facing, p. 116); W. George, undated, p. 13 (repr.); J. Meier-Graefe, 1929, p. 414 (repr. No. 278); *L'Atelier de Renoir*, vol. II, No. 675 (repr. pl. 212).

Renoir, *Tilla Durieux*,
New York,
Metropolitan Museum.

# Pierre-Auguste Renoir

## 100
## *Woman in Hat*

(Femme au chapeau)

Oil on canvas. H. 26 cm.; W. 26 cm.
Signed on upper right in brown: Renoir
RF 1963-21

Renoir painted countless portraits of women, including several depicting women wearing hats. The artist made extensive use of this accessory in the composition and chromatic effects of his paintings. This very small picture can be compared with other portraits of *Woman in Hat* of equally small size (*Young Girl in Straw Hat*, 20 × 17 cm., Sotheby auction, 1 December 1965, No. 19; *Woman Resting her Chin in her Hands*, 25 × 23 cm., Galliéra sale, 16 June 1964, No. 152; *Head of Woman*, 28.5 × 22 cm., Sotheby auction, 2 December 1981, No. 33). In these, as in the *Woman with Hat* (51 × 41 cm., Christie's, 30 March 1981), and the Half-length *Portrait of a Woman* (32 × 38 cm., Christie's, 29 March 1982), can be seen the same wide, faintly labored, even slightly inconsistent brushstrokes and the scumble that reveals the texture of the canvas, which are characteristic of Renoir's last works and which are grounds for dating this portrait as of the period 1915-1919. In 1910, Renoir had already used a broad-brimmed, deep-crown hat worn by the woman in the foreground of the composition entitled *Claude Renoir and the Two Maids* (M. Drucker, 1945, No. 127).

Paul Guillaume owned another portrait of a woman entitled *The Naked Shoulder* (33 × 30 cm., sale at Galerie Georges Giroux, Brussels, 11 March 1949), featuring the same stylistic particularities, as well as the round, rather soft face, the unfocussed gaze and the fleshy lips of the model in *Woman in Hat*.                                    H.G.

*Collections:*
A. Vollard (?); Paul Guillaume; Mrs. Jean Walter.

*Exhibitions:*
1966, Paris, No. 39 (repr.).

# Pierre-Auguste Renoir

## 101
## *Woman Leaning on her Elbow*
(Femme accoudée)

Oil on canvas. H. 23 cm.; W. 32 cm.
Signed on lower right in brown: Renoir
RF 1963-28

This portrait of a *Woman Leaning on her Elbow* appears below and to the right of a painting containing several motifs, reproduced in *L'Atelier de Renoir* (volume II, plate 134, No. 413, "Heads of Women and Landscapes," 52 × 56 cm.). Above it is a half-length portrait of the same model in a profile view, her right hand reaching forward toward the spectator. This canvas therefore was cut up on the basis of its various motifs after Renoir's death.

The *Woman Leaning on her Elbow* compares with the *Woman in Hat* in the Walter-Guillaume collection (No. 100) by its stylistic characteristics, by its long, light brushstrokes whose uneven pressure reveals the texture of the canvas, by the blurred image of the model, by the handling of the face, by the identical rendering of the eyes, nose and mouth, and by the small size of the canvas; both

these works belong to the last few years of Renoir's career. In *L'Atelier de Renoir*, there is a reproduction of a very similar figure (*Woman in Green Blouse Leaning on her Right Elbow*, reproduction No. 620), dated 1917 by the author, whereas the M. Gangnat collection contained a *Woman Leaning on her Elbow* in which the model was dressed in red, in a very small format (18 × 20 cm.), dated 1911 in the sales catalogue (M. Gangnat auction, 1925, No. 50). The pose of a woman resting on one elbow also appeared in a composition of Renoir's later years, entitled *The Concert* (Ontario Gallery of Art, Toronto, gift of the Reuben Wells Leonard Estate), in which a young woman is depicted with her right elbow resting on a small, round table and her head in her hand, listening meditatively to a mandolin player seated at her feet.                          H.G.

*Collections:*
In Renoir's studio at his death; Paul Guillaume (in 1929); Mrs. Jean Walter.

*Exhibitions:*
1929, Paris; 1966, Paris, No. 42 (repr.); 1969, Troyes, Musée des Beaux-Arts, *Renoir et ses amis*, No. 23.

*Literature:*
W. George, undated, p. 16 (repr.); *L'Atelier de Renoir*, vol. II, No. 413 (pl. 134).

# Henri Rousseau, called Le Douanier

Laval, 1844-Paris, 1910

## 102
### The Storm-tossed Vessel
(Le navire dans la tempête)

Oil on canvas. H. 54 cm.; W. 65 cm.
Signed with brush on lower left, in yellow: Henri Rousseau
RF 1960-27

This painting is a fairly unusual work in Rousseau's production. The artist had let it be thought (and Apollinaire claimed to have been taken in by this fable, of which he was a propagator) that he had participated in the French military expedition to Mexico (1862-1867), whereas in actuality he had never traveled, and in all probability never went aboard a ship. A large number of the works of this confirmed Parisian city dweller are, by a kind of compensatory effect, an invitation to travel and to escapism.

Rousseau no doubt got the elements for this curious composition from a street-fair stand representing a ship riding into a storm, or from a diorama at the 1889 world's fair. This would explain the appearance of the ocean waves, which look as if they had been punched out of a sheet of metal: they are faintly reminiscent of those in Hokusai's famous wood-block print. For the ship itself, the source was probably a picture from an illustrated magazine. In this vessel, Y. Le Pichon (p. 123) has discerned the characteristic silhouette of the cruiser Entrecasteaux, with its off-centered third smokestack; it was launched in 1896.

Whatever his models, here, once again, Rousseau has interpreted them freely. In addition, this painting is further evidence of his interest in the innovations of his time. For example, over a long period, Rousseau remained the only painter who had ventured to depict the Eiffel tower (if we except Seurat, who produced a rough sketch that was recently acquired by the California Palace of the Legion of Honor in San Francisco), as well as dirigible balloons and airplanes. In this depiction of a seagoing vessel, with flags flying, sailing into the storm, Rousseau renewed his thematics by exalting a prestigious achievement of France's national industry and military forces.        M.H.

*Collections:*
A. Vollard, Paris; Paul Guillaume (1931); Mrs. Jean Walter.

*Exhibitions:*
1933, Basel, No. 34; 1935, Paris, Petit Palais, No. 414; 1935, Paris, Galerie des Beaux-Arts show, No. 123; 1951, New York, No. 1; 1961, Paris, No. 20; 1964, Rotterdam, Paris, No. 9 (repr.); 1966, Paris, No. 43 (repr.); 1981, Tbilisi-Leningrad, No. 42 (repr.); 1982, Paris, Salon des Indépendants (repr.); 1984-1985, Paris, New York, No. 15 (color repr.).

*Literature:*
A. Basler, 1927, pl. 35; C. Zervos, Paris, 1927, pl. 29; W. George, "Le miracle de Rousseau," *Les Arts à Paris*, No. 18, July 1933, fig p. 11; R. Grey, 1943, pl. 61; J. Bouret, 1961, pp. 10 and 256, fig. 110, p. 200; D. Vallier, 1961, pp. 42, 43, 132, fig. 54, p. 307; D. Vallier, 1970, new edition in 1981, figure and commentary, 57, pl. XXIII; L. and O. Bihalji-Merin, Dresden, 1971, fig. 9, p. 44; A. Jakovsky, "Le Douanier Rousseau savait-il peindre?" *Médecine de France*, January 1971 (repr.); V. Nezval, Insita 4, Bratislava, 1972, p. 79; C. Keay, 1976, p. 128 (repr.); F. Elgar, Paris, 1980, pl. 22; Y. Le Pichon, 1981, fig. p. 123.

# Henri Rousseau

## 103
### *Chair Factory in Alfortville*
(La fabrique de chaises à Alfortville)

Oil on canvas: H. 73 cm., W. 92 cm.
Signed on lower right: Henri Rousseau
RF 1963-32

## 104
### *Chair Factory*
(La fabrique de chaises)

Oil on canvas. H. 38 cm.; W. 46 cm.
Signed on lower right: Henri Rousseau
RF 1960-28

In Henri Rousseau's works, the landscapes of suburban Paris are generally based on first-hand, careful observation of a seemingly insignificant site; in this painting, it is a chair factory in Alfortville, a suburb southeast of Paris, which he infuses with the harsh poetry of a theatre set for a naturalist play, contrasting with the exotic charm of his tropical landscapes. This is one of the few pictures of a fairly large size that he painted of a townscape. It was done with particularly painstaking care, notably as concerns the sky, in the depiction of which Rousseau displays mastery of the art of traditional painting. The shaping of the clouds, the tonal relationship between their color and the blue of the sky are nearly the same as in Poussin's skies (a close-up comparison clearly confirms this fact), and, as in the case of Poussin's works, a recent cleaning has greatly attenuated the yellowing of the painting.

The starkly rigid lines of the buildings are represented with what amounts to schoolboy diligence, with no consistent abidance by the principles of linear perspective. However, the principal axes are arranged in accordance with the golden section. The curving edge of the sidewalk and of the banks of the Seine are the only features that soften and enliven the composition; the only figures are those of a few passersby and an angler.

There is a temptation to view the small version (No. 104) as a preparatory sketch for the large painting (No. 103), which, by its careful brushwork and big size, can certainly be identified as the painting presented at the 1897 Salon des Indépendants. However, the size of the smaller version is distinctly larger than that of the other known sketches for this work. It is hence more plausible to view it as a copy, painted several years afterwards, when Rous-

seau's success was leading him to repeat certain earlier compositions.

It differs from the larger version in several ways: lower line of the horizon, modifications in the outlines of the roads and the river banks, different locations for the figures; all these details enabled Rousseau to better suggest perspective.

M.H.

---

103

*Collections:*
Paul Guillaume (1931); Mrs. Jean Walter.

*Exhibitions:*
1897, Paris, Petit Palais, No. 417-d, Salon des Indépendants; 1931, New York; 1933, Basel, No. 16; 1935, Paris; 1935, Paris, Galerie des Beaux-Arts exhibition, No. 122; 1937, Paris, No. 3; 1937, Zurich, No. 3; 1950, Paris, Galerie Charpentier, *Autour de 1900*, No. 153 (repr.); 1961, Paris, No 77 (repr.); 1964, Rotterdam, Paris, No. 8; 1966, Paris, No. 45 (repr.); 1980, Athens, No. 34 (repr. p. 180); 1981 Tbilisi-Leningrad, No. 43 (repr.); 1982, Tokyo, Bridgestone Museum-Hiroshima, Municipal Museum, *Figurations révolutionnaires de Cézanne à aujourd'hui*, No. 3 (color repr.); 1984-1985, Paris, New York, No. 18 (color repr.).

*Bibliographie:*
H. Kolle, 1922, p. 17; F. Fels, "En marge de l'exposition Rousseau à la Marie Harriman Gallery, New York. Exposition de toiles réunies par Paul Guillaume et Marie Harriman," *Formes*, No. 11, January 1931; W. George "Le miracle de Rousseau," *Les Arts à Paris,*" No. 18, July 1931 (repr. p. 5); P. Courthion, *Henri Rousseau dit Le Douanier*, Geneva, 1944, pl. 37; D. Vallier, 1961, fig. 146 (repr.); J. Bouret, 1961, fig. 106, p. 198; H. Certigny, 1961, p. 17; D. Vallier, 1970, new edition in 1981, pl. XX, figure and commentary No. 103; A. Jakovski, "Le Douanier Rousseau savait-il peindre?", *Médecine de France*, No. 218, 1971, repr.: P. Descargues, 1972, p. 37 (repr.), p. 86; D. Larkin, 1975, pl. 14; C. Keay, 1976, p. 128 (repr.); F. Elgar, 1980, fig. 18; Y. Le Pichon, 1981 (repr. p. 120).

103

104

104

---

*Collections:*
Paul Guillaume (1931); Mrs. J. Walter.

*Exhibitions:*
1933, Basel, No. 20; 1935, Paris, G.B.A. exhibition, No. 124; 1951, New York; 1960, Paris, M.N.A.M., *Les sources du XXᵉ siècle. Les Arts en Europe de 1884 à 1914*, No. 621; 1964, Salzburg; 1966, Paris, No. 44 (repr.); 1982, Paris, Salon des Indépendants, unnumbered.

*Literature:*
W. George, "Le miracle de Rousseau," *Les Arts à Paris*, No. 18, July 1931, fig. p. 7; R. Grey, 1943, pl. 82; J. Bouret, 1961, fig. 11, p. 81; D. Vallier, 1961, p. 141, fig. 147; J. Cassou, E. Langui, N. Pevsner, *Les sources du XXᵉ siècle*, Paris, 1961, fig. 115; D. Vallier, 1970, new edition 1981, fig. and commentary 103-B; C. Keay, 1976, inset color plate; 1984, Paris, not listed in catalogue (black and white repr. p. 146).

# 105
## *The Cliff*
(La falaise)

Oil on canvas. H. 21 cm.; W. 35 cm.
Signed on lower letf: Henri Rousseau
RF 1960-29

This small painting, handled with light, thin applications of paint, is one of Rousseau's few "seascapes." It has been suggested by M.-T. Lemoyne de Forges (1966 catalogue, No. 46) that Rousseau may have drawn his inspiration from Claude Monet, who happened to have just exhibited a series of paintings entitled *Cliffs at Pourville*, at the Georges Petit Gallery, in 1891. Catton Rich (1946, p. 49) and Y. Le Pichon (1981, p. 122) claim that there is a hint of Courbet's influence. Le Pichon has reproduced a detail of a cliff with boats by Courbet (entitled *Seashore, Cliff at Etretat*, Fernier II, No. 879), the design of whose composition is repeated almost exactly, but in reverse. The Normandy coast cliffs inspired such a large number of artists in the late ninetenth century that Rousseau, concerned with varying his thematics, had no need to copy any specific predecessor in order to deal with this motif.

D. Vallier (V4) excludes this painting from Rousseau's works. Despite a certain weakness of execution, especially in the figures, we, along with other scholars, believe it to be authentic. Moreover, this painting has a kind of monumental dignity that is out of keeping with its small size. The fact that there are only very few certified authentic Rousseau paintings devoted to a similar subject makes a decision difficult, and laboratory examinations have failed to adduce any decisive findings.          M.H.

*Collections:*
Paul Guillaume (in 1929); Mrs. Jean Walter.

*Exhibitions:*
1931, New York; 1933, Basel, No. 12; 1936, Paris, No. 128; 1950, Venice, No. 21; 1951, New York; 1961, Paris, No. 17; 1964, Rotterdam-Paris, No. 7 (repr.); 1966, Paris, No. 46 (repr.).

*Literature:*
*Les Arts à Paris*, January 1929, No. 16, fig. p. 23; C. Roger-Marx, "La maison d'un collectionneur," *L'Art vivant*, 1935, fig. p. 191; D. Catton-Rich, New York, 1946, p. 49; J. Bouret, 1961, fig. 92, p. 192; D. Vallier, 1970, new edition 1981, fig. and commentary V4; H. Certigny, 1971, pp. 92-93; A. Jakovsky, "Le Douanier Rousseau savait-il peindre?", *Médecine de France*, January 1971, (repr.); C. Keay, 1976, p. 123 (repr.); F. Elgar, Paris, 1980 (color fig. 21); Y. Le Pichon, 1981, p. 122 (repr.).

# Henri Rousseau

## 106
## *The Anglers*
(Les pêcheurs à la ligne)

Oil on canvas. H. 46 cm.; W. 55 cm.
Signed on lower left: H. Rousseau
RF 1963-31

Rousseau was highly concerned with finding models or guaranteed subjects in the art of the past, and also very mindful of the technical discoveries of his day; he portrayed dirigibles and airplanes on several occasions. He had "seen a reproduction of Goya's *The Balloon*, had read Jules Verne's tale entitled *Five Weeks in a Balloon*, published in *Le Musée des Familles*, and had observed Bartholdi's monument to the memory of the aeronauts of the siege of Paris. The grand prix balloon race in 1900, the test flights of Santos Dumont in 1901 were familiar to him... as were the flights of the *Lebaudy* and *Patrie* balloons over Meudon in 1906, and the exploits of Blériot, Voisin, Farman and Delagrange, all of which were front-page news" (Le Pichon, pages 98-99). However, he probably did not know *The Balloon* painted by Puvis de Chavannes. Rousseau, imitated only by his great admirer Robert Delaunay and by Roger de La Fresnaye, dared to introduce into his paintings both the "flying machines" and the Eiffel tower, which were symbols of escapism but also of communication between men.

The biplane shown here is that of Wilbur Wright, demonstrated in France in 1908; it recurs in several other Rousseau paintings, notably twice in company with the balloon *Patrie*, represented in the form in which it flew as early as 1907 (D. Vallier, 1951, No. 118). The present painting is hence of a date close to 1908, perhaps slightly posterior. The actual landscape consists of a sort of clutter of elements, which Rousseau uses rather like the pieces of a puzzle, and their choice and positions vary from one picture to the next: houses with carefully aligned windows, factory chimneys, trees, and anglers, whose dark figures stand out against the light. The middle ground is occupied by a curiously incurvated beach, whose characteristic shape occurs in several of Rousseau's paintings. Here, with the tiered arrangement of the houses on the right, he uses it to suggest depth.                                        M.H.

*Literature:*
A. Basler, Paris, 1927, pl. 22; C. Zervos, *Rousseau*, 1927, pl. 28; W. George, "Le miracle de Rousseau," *Les Arts à Paris*, No. 18, July 1931, p. 9 (repr.); R. Grey, 1943, pl. 80; J. Bouret, 1961, fig. 33 p. 124; D. Vallier, 1961, No. 120; D. Vallier, 1970, new edition 1981, No. 208 (repr.); V. Nezval, *Insita 4*, Bratislava, 1972, p. 79; C. Keay, 1976, inset color plate; B. Dorival, "Robert Delaunay et l'œuvre du Douanier Rousseau," *L'œil*, No. 267, October 1977, pp. 19-20, footnote 8; F. Elgar, 1980, fig. 44; H. Certigny, "Le Douanier Rousseau et la source du centenaire de l'Indépendance," *L'Œil*, No. 309, April 1981, fig. No. 4, p. 64.

"Gala aviation week," supplement to
*Le Petit Journal*, 5 september 1909.

## 107
## *Strollers in a Park*
(Promeneurs dans un parc)

Oil on canvas. H. 46 cm.; W. 55 cm.
Signed on lower left with brush in white: H. Rousseau
RF 1963-30

By its subject and its size, this painting belongs to a small group of urban landscapes combining houses and a curtain of greenery. The figures of a few strollers lend animation to the scene without suggesting any precise anecdote. The sundry titles assigned to this painting are vague, except the one given by A. Basler (1927, *A Scene in Viroflay*), which has been neither confirmed nor infirmed.

D. Vallier (No. 204) deems this to be "a hastily turned out work, surely prompted by the demand." Rousseau, to whom success came late in life, no doubt indulged himself by painting pictures in which his creativeness did not always emerge. However, he remained consistently able to confer his distinctive stamp along with a personal meaning —legible, albeit perhaps unconscious— on the most ordinary, unpicturesque scene. The closed-in space shown here, with its opaque walls, is not a Van Gogh-style prison yard.

In this painting, it is true, Rousseau did not introduce a balloon, an aeroplane or the distant outline of the Eiffel Tower, three symbols he frequently used to interpret an invasion skywards. But the presence of the open door on the right, the expanse of foliage looming beyond the archway or tunnel, the variety and the isolation of the figures are sufficient to suggest a peaceful rather than a prison-like atmosphere.

M.H.

*Collections:*
A. Vollard, Paris; Paul Guillaume (in 1931); Mrs. Jean Walter.

*Exhibitions:*
1923, Prague, *Vystava Francouszského uméni XIX. a XX Stoleti*, No. 230; 1931, New York; 1933, Basel, No. 33; 1935, Paris, Petit Palais, No. 418; 1937, Paris, No. 19; 1937, Zurich, No. 14; 1944, Paris No. 15; 1950, Venice, No. 8; 1957, Paris, Galerie Charpentier, *Cent Chefs-d'œuvre de l'art français, 1750-1950*, No. 84; 1960, Paris, Maison de la Pensée française, *La peinture naïve française du Douanier Rousseau à nos jours*, No. 53 (repr.); 1961, Paris, No. 19 (repr.); 1964, Rotterdam-Paris, No. 19 (repr.); 1966, Paris, No. 50 (repr.); 1966, Paris, No. 50 (repr.); 1979, Paris, Palais de Tokyo, *Le paysage de Corot à Bonnard*, unnumbered.

*Literature:*
A. Basler, 1927, pl. 25; C. Zervos, Paris, 1927, pl. 32; W. George, "Le miracle de Rousseau," *Les Arts à Paris*, No. 18, July 1931, fig. p. 8; R. Grey, 1943, pl. 51; P. Courthion, Geneva, 1944, pl. 44; J. Bouret, 1961, fig. 40 p. 139; D. Vallier, 1961, fig. 117; D. Vallier, 1970, new edition 1981, fig. 204, pl. 38; A. Jakovsky, "Le Douanier Rousseau savait-il peindre?," *Medecine de France*, January 1971 (repr.); D. Larkin, 1975, fig. 22; C. Keay, 1976, p. 154 (repr.); F. Elgar, Paris, 1980, fig. 41; Y. Le Pichon, 1981, p. 96 (repr.).

# 108
## *Child with Doll*
(L'enfant à la poupée)

Oil on canvas. H. 67 cm.; W. 52 cm.
Signed on lower right in black paint: H. J. Rousseau
RF 1963-29

Like many of Rousseau's figures, this child is depicted full face as regards her head and torso. The same frontality and the same reduction to the space (did Rousseau get the idea from Gauguin?) are observed in the face, the collar, the doll and the daisy that the child is clasping. The evenly-patterned distribution of the polka dots on the dress abolishes volumes, as in Bonnard's figures at the height of the Nabi period (*The Checkered Blouse*, 1892, Paris, Musée d'Orsay).

Rousseau always experienced considerable difficulty in "setting" his figures on the ground. D. Vallier notes, however, that this painting shows progress as compared with the one entitled *Child with Rocks* (National Gallery, Washington, D.C.). The child's legs look as if they are sunk down into a carpet of grass sown with tiny flowers, which bears a resemblance to late medieval tapestry designs, with which Rousseau was familiar. The decreasing sizes of the white, red and black flowers, as well as the increasingly darker shadings of green, suggest the perspective of distance. The important use of the color red is of infrequent occurrence in Rousseau's work. It is even totally absent from many of his canvasses.

The face is handled with a degree of application that verges on awkwardness. We propose that this is the same face, at a slightly later age, as the one in the model for *Child with Punchinello* (DV 145, Winterthur, Kunstverein), which D. Vallier claims can be identified with a picture exhibited at the 1903 Salon des Indépendants, entitled *To Fête Baby*. In this case, the picture shown here could be dated circa 1904-1905. Only four children's portraits by Rousseau are known. In addition to those noted above, he depicted a seated infant (DV 177, 60 × 49 cm., Sotheby auction, New York, 18 February 1982, No. 15). Rousseau seems to have attached importance to this painting. He gave a photograph of it to his friend Max Weber, the painter, when the latter left Paris in late 1908 (cf. S. Leonard, *Rousseau and Max Weber*, New York, 1970, page 20, footnote 31). M.H.

*Collections:*
Wilhelm Uhde, Paris; Uhde sale, Drouot auction house, 30 May 1921 (wartime sequestration), No. 57, repr.; J. Quinn, New York; Paul Guillaume (in 1927); Mrs. Jean Walter.

*Exhibitions:*
1933, Basel, No. 35; 1935, Paris, G.B.A. exhibition, No. 129; 1936, New York, Museum of Modern Art, No. 248; 1937, Paris, No. 5 (repr.); 1944, Paris, No. 13 (repr.); 1949, Paris, Galerie Charpentier, *L'Enfance*, No. 184 (repr.); 1950, Venice, No. 7; 1951, New York, No. 12; 1960, Paris, Galerie Charpentier, No. 90 (repr.); 1961, Paris, No. 13 (repr.); 1964, Rotterdam-Paris, No. 13 (repr.); 1966, Paris, No. 48 (repr.); 1981, Tbilisi-Leningrad, No. 44 (repr.); 1982, Paris, unnumbered; 1983, Paris, Centre Georges-Pompidou, M.N.A.M., *Hommage à Wilhelm Uhde*, no catalogue; 1984-1985, Paris, New York, No. 34 (color repr.).

*Literature:*
W. Uhde, Paris, 1911, p. 47; W. Uhde, *Rousseau*, Paris, 1914, pl. 6; H. Kolle, 1922, pl. 4; C. Zervos, Paris, 1927, pl.19; A. Basler, 1927, pl. 11; W. George, undated, p. 55, fig. p. 58; R. Grey, 1943, pl. 11; C. Gerraton, "Laurier et topinambours, une fort simple explication de l'art exotique du Douanier Rousseau," *Les Arts*, 9 September 1949, p. 1, fig. p. 5; J. Bouret, 1961, fig. 169 p. 222; D. Vallier, 1961, pl. 105; C. Roger-Marx "Les enchantements du Douanier Henri Rousseau à la Galerie Charpentier, un ensemble jamais réuni," *Le Figaro littéraire*, 11 November 1961 (repr.); S. Léonard, *Rousseau and Max Weber*, New York, 1970, footnote 31, p. 20; D. Vallier, 1970, new edition 1981, fig. and commentary 207, pl. XLII; L. and O. Bihalji-Merin, Dresden, 1971, p. 22, fig. 29; D. Larkin, 1975, pl. 26; C. Keay, 1976, p. 147 (repr.); F. Elgar, Paris, 1980, fig. 42; Y. Le Pichon, 1981 p. 62 (repr.).

Le Douanier Rousseau, *Child with Puppet*, Winterthur, Kunstmuseum.

# Henri Rousseau

## 109
## *The Wedding Party*
(La noce)

Oil on canvas. H. 163 cm.; W. 114 cm.
Signed on lower right with brush in black:
Henri Julien Rousseau
RF 1960-25

In the abundant literature dealing with Rousseau's sources and work methods, this painting, although it is one of his best known, is almost never mentioned. Neither the identity of the figures, of whom this is clearly a set of portraits, nor the photograph from which Rousseau probably took his inspiration have been found.

The composition is one of the most ambitious ever undertaken by Rousseau, since it constitutes a large-sized group portrait in which the faces are distinctly individualized and the tree species sharply differentiated. As in *Old Man Junier's Carriage* (No. 110), the cut-out figure of a dog occupies the foreground. The main lines of the design form a St. Andrew's cross, the center of which is located exactly on the bow of the bride's sash. The static pattern of arrangement is roughly the same as in *The Soccer Players* (New York, Guggenheim Museum). The trees suggest a certain perspective by their arrangement and by the decreasing sizes of the trunks and leaves, as if Rousseau had sought to break away from the painted backdrops that were customarily placed behind groups photographed in studio interiors. On the other hand, these immobile figures are presented on a single plane, in the form of flat silhouettes devoid of depth, in an arrangement somewhat reminiscent of Manet's *The Balcony*, which had been exhibited in the Musée du Luxembourg since 1896 as part of the Caillebotte bequest, and with which Rousseau was familiar. In the Manet painting, there is also a dog in the foreground. X-ray examination has disclosed several major alterations: originally, the grandmother's dress, on the right, extended as far as the dog, and the bridal veil was painted over the other already completed figures. This type of procedure, i.e. failure to make provision for accommodating the elements of a painting that are yet to be added, is typical of the working methods of an inexperienced artist.
M.H.

Collections:
Jastrebzoff (Serge Férat), Paris; Paul Guillaume (in 1929); Mrs. Jean Walter.

Exhibitions:
1905, Paris, Salond es Indépendants, No. 3589; 1911, Paris, Salon des Indépendants, No. 1; 1923, Paris, Galerie Paul Rosenberg, *Henri Rousseau*, No. 5; 1926, Paris, No. 3188; 1931, New York; 1933, Basel, No. 31 (repr.); 1935, Paris, Petit Palais, No. 411; 1935, Paris, G.B.A. exhibition, No. 121 (repr.); 1937, Paris, No. 6 (repr.); 1944, Paris, No. 3 (repr.); 1946, Paris, No. 77 (repr.); 1950, Venice, No. 9; 1951, New York, No. 13; 1961, Paris, No. 75 (repr.); 1966, Paris, No. 47 (color repr.); 1978, Paris, Centre Georges-Pompidou, M.N.A.M., *Paris-Berlin, 1900-1930*, No. 320 (repr.); 1984-1985, Paris, New York, No. 28 (color repr.).

Literature:
F. Lepeseur, *La Rénovation esthétique*, June 1905; W. Uhde, *Henri Rousseau*, Paris, 1911, pl. 8; G. Apollinaire, "Les Indépendants," *L'Intransigeant*, 20 April 1911; W. Kandinsky, "Uber die Formfrage," *Der Blaue Reiter*, Munich. 1912, p. 231; W. Uhde, *Rousseau*, 1914, pl. 8; H. Kolle, 1922, pl. 5; R. Grey, 1924 (repr.); A. Basler, 1927, pl. 3; A. Salmon, Paris, 1927, pl. 20; P. Soupault, Paris, 1927, fig. 17; C. Zervos, Paris, 1927, pl. 93; A. Basler, Paris, 1929, pl. 41; *Les Arts à Paris*, No. 16, January 1929 (repr.); F. Fels, "En marge de l'exposition Rousseau à la Marie Harriman Gallery, New York. Exposition de toiles réunies par Paul Guillaume et Marie Harriman," Formes, No. 11, January 1932, No. 21; R. Huyghe, "La peinture d'instinct, introduction," *L'Amour de l'Art*, No. 8, October 1933, p. 188, fig. 236; R. Grey, 1943, pp. 48-49, pl. 3; P. Courthion, Geneva, 1944, pl. 20; *L'Amour de l'Art*, No. 7, July 1946, repr. p. 208; W. Uhde, *Cinq maîtres primitifs*, Paris, 1949, repr. p. 32; H. Perruchot, *Le Douanier Rousseau*, Paris, 1957, pl. VII; W. George, *Arts*, 1969; H. Certigny, *La vérité sur le Douanier Rousseau*, Paris, 1961, repr. facing page 246, pp. 455-456; J. Bouret, 1961, p. 50, p. 113, fig. 27; D. Vallier, 1961, pl. 98; *Musées et Collections publiques de France*, 1966, No. 1 (color repr.); 5. Léonard, *Rousseau and Max Wéber*, New York, 1970, p. 40, pl. 9, p. 75; D. Vallier, 1970, new edition 1981, No. 167; L. and O. Bihalji-Merin, Dresden, 1971, p. 93, fig. 35; A. Jakovski, "Le Douanier Rousseau savait-il peindre?," *Médecine de France*, No. 218, 1971, repr.; R. Nacenta, *Les Naïfs*, Paris, 1973, pl. and commentary No. 2; D. Larkin, 1975, color repr. No. 19; I. Niggli, *Naïve Art Yesterday and Today*, Niederteufen, 1976, fig. 74, p. 47; C. Keay, 1976, pp. 28, 29, 35, inset color plate; F. Elgar, Paris, 1980 (color repr. No. 36); Y. Le Pichon, 1981, pp. 38-39 (color repr.).

# Henri Rousseau

## 110
## *Old Man Junier's Carriage*
(La carriole du Père Junier)

Oil on canvas. H. 97 cm.; W. 129 cm.
Signed and dated on lower left with brush, in white:
Henri J. Rousseau, 1908
RF 1960-26

This painting is an homage to the neighborhood friendships that are known to have figured importantly in Rousseau's existence.

Claude Junier (not "Juniet") (1857-1932) and his wife
ran a grocery store at 74, Rue Vercingétorix, at the corner
of Rue Perrel, where Rousseau lived. The neighbors became friends, and, in 1908, Rousseau painted their portrait, doubtless commissioned by them. In the painting,
Junier and Rousseau himself are depicted on the front seat
of the carriage, while in the back are seated Madame
Junier, with, on her right, her niece Lea Junier and, on her
lap, the daughter of her nephew. (The childless Juniers had
taken the children of his late brother into their home. It is
through information provided by his grand-nephew
A. Labrosse, in 1961, which had never been used by Rousseau scholars, that the story behind this painting and the
identity of the figures became known.) Claude Junier, who
was also a horse trainer, was particularly proud of his
white mare, Rosa. Equally noteworthy is the presence of
three dogs. Such an assembly of domestic animals is of rare
occurrence in Rousseau's works.

This painting is one of those for which the greatest
amount of information is available concerning Rousseau's
photographic "sources." Two photographs have been frequently reproduced (most recently, displayed side by side
by Y. Le Pichon, p. 58). One of them —paint-splattered—
belonged to Robert Delaunay, while the other was in the
J.J. Sweeney collection; a third was revealed in a confiden-
tial account (A. Labrosse, 1961). These photographs were
the record of an excursion to Clamart (on the outskirts of
Paris). The three of them were taken with the position of
the carriage and the camera angle unchanged. The horse
has not moved, either; however, in each photograph, the
people and the dogs are in different positions.

Rousseau used these photographs to make an overall
layout design that he filled in after his own fashion (D. Vallier thinks that he even made use of a pantograph). Thus,
he eliminated the tree behind the horse's head, and re-
interpreted the vegetation. The figures are arranged in a
manner unlike any of those shown in the three photographs. Were there possibly other photographs? In all

Photograph taken by Anna Junier in 1908
that was used by Rousseau,
showing traces of paint.

Photograph taken by Anna Junier in 1908.

Photograph taken by Anna Junier in 1908.

# Henri Rousseau

likelihood, Rousseau rearranged the scene to suit his own fancy. While the figures are carefully grouped, the overall composition is exceptionally uncrowded. The accentuated main lines of the structure follow the vertical and the horizontal axes.

According to the valuable testimony of Max Wéber (quoted by Catton Rich, 1946, page 52), who witnessed the progress of this picture while it was being painted, Rousseau finished at the place where the black dog stands beneath the carriage. "When Wéber enquired whether he did not think that the dog might be too large for the amount of space allowed, Rousseau, gazing pensively at his canvas, answered that that was the way it had to be."

D. Vallier also points out that Rousseau committed his biggest error of perspective (incorrect placing of the spokes and hub of the left wheel) at the place occupied by the dog in the Delaunay photograph, and that he decided to leave it empty. There are several details of error in traditional perspective, in particular the body of the carriage, in which the occupants are carefully portrayed full-face, as in *The Wedding Party* (No. 109). On the other hand, Rousseau attempted to express distance perspective by the edge of the sidewalk and the paved gutter that run across the lower part of the composition.                                      M.H.

*Collections:*
Claude Junier; P. Rosenberg, Paris; A. Villard, Paris; Paul Guillaume (in 1927); Mrs. Jean Walter.

*Exhibitions:*
1911, Paris, Salon des Indépendants, No. 46; 1923, Prague, *Vystava Francouzského uméni XIX a XX stoleti*, No. 226 (repr.); 1926, Paris, No. 3184; 1927, London, Lefevre Gallery, *Henri Rousseau*, No. 8; 1933, Basel, No. 51 (repr.); 1935, Paris, Petit Palais, No. 412; 1936, New York; 1937, Paris, No. 1 (repr.); 1937, Paris, No. 2 (repr.); 1944, Paris, No. 4 (repr.); 1950, Venice, No. 16; 1951, New York, No. 18; 1961, Paris, No. 76 (repr.); 1966, Paris, No. 51 (repr.); 1981, Paris, unnumbered; 1984-1985, Paris, New York, No. 39 (repr.).

*Literature:*
A. Soffici, La Voce, 15 September 1910, reprinted in "La France jugée à l'étranger: Le peintre Henri Rousseau," *Mercure de France*, 16 October 1910; W. Uhde, 1914, pl. 14; G. Apollinaire, "Henri Rousseau, Le Douanier," *Les soirées de Paris*, 15 January 1914, fig. p. 63; H. Kolle, 1922, pl. 17, p. 17; R. Grey, 1924 (repr.); F. Lehel, *Notre art dément*, Paris, 1926, pl. 25; A. Salmon, Paris, 1927, fig. p. 34; A. Basler, Paris, 1927, pl. 13; C. Zervos, Paris, 1927, pl. 13; P. Soupault, Paris, 1927, p. 37, fig. 32; *Les Arts à Paris*, No. 13, June 1927, pl. p. 7; A. Basler, 1929, pl. 37; W. George, undated, p. 55, pl. p. 59; J. Combe, "Un Douanier Rousseau au XVIIᵉ siècle," *L'Amour de l'Art*, No. 12, December, 1931, p. 487, fig. 38; W. Uhde, "Henri Rousseau et les primitifs modernes," *L'Amour de l'Art*, No. 8, October 1933, p. 189, fig. 237; M. Morsel, "French Masters of the Twentieth Century in the Valentine Show," *Art News*, 11 January 1936 (cover repr.); C.J. Bulliet, *The Significant Moderns*, New York, 1936, pl. 132; R. Huyghe, *Les Contemporains*, Paris, 1939, pl. 94; D. Catton Rich, New York, 1942, pp. 50, 52, fig. p. 53; R. Grey, 1943, pl.6; M. Buzzichini, *Henri Rousseau*, Milan, 1944 (color repr.); W. George, *Arts*, 1959, repr.; J. Bouret, 1961, p. 43, fig. 42 p. 143; D. Vallier, 1961, pl. 136; H. Certigny, 1961, pp. 330-331, repr. facing p. 327; A. Labrosse, *Montmartre*, undated, No. 1 (repr.); T. Tzara, "Le rôle du temps et de l'espace dans l'œuvre du Douanier Rousseau," *Art de France*, 1962, No. 2, p. 326; P. Courthion, *Dictionnaire de la peinture moderne*, Paris, 1963, fig. pp. 320-321; L. Cheronnet, "La légende dorée du Douanier Rousseau," *Médecine, Peintures*, No. 74, October 1964, unpaginated, pl. X; M.T. de Forges and G. Allemand, *Revue du Louvre*, 1966, p. 1 p. 57, fig. p. 60; S. Léonard, *Henri Rousseau and Max Wéber*, New York, 1970, p. 29; D. Vallier, "L'emploi du pantographe dans l'œuvre du Douanier Rousseau," *La Revue de l'Art*, 1970, No. 7, p. 96, fig. p. 97; D. Vallier, 1970, new edition 1981, commentary and fig. 212, color pl. XLVIII; L. and O. Bihalji-Merin, Dresden, 1971, pp. 25 and 66, fig. 34; P. Descargues, 1972, color pl. p. 97; V. Nezval, *Insita 4*, Bratislava, 1972, p. 81; R. Nacenta, *Les Naïfs*, Paris, 1973, color pl. and commentary 3; D. Larkin, 1975 (color pl. 25); I. Niggli, *Naïve Art Yesterday and Today*, Niederteufen, 1976, fig. 78 p. 48; C. Keay, 1976, p. 34, inset color pl.; C. Lonzi, *Le Douanier Rousseau*, 1979 (color pl. IX; D. Vallier, *Henri Rousseau Le Douanier, un dossier*, 1979, fig. p. 81; F. Elgar, 1980, fig. 50; Y. Le Pichon, 1981, pp. 57-58 (color pl.).

# Alfred Sisley

Paris, 1839-Moret-sur-Loing, 1899

## 111

### The Way from Montbuisson to Louveciennes

(Le chemin de Montbuisson à Louveciennes)

Oil on canvas. H. 46 cm.; W. 61 cm.
Signed and dated on lower right: Sisley 75.
RF 1960-47

In an article on the Exhibition of 1874, held at Nadar's premises on Boulevard des Capucines, a critic commented on the extent to which Sisley had innovated "by achieving the absolute expression of the school's ambitions in landscapes." He added: "I know of no other painting, either past or present, which so completely and perfectly conveys the physical impression of the plein air atmosphere. This is something utterly new in painting, and it behooves us to take due note thereof" (Ernest Cheneau, *Paris-Journal*, 7 May 1874). Working without respite, Sisley continued to render these new plein-air impressions in landscapes of the Ile-de-France area, an inexhaustible source of his inspiration. In accordance with his accustomed practice

(*View of Saint-Martin Canal*, 1870, Musée d'Orsay, *The road seen from the way to Sèvres*, 1873, Musée d'Orsay, virtually contemporary with *Along the Way from Montbuisson to Louveciennes*), in this present work, which dates from around the time of the 1874 Exhibition, the artist juxtaposes the receding perspective of the foreground and the strongly asserted presence of the sky: "The sky cannot be merely a background. Not only does it contribute to providing depth through its various planes... but it also imparts movement by its form, by its arrangement in relation to the effect or to the composition of the painting... When I begin a painting, I always do the sky first."     H.G.

*Collections:*
Georges Viau; Knoedler, New York; private collection; Wildenstein; purchased by Mrs. Jean Walter in 1953.

*Exhibitions:*
1917, Paris, Galerie Georges Petit, *Alfred Sisley*, No. 59; 1966, Paris, No. 17 (repr.); 1980, Athens, No. 36 (color repr.); 1981, Tbilisi-Leningrad, No. 45 (repr.).

*Literature:*
F. Daulte, *Alfred Sisley, Catalogue raisonné de l'œuvre peint*, Paris, 1959, No. 165.

# Chaim Soutine

Smilovichi, 1893-Paris, 1943

## 112
## *Gladioli*
(Glaïeuls)

Oil on canvas. H. 56 cm.; W. 46 cm.
Signed on lower left with brush, in red: Soutine.
RF 1963-95

Prior to 1917, Soutine's first flower bouquets, painted while he was living in La Ruche or in the Cité Falguière, were inserted into still lifes cluttered with sundry objects arranged on a chair or armchair: *Bouquet of Flowers on an Armchair* (private collection); *Flowers on a Chair* (New York, Josten Collection); *Apples, Jug, Chair and Flowers* (New York, Dr. Harry Austin Blutman Collection). Soutine handled this theme in the same manner as van Gogh — *The Yellow Chair* (London, National Gallery) and *Gauguin's Armchair* (Amsterdam, van Gogh Museum — and as Matisse, in 1919, in his *Chair with Peaches* (Soleure, J. Muller Collection).

Other compositions more strongly suggest the influence of the overall design used by Cézanne, including walls covered with wallpaper, cloths folded on a table, fruits and flowers. Soutine's *Flowers and Fruit* (Paris, Henri Epstein) and *Still Life with Oranges* (Paris, Roger Bernheim) can be likened to certain Cézanne works such as *Tulips* (Chicago Art Institute) and *Flowers and Fruits* (No. 4).

The narrative theme soon became indistinct; the surface of the painting was occupied entirely by the bouquet, whose movement and colored material became the center of interest — bouquets of lilacs, carnations, and, especially, gladioli, of which there are some fifteen examples. The vase participated in the overall color vibrations of the still life against a much more subdued dark background. Originally centered, and occupying the upper part of the picture (*Gladioli*, Brooklyn Museum), the vase was subsequently moved to the right, as in most of Soutine's works of that period, and the bouquet thus occupied a major part of the pictorial surface.

Soutine's first gladiolus bouquets were portrayed in muted colors achieved by thinly applied paint through which the canvas texture occasionally appeared. After his first few stays in southern France, he began to develop a new manner of viewing, and modified his technique. He applied the paint more thickly in order to render the surging forth of the flowers, as in this present painting, thereby foreshadowing the technique of the landscape of his Céret period; this makes it possible to pinpoint this bouquet at circa 1918-1919. The impasto around the stems sets off the brisk, angular character of the brushstroke.

This painting was remounted and underwent a number of modifications. As seen in a Giraudon photograph taken in 1926, the painting originally was unsigned; after it had been mounted onto a new canvas, the signature was affixed onto the lower left part and the vase retouched; the canvas was enlarged along its lower space, so that the vase no longer rests on the base of the painting but seems to be floating in a vacuum. Who was responsible for the restoration? Zborowski or Henri Bing, the subsequent owner? P. Courthion claims that, according to Henri Bing, Soutine, who often did not sign his works, had granted signature rights to Zborowski, Van Leer and Bing. René Gimpel, referring to this matter in his *Mémoires d'un collectionneur*, implies that there was reluctance about asking Soutine to sign paintings, since once they were entrusted to him for this purpose he was addicted to altering them, frequently to their disadvantage, and there was the ever-present risk that he might attempt to destroy a painting.

C.G.

*Collections:*
L. Zborowski, Paris; H. Bing, Paris; Paul Guillaume (in 1929); Mrs. Jean Walter.

*Exhibitions:*
1935, Springfield, Mass.; 1952, Venice, No. 30; 1959, Paris, No. 13; 1965, Paris, Galerie Charpentier, *Les jardins et les fleurs de Breughel à Bonnard*, No. 122; 1966, Paris, No. 124 (repr.); 1973, Paris, No. 5 (repr.).

*Literature:*
W. George, 1928 (pl. 8); W. George, undated, p. 160 (repr.), p. 161; W. George, "Les peintres juifs, II: Soutine et la violence dramatique," *L'Amour de l'Art*, No. 6, June 1933, fig. 188; M. Wheeler, *Soutine*, New York, 1950, p. 46 (concerning the gladioli in general); W. George, 1959; H. Serouya, Paris, 1967 (pl. 2); P. Courthion, 1972, p. 192, fig. B; R. Cogniat, 1973, p. 56; E. Dunow, "Soutine Still Lifes," *Chaim Soutine, 1893-1943*, London, 1981, p. 73 (concerning the gladioli in general).

# Chaim Soutine

## 113
## *Houses*
(Les maisons)

Oil on canvas. H. 58 cm.; W. 92 cm.
Signed on lower left, with brush, four letters in red and three letters in blue: Soutine.
RF 1960-49

The painting entitled *Houses* represents the last stage in the landscape of Céret. This painting may be assumed to depict the cluster of buildings photographed in Céret in 1967 by Maurice Tuchman (Soutine Exhibition, Los Angeles, 1968, page 24, figure 11), used by Soutine one year earlier in his *View of Céret*, in which the brushwork is so much more turbulent.

Here, the composition is horizontal; a leftward movement of rooftops is balanced by a mountainous background on the right. The brushstroke is angular, handled less violently than in the landscapes of the early Céret period. The houses press tightly against one another and form an impenetrable wall to our gaze. They offer an anthropomorphic view of malleable blocks, loosely awry on their bases, that become distorted as they reach disproportionately upward, in a strict pattern of rooftops whose corners stretch out broadly so as to almost wholly absorb the sky. The forms on the right disintegrate until they become virtually mere abstract patches of color.

This unrealistic, arbitrary deformation of the elements portrayed is clearly reminiscent of van Gogh, and also of the Brücke painters, Kirchner and Heckel in particular.

C.G.

*Collections:*
Paul Guillaume; Mrs. Jean Walter.

*Exhibitions:*
1959, Paris, No. 5; 1960, Paris, No. 94; 1966, Paris, No. 125 (repr.); 1980, Athens, No. 38, repr.; 1981, Tbilisi-Leningrad, No. 47 (repr.).

*Literature:*
P. Courthion, 1972, p. 188, fig. B.

# Chaim Soutine

## 114
## *Landscape*
(Paysage)

Oil on canvas. H. 92 cm.; W. 65 cm.
Signed on lower right with brush, in green: Soutine.
RF 1963-84

In this *Landscape*, Soutine's colors take on vividness, and a tree emerges as a protective element, here surrounding the small cluster of houses. Soutine was born in a forest region where trees were worshipped by traditional rites; from these, he retained a security-inducing image. The tree was a recurrent element in his landscapes; however, after being soothing and familiar, as in the landscapes of Cagnes and Vence, where it was of the same height as the houses, it eventually became majestic in the paintings of Soutine's last few years, and occurred in the form of groups — trees lining lanes or planted in clumps. The tree, taller and slenderer, was set off from the other elements in the landscape, which it clearly dominated: *Flight of Stairs, Chartres*, 1933 (New York, Jack I. Poses Collection), *Avenue (Alley of Trees)*, *Avenue of Poplars, Civry* and *Autumn at Champigny* (Paris, Mme. Castaing Collection).

Near the trees, the walls of the houses capture the light in large yellow patches that contrast with the curving, multicolored brushstrokes that are briskly applied to the pattern of artistic disarray, wherever it involves the denser texture of vegetation and tree foliage. A winding path twists its way up to the huddle of buildings, and the sky overwhelms the scene with its blue mass penetrating the houses through the windows, creating a strange mood. The lower parts of the houses lilt with an undulating motion, and the perspective stops in the foreground, with the climbing pathway. These features combine to foster the feeling of a dream world blended with fantasy, evoking other landscapes in which Soutine enlivened the surface of his canvas with an equally palpitating colored mass, such as *Street at Cagnes* (Paris, Galerie Pétridès) and *The Old Mill* (New York, Museum of Modern Art).     C.G.

*Collections:*
Paul Guillaume; Mrs. Jean Walter.

*Exhibitions:*
1959, Paris, No. 25; 1966, Paris, No. 126 (repr.).

*Literature:*
R. Negri, *L'Arte Moderna*, Milan, 1967, p. 206 (color repr.); M. Tuchman, *Chaim Soutine, 1893-1943*, Los Angeles, 1968, p. 29 (concerning the landscapes of Cagnes in general); P. Courthion, 1972, p. 218, fig. A.

# Chaim Soutine

## 115
### *The Fiancée*

(La fiancée)

Oil on canvas. H. 81 cm.; W. 46 cm.
Signature brushed in vertically in red, on lower right: Soutine.
RF 1960-51

Considerable uncertainty prevails concerning the anecdotal content of *The Fiancée*. It was probably painted at Cagnes, as were several portraits of women that display the curvilinear brushstroke which was Soutine's "trademark" at the time. The whiteness of the gown fascinated him in exactly the same way as the cooks' white coats, and is more specifically reminiscent of *The Pastry Cook*, in the Joseph H. Hazen Collection (Soutine exhibition, Perls Gallery, 1969, No. 8, reproduction). Like the young woman shown here, the hunched-shouldered pastry cook is depicted against a background of dark green wall hangings. On all sides, the whiteness is modulated with broad, oval brushstrokes that, in the portrait of the fiancée, strongly emphasize the emaciated neck and throat. In both portraits, the faces, drawn out lengthwise, look even longer because the canvas barely accommodates the pastry cook's hat and the woman's hair. The dissymmetry of the face is echoed by that of the body: the left side, handled with suppleness, extends up higher than the right side, where the arms rest stiffly on the chairback. The background is filled in with an application of rounded brushstrokes that, in vertical movements, contribute to further elongating the face.

There is a half-length preparatory study for *The Fiancée*, portrayed with the back of her neck resting against the back of a dark red armchair — as in *The Pastry Cook*, in the Joseph H. Hazen Collection — in which the woman's figure stands out against a green background and attests to the detailed work involved in elaborating the rigidly fixed face. On the basis of this study, Soutine preferred to depict the model standing, leaning on a chair, as in his *Woman with Chair* (P. Courthion, 212 E, Sotheby auction, London, 2 December 1981, No. 52, color reproduction), in order to concentrate his attention on rendering the dress in contrast with the harshness of the figure.    C.G.

*Collections:*
Paul Guillaume, Mrs. Jean Walter.

*Exhibitions:*
1952, Venice, No. 33; 1959, Paris, No. 36; 1966, Paris, No. 128 (repr.).

*Literature:*
P. Courthion, 1972, p. 214, fig. E.

# Chaim Soutine

## 116
### *Fallen Tree*
(Arbre couché)

Oil on canvas. H. 60 cm.; W. 81 cm.
Unsigned.
RF 1963-91

Soutine was ever reluctant to express depth of field by the usual means. In the present painting, he somehow superposes two fields without depth — in the foreground, a tree lying prone as if it had been uprooted by the wind, looking as if it were floating through space, and, in the background, houses in a jumbled pattern.

The composition is designed laterally to follow the tree's movement, which, in the artist's vision, sweeps the road and the slope along in a widening arc. The houses cluster together amid a swirl of greenery. The single element that emerges in opposition to the overall movement is a somewhat stiffly-poised seated figure on the right, the blueness of whose clothing echoes that of the scattered patches of the sky's mass where it attempts to break through.                                                    C.G.

*Collections:*
Paul Guillaume, Mrs. Jean Walter.

*Exhibitions:*
1952, Venice, No. 25; 1959, Paris, No. 39; 1966, Paris, No. 129 (repr.); 1973, Paris, No. 13.

*Literature:*
M. Castaing and J. Leymarie, Paris and Lausanne, 1963, p. 32; H. Serouya, Paris, 1967, pl. 18; P. Courthion, 1972, p. 220, fig. E; R. Cogniat, 1973, fig. p. 13.

# Chaim Soutine

## 117

## *Portrait of a Man (Emile Lejeune)*

(Portrait d'homme [Emile Lejeune])

Oil on canvas. H. 55 cm.; W. 46.5 cm.
Signed with brush, in blue, on lower right: Soutine.
RF 1963-94

Soutine continued to paint portraits throughout his artistic career, in counterpoint to his embracing and abandoning of various other themes at determined dates. There is no evidence of any group portraits among his works; his portraits were consistently individual, with the model viewed from every level of the body, full face or in profile, with relatively few accessories, generally just a chair. Nor did Soutine accept portrait commissions. He enjoyed painting his friends and certain acquaintances, and anecdotes abound concerning his obstinacy in persuading a person whose expression interested him to sit for him during the many long hours that he required.

Soutine's earliest portraits (including one of a little boy dated 1914-1915) already contain evidence of the features that would be his trademark in the works of his maturity: awkwardness and heaviness of arms and hands, facial distortions designed to emphasize whatever it was in his model's personality, that had attracted the artist, and painstaking depiction of the fabrics in clothing. However, he gradually evolved, so as to provide a greater amount of uncrowded space around the figure: the arms were depicted farther away from the body, thereby providing a more natural relationship between the figure and the background.

We know the identities of the models for certain of his portraits, including Miestchaninoff, Richard and Kikoine, who were friends and fellow artists; Madeleine Castaing, his protectress; and Maria Lani, for whom he painted what was perhaps his only commissioned portrait; plus his self-portraits. The identities of the other portrait models, doubtless friends of his, are unknown. In fact, Soutine was not bent on achieving physical likenesses; rather, he chose his models on the basis of their expressions or of their friendship with him. For example, there is the portrait of Udo Einsild, which became *The Boy in the Blue Suit* (private collection), and also the portrait shown here, exhibited and reproduced under the title of *Portrait of a Man*, which purportedly represents the painter Emile Lejeune.

Emile Lejeune was born in 1885 in Geneva of a Swiss father and a French mother; he settled in the Montparnasse area, where he rented a large studio at 6, Rue Huyghens, the site of many exhibitions, including a show of African art organized by Paul Guillaume, plus poetry readings by Guillaume Apollinaire and Jean Cocteau, and musical evenings with the Groupe des Six. In the course of his travels through Provence, Lejeune decided to settle in Cagnes with his family. Soutine's two portraits of Lejeune date either from the end of his period of residence in Paris or from the early days of his stay in Cagnes (1922). In the first portrait (Courthion, catalogue 213-A, former Bing Collection), the face is handled indistinctly; the man gazes out from behind spectacles, he is wearing a bow tie instead of a necktie, but is depicted with distortions similar to those in the present portrait. The neck is stretched disproportionately and is prolonged by a tightening of the upper part of the jacket accentuated by the necktie that encloses the shirt, and also by a tightening of the lower part of the face, with its pointed chin. The fine-lipped mouth beneath the carefully clipped mustache and the two small eyes are brightened by vivid, lightly applied brushstrokes in many colors. A contrast emerges between the lower part of the face, which is very present and carefully outlined, and the excessively rounded eyes, whose blueness is half-absorbed by the pigmentation of the area surrounding them, conveying a far-off gaze, and provoking an expression of evasiveness that is frequent in the faces of Soutine's models.

C.G.

*Collections:*
Paul Guillaume; Mrs. Jean Walter.

*Exhibitions:*
1959, Paris, No. 64; 1966, Paris, No. 138 (repr.).

*Literature:*
P. Courthion, 1972, p. 213, fig. B; R. Cogniat, 1973, p. 21 (repr.).

# Chaim Soutine

## 118
## *The Village*
(Le Village)

Oil on canvas. H. 73.5 cm.; W. 92 cm.
Unsigned.
RF 1963-88

Soutine eventually grew tired of the landscape around Cagnes. In late 1923 or early 1924, he wrote to Zborowski as follows: "I want to get away from Cagnes, a landscape that I cannot abide..." He asked Zborowski to arrange for him to return to Paris, and, to while away the time, he traveled through the back country; he discovered the vineyards of La Gaude, just above Vence, which revived his interest in paintings of trees and houses with roads rising toward them. On several occasions, he set up his easel on the heights of La Gaude, near Saint-Jannet, where he produced the present scene, as well as a *Landscape* (Columbus, Ohio, Dr. Howard Sinak Collection), in which the central part of the houses between the tree and the house in the upper portion is more important; a view halfway up a hillside (Avignon, former collection of Mrs. Charles Pomaret); and a close-up, set off to the right, in which a series of small houses emerges along the road (Paris, Galerie Katia Granoff). In the picture shown here, the artist's interior landscape superimposes on the motif an intense affective dimension to which a tranquillizing note is contributed by the tree and the high-standing house.

Several roads give the effect of leading into this hilltop village, whereas in reality there is no perspective; the central tree penetrates all the spaces and its tall branches frame the most distant buildings. The vegetation in the foreground and the tree's foliage, which absorb a major share of the sky, are done with a circular brushstroke and thickly applied paint. The houses are distorted, not at their bases, but as if they followed the contortions of the rocky pathways that are enlivened with vividly silhouetted figures. The composition as a whole uses an extremely rich palette of colors. Here Soutine directly opens up the way for the Cobra group and for the American Abstract Expressionists of the 1950s (de Kooning, in particular). C.G.

*Collections:*
Paul Guillaume; Mrs. Jean Walter.

*Exhibitions:*
1945, Paris, Galerie Charpentier, *Paysages de France*, No. 97 (repr.); 1959, Paris, No. 49; 1966, Paris, No. 130 (repr.); 1981, Moscow, Pushkin Museum, *Moscow-Paris, 1900-1930*, p. 310.

*Literature:*
H. Serouya, Paris, 1967, pl. VI; P. Courthion, 1972, p. 231, fig. A.

# Chaim Soutine

## 119
## *The Little Pastry Cook*
(Le petit pâtissier)

Oil on canvas. H. 73 cm.; W. 54 cm.
Signed on lower right in red with brush: Soutine.
RF 1963-98

It was the portrait of a pastry cook that determined Soutine's career; with *The Little Pastry Cook*, the present collection reveals one of this artist's most successfully achieved works.

At a time when he was looking for works by Modigliani, Paul Guillaume discovered one of Soutine's paintings, thanks to Michel Georges-Michel *(op. cit.)*, a novelist and art critic who had already devoted an article to Soutine. This painting represented "an extraordinary, fascinating, real, truculent pastry-maker, afflicted with huge, superb, unexpected and exactly right ears: a masterpiece! I bought it, and Dr. Barnes saw it at my place. 'It's a peach!' he exclaimed. His spontaneous delight at viewing this painting decided Soutine's sudden good luck, and made him overnight into a well-known painter, much sought after by art lovers, a personage no longer to be scoffed at in Montparnasse, a hero." *(Les Arts à Paris, loc. cit.)* It also marked the onset of fruitful collaboration between Paul Guillaume and Dr. Barnes, which continued over several years. It is customary to connect this famous anecdote with the painting in the Paul Guillaume collection. However, the record shows that in 1928, this painting was still in the Zborowski collection under the title of *Cook's Boy*, according to the brief article published that same year by Waldemar George. From the Zborowski collection, Paul Guillaume owned one of the first of the pastry cook paintings done in Cagnes (1921-1922, Courthion, catalogue 214-B, 1973 exhibition, No. 15, private collection, reproduced opposite). But this latter painting is too severe to correspond to the description quoted above. Rather, the description refers to the painting purchased by Dr. Barnes, now at the Barnes Foundation, in Merion, Pennsylvania. In this painting, in fact, all the forms are handled as round shapes, starting with the round-faced figure with a turned-up, ball-like chin, his mouth open in a half-circle, his rounded cheekbones, his absence of a neck, and his jacket bunched over rounded shoulders that further exaggerate the curve of his elbows. The sharply-marked buttons echo the circular brushstrokes of the background, handled in much the same manner as the face. The right ear is in its correct place; however, the left ear protrudes out toward the top of the rippled chairback, a disproportionate appen-

Soutine, *Pastry Cook*,
Merion, Penns., Barnes Foundation.

Soutine, *The Little Pastry Cook in Cagnes*,
Paris, private collection.

# Chaïm Soutine

dage that seems to concentrate upon this figure all the derision conveyed by his outfit that fails to impart a personality to him.

By contrast, the young pastry cook depicted here is an angular figure. The artist assigned greater importance to the quality of the skin's pigmentation than to the facial expression. In fact, the face, with its distortions starting at the base of the nose, the high, bushy eyebrows on a low forehead, the half-open mouth, the design of the eyes with their absent gaze, denotes the intention to depict inward withdrawal. The introversion of the individual is underlined by the immobility of the figure in an armchair with a monumental backrest, and by the background, which is handled as a draped arrangement whose obliques divide the space into various warm tones. The hands emerge from the sleeves looking as if they were swollen. The figure's pyramidal composition occupies all the lower part of the picture and gives it great stability, accentuated by the positions of the forearms, firmly resting on the chair arms, as well as the well-developed epaulettes of the jacket. The texture of the fabric is modulated by flat patches of white with multicolored tinges set off by the red handkerchief that is clutched tightly between the two hands, with the same gesture as in the later portrait entitled *The Chambermaid* (Lucerne, Kunstmuseum): this is a masterpiece in the field of investigation of colored matter.

Pierre Courthion erroneously reproduced this painting twice with dates five years apart; the correct date is 1922; it corresponds to the technique that was employed for *The Pastry Cook* painted in Cagnes (Courthion, catalogue 214-B), in which the face betrays an extreme melancholy beneath a devious gaze. Another portrait of a *Little Pastry Cook* (New York, Joseph H. Hazen Collection) recalls the technique used in the painting entitled *The Fiancée*, showing a figure with high shoulders and color applied with oval brushstrokes. Each one of these faces, either by its brooding sadness — as in *The Little Pastry Cook* (Courthion, catalogue 255 I, New York, Lee A. Ault Collection) — or by its overtones of gravity, represents the uneasy infelicity that had attracted the artist's attention, even when they are tinged with humor or fantasy, as in the case of *The Pastry Cook* (Courthion, catalogue 213-A, Barnes Foundation, Merion, Pennsylvania) or *The Large Pastry Cook* (Courthion, catalogue 256-A, Portland Art Museum, Portland, Oregon), which points up a fundamental aspect of Soutine's character. 
C.G.

*Collections:*
L. Zborowski, Paris; Joss Hessel, Paris; Paul Guillaume; Mrs. Jean Walter.

*Exhibitions:*
1945, Paris, No. 12; 1945, Paris, Galerie Charpentier, *Portraits français*, No. 162; 1946, Paris, No. 84; 1950, New York-Cleveland, p. 73, p. 77 (repr.); 1952, Venice, No. 9 (pl. 55); 1959, Paris, No. 38 (repr.); 1966, Paris, No. 127 (repr.); 1973, Paris, No. 12 (repr.); 1980, Athens, p. 171, fig. 39, p. 172, p. 183, pl. 39; 1981, Tbilisi-Leningrad, No. 48 (repr.).

*Literature:*
*Les Arts à Paris*, January 1923, No. 7, pp. 5-7; W. George, Paris, 1928, pl. 5; M. Wheeler, *Soutine*, New York, 1950, p. 73 (repr. p. 77); J. Lassaigne, 1954, Paris, pl. 7; M. Georges-Michel, 1954, pp. 172-175; W. George, 1959 (repr.); *Goya*, September-October 1959, No. 32, repr. p. 93; M. Castaing and J. Leymarie, Paris, 1963, p. 19 (repr.); pp. 20-21; M. Ragon, *L'expressionnisme*, Lausanne, 1966, p. 194 (repr.); H. Serouya, Paris, 1967, pl. 5; M. Tuchman, *Chaïm Soutine*, Los Angeles, 1968, pp. 35-36; P. Courthion, 1972, p. 255, fig. H and p. 223, fig. C (by mistake, reproduced twice); R. Cogniat, 1973, pl. p. 33; *Goya*, July-August 1973, No. 115, rep. p. 33; C. Constans, *Le Vingtième Siècle*, vol. 2, Paris, 1982, No. 64 (repr.).

Soutine, *The Chambermaid*,
Lucerne, Kunstmuseum.

# Chaim Soutine

## 120
### Side of Beef and Calf's Head
(Bœuf et tête de veau)

Oil on canvas. H. 92 cm.; W. 73 cm.
Signed with brush in red, on lower right: C. Soutine.
RF 1963-86

Maurice Tuchman has recorded the following story told by Emil Szittya, Soutine's friend and biographer, as related by the artist: "One day as I was watching the butcher, I saw his knife slit the throat of a bird and drain it of its blood. I tried to cry out, but his joyful expression stifled the cry in the back of my throat." Soutine rubbed his throat and continued: "I still feel that cry right here. As a child, when I used to draw cruel portraits of my teacher, I attempted to get rid of that cry, but in vain. Whenever I painted an animal carcass, it was again this cry that I was striving to set free. I still haven't succeeded in doing so." To these youthful fantasies there must, of course, be added the reminiscence of Rembrandt, for whom Soutine felt the keenest admiration.

Soutine painted a number of skinned sides of beef, and they include some of his largest-sized canvasses: for example, *The Ox* (2.02 m. × 1.14 m., Courthion, catalogue 241-C, Grenoble, Musée de Peinture et de Sculpture); *The Ox* (1.15 m. × 66 cm., Courthion, catalogue 240-A, color reproduction, Buffalo, New York, Albright-Knox Gallery; *Beef Carcass* (1.16 m. × 81 cm., Courthion, catalogue 238-D, in which it is entitled *Skinned Calf*, Minneapolis Institute of Arts, gift of Mr. and Mrs. Donald Winstone and anonymous donor); and *The Skinned Ox* (82 cm. × 75 cm., Geneva, Petit Palais).

The composition of the painting shown here is more complex than that of the preceding ones: a calf's head suspended from a butcher's hook and an ox quarter whose upper part, dangling from two hooks, lets the leg finish on the right the diagonal begun on the left by the calf's head. This design displays an obvious concern with construction, in which the head — with yellow color dominating — is handled with brushstrokes applied by hatching, smaller but more even than those of the ox, with the ultimate effect of making the head seem longer.

Unlike Soutine's other sides of beef, this one is depicted in a side view, broadly spread out, as if it had been flattened beforehand in order to fill up the canvas. The colors stand out strongly against the dark background. Within, throughout the mass of the ox quarter, there is a profoundly agitated brushstroke applied in wide green, yellow and red hatchings, which crisscross and intersect one another in an effect of great artistic disarray. Their purpose is not to mark volume; in fact, there is no effect of mass; rather, there is a billowing swirl of colors that contrasts with the head.

The paintings of skinned carcasses were done in 1925, when Soutine had a studio on the Rue du Saint-Gothard, where he had carcasses delivered to him, over which he poured blood when they began to lose their color.

C.G.

*Collections:*
Paul Guillaume; Mrs. Jean Walter.

*Exhibitions:*
1952, Venice, No. 71; 1959, Paris, No. 45; 1963, London, No. 28 (fig. 18); 1966, Paris, No. 131 (repr.); 1978, Paris, No. 125; 1981, Münster-Tübingen, No. 15 (repr.).

*Literature:*
D. Sylvester, *Chaim Soutine, 1893-1943*, London, 1963, Commentary 28; W. George, "Présence et Primauté d'Eugène Delacroix," exhibition entitled *L'Héritage de Delacroix*, Paris, 1964, unpaginated; M. Tuchman, *Chaim Soutine, 1893-1943*, Los Angeles, 1968, p. 15; P. Courthion, 1972, p. 242; fig. A.

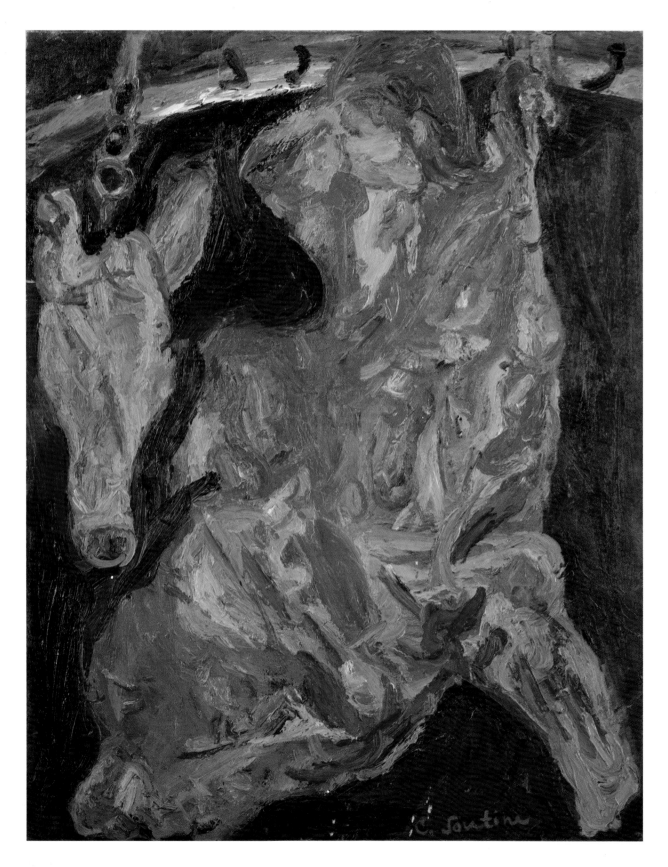

# Chaim Soutine

## 121
## *The Plucked Chicken*
(Le poulet plumé)

Oil on canvas. H. 67 cm.; W. 40 cm.
Signed with brush in blue on lower right: Soutine.
RF 1963-93

The painting entitled *The Plucked Chicken*, dated 1925 by Courthion, is one of the series depicting plucked chickens and rabbits developed by Soutine concurrently with his portraits of individuals in uniform. This theme harks back to the artistic tradition of the seventeenth and eighteenth centuries: now descriptive, it belongs to still lifes with complex subjects; now anecdotal, it is linked to the spoils of hunting. In Soutine's early still lifes, we find compositions depicting food, in which poultry is combined with fruits or with kitchen utensils: *The Chicken on the Table* (Dr. Lucien Kléman Collection), *Still Life with Turkey* (Pierre Lévy Bequest, Musée de Troyes). However, these still lifes soon began taking on a wholly different appearance, and the carcasses laid on a table became immolated victims suspended from hooks, thereby evoking scenes of the Day of Atonement, on Yom Kippur Eve, which the artist had witnessed as a child, and in which the poultry dangles twirling above the penitent's head to cleanse him of his sins as it turns. Soutine was not seeking for a scapegoat, as in the shtetl tradition; rather, he was endeavouring to free himself from his own anguish over death and suffering; the reading of this theme, to which he assigned major importance during the years that he dealt with it, points up the artist's hope of redemption through the ardour with which he dynamized the immolated animal's flesh with his colored matter.

In this painting, the plucked chicken dangles by its neck above an overturned table that separates it from all the elements of life. Its body looms forth in its many colors, with scattered dark blue tinges that are concentrated around the animal's neck, to which the feathers are still attached, thus setting it apart from the head. The head is rendered in a muted blue, absorbing the colored hues of the beak, which protrudes in a disproportionate extension, like some final vestige of energy. The wood and metallic elements in the background are absorbed by paint applied in swirling strokes, in which white blends with blue to trigger a certain dynamism.                                        C.G.

*Collections:*
Paul Guillaume; Mrs. Jean Walter.

*Exhibitions:*
1937, Paris, No. 46; 1945, Paris, No. 30; 1959, Paris, No. 83; 1966, Paris, No. 132 (repr.).

*Literature:*
P. Courthion, 1972, p. 244, fig. A.

# Chaim Soutine

## 122
## *The Rabbit*
(Le lapin)

Oil on canvas. H. 73 cm.; W. 36 cm.
Slanting signature, done with brush, in red, on lower right: Soutine.
RF 1963-90

*The Rabbit* belongs to a series of hares and rabbits suspended by one paw against backgrounds that can be either a clearly defined blue, as in *Hare with Green Shutter*, in the Pierre Lévy Bequest (Musée de Troyes), or a dark background that fades away into indistinctness behind the carcass. There is a hanging red jug, rendered with the same brushstroke and located in the same plane as the rabbit. The full weight of the body bears down on the animal's head. Here, Soutine has created an atmosphere that is completely different from the one in his poultry paintings. Although the dilated white eyes are a reminder that the animal is dead, the beholder cannot fail to note the extreme care and interest devoted to depicting its fur; with small strokes of sparkling white, the artist reveals the softness of the fur on the paws, neck and belly; similarly, the thick white of the tail brings out the density of the fur and the pleasure enjoyed by the artist as he dwelt on this detail.

Soutine had come a long way since the days when he depicted the scraggy rabbits on food-laden tables in his earliest paintings. The extremely free brushwork, with paint applied in long, comma-shaped strokes, foreshadows the painters of the Cobra group. The many colors that compose the fur infuse new energy into the painting, which continues a traditional still-life theme. C.G.

Soutine, *Hare with Green Shutter*, Troyes, Musée d'Art Moderne Denise and Pierre Lévy Bequest.

*Collections:*
Paul Guillaume; Mrs. Jean Walter.

*Exhibitions:*
1959, Paris, No. 82; 1966, Paris, No. 133 (repr.).

*Literature:*
P. Courthion, 1972, p. 243, fig. A; R. Cogniat, 1973, p. 39 (repr.); J. Lanthemann, *Catalogue raisonné de l'œuvre dessiné de Soutine*, 1981, p. 30 (repr.).

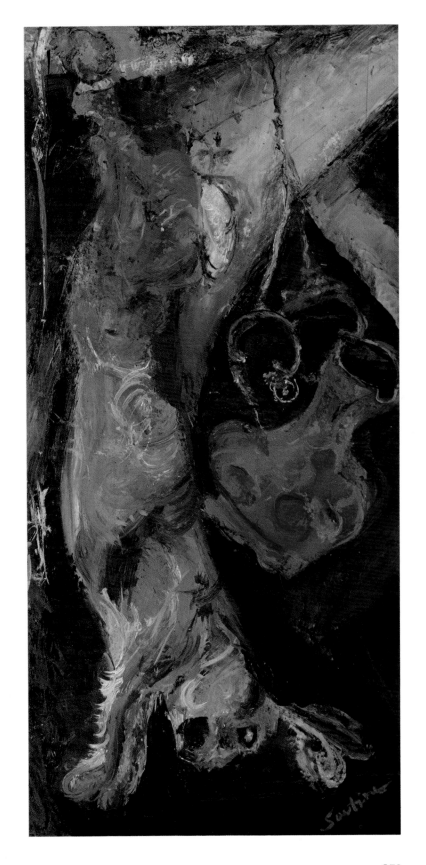

# Chaim Soutine

## 123
## *The Turkey*
(Le Dindon)

Oil on canvas. H. 80 cm.; W. 65 cm.
Unsigned.
RF 1963-81

*The Turkey* contrasts, by an impression of mass, with the stringy body of the *Plucked Chicken* (No. 121), and its midnight blue plumage obtrudes upon the lower part of the painting, stretching up poignantly along a diagonal line.

This painting is distinctly less luminous than *The Plucked Chicken*, and the muted tone of the background contributes to attracting our attention to the animal's body, whose head is absorbed in the scramble of the paint which holds the eye; the blue neck feathers no longer divide the body from the head: rather, they denote the difficulty of the transition from life to death. Yellow dominates the brushstrokes on the body, which rests heavily in a position of withdrawal, in which suffering occupies our full attention, creating an atmosphere fraught with heaviness. C.G.

*Collections:*
Paul Guillaume; Mrs. Jean Walter.

*Exhibitions:*
1929, Paris; 1935, Paris, No. 140; 1945, Paris, No. 17; 1952, Venice, No. 29; 1959, Paris, No. 73; 1966, Paris, No. 135 (repr.).

*Literature:*
W. George, undated, p. 157 (repr.); R. Negri, *Arte Moderna*, Milan, 1967, p. 218 (repr.); P. Courthion, 1972, 244, fig. G.

# Chaim Soutine

## 124
### Turkey and Tomatoes
(Dindon et tomates)

Oil on canvas. H. 81 cm.; W. 49 cm.
Slanting signature, done with brush in red, on lower right: Soutine.
RF 1963-89

By its composition, this work bears a certain resemblance to *The Plucked Chicken*, except that here, the bird is suspended along a diagonal and, as was correctly pointed out by M. Bundorf in the 1966 catalogue, Soutine "placed it in an oblique line, as if he had wished to capture the animal during one of the phases of an oscillatory movement." A triangular expanse on the lower left is lightened by a luminous piece of cloth on which tomatoes are heaped. Their rosy tint is reflected on the bird, and, together with a luminous yellow, creates a new energy. Only the feet, suffused with a lugubrious blue that gradually conceals the initial yellowish green, and with a voluminous black patch in the lower part, are reminders of the presence of death conveyed by the head; the latter is handled in shades of grey and blue; it is surmounted by the crest, rendered by black hatching, on which a few red traces are still visible, the last vestige of life.

Yet this still life is less emotionally appealing than the other paintings of birds in the collection: the head, showing the eye, stands out more sharply from the background, the brushstrokes are more rounded and even, and the mordantly defined contour lines define the animal and give it a more deliberately delineated look. C.G.

*Collections:*
Paul Guillaume; Mrs. Jean Walter.

*Exhibitions:*
1952, Venice, No. 31; 1959, Paris, No. 72; 1966, Paris, No. 134 (repr.); 1978, Paris, No. 124; Tbilisi-Leningrad, No. 49 (repr.); 1982, Lucerne, No. 101 (repr.).

*Literature:*
Goya, September-October 1959, No. 32, repr. p. 94; P. Courthion, 1972, p. 248, fig. A; Y. Le Pichon, *Les peintres du bonheur*, Paris, 1983, fig. 3, p. 253.

# Chaim Soutine

## 125
## *The Table*
(La table)

Oil on canvas. H. 81 cm.; W. 100 cm.
Signed on lower left with brush in red: Soutine.
RF 1963-82

In this painting, Soutine returned to a theme to which he had devoted considerable attention during his first few years in Paris (1914-1915), but here, he no longer infuses it with the poignant appeal inspired by hunger. This composition is reminiscent of one painted by Cézanne during the early, Expressionist part of his career, entitled *Loaf of Bread and Leg of Lamb* (Venturi, No. 63, Zurich, Kunsthaus), but Soutine remains faithful to his own particular thematics.

In order to give greater impact to the sides of beef, he grouped them in a reduced space in which, together with the other objects in the composition — a wine bottle that is as sturdily ensconced on its base as a Soutine tree, a compote dish that is seemingly dancing on its incurvated, unnaturally frail stem, a coffee pot and another wine bottle — they form a triangle. An entire portion of the table is empty, but to enable the other part to accommodate the objects thus grouped, he draws it out and curves it forward. What appears to be a side of venison barely touches the table, and only the second piece of meat actually rests its full weight on the table. Both are animated by a scramble of curvilinear brushstrokes in which red dominates — not the red of blood, but that of the artist's creative impetuousness, echoed by a strengthening outline around the compote dish and the upper part of the table drawer.        C.G.

*Collections:*
Paul Guillaume, Mrs. Jean Walter.

*Exhibitions:*
1959, Paris, No. 17; 1966, Paris, No. 136 (repr.).

*Literature:*
P. Courthion, 1972, p. 184, fig. C.; *Goya*, July-August 1973, No. 115, repr. p. 33.

# Chaim Soutine

## 126
### *Still Life with Pheasant*
(Nature morte au faisan)

Oil on canvas. H. 64.5 cm.; W. 92 cm.
Signed with brush in black, on lower right: Soutine.
RF 1963-83

This *Still Life with Pheasant* is from another series of paintings of fowls; the pheasant and the cloth on which it lies belong to a limp universe. Recumbent in its white shroud, the carcass has shed all signs of any vital energy. To its inertia, the pitcher opposes its vividly bulging forms, attenuated by an enigmatic object which could be a long-handled spoon propped against the pouring lip, thereby interrupting the figuration. On the forward-right-tilting table, the pheasant is delineated by the forms and also by the purplish red of the bell pepper in the lower part, as well as by the circular yellow brushstrokes massed in the upper part. The brushwork on the pheasant's carcass is mordantly executed, and in places the paint is applied in a thick impasto, in an array of colors and in variegated curvilinear and comma-like shapes whose swarmingly crowded density surges forth to compensate for the lost energy. A new dynamism is spawned by the concentration of a multifarious array of elements that thus emerge in mutual opposition around this composition.                                C.G.

*History of ownership:*
Paul Guillaume; Mrs. Jean Walter.

*Exhibitions:*
1942, Geneva, Galerie Georges Moos, *Exposition d'art français depuis 1900*, No. 59; 1946, Paris, Galerie Charpentier, *La vie silencieuse*, No. 64; 1952, Venice, No. 32; 1959, Paris, No. 65; 1966, Paris, No. 137 (repr.); 1981, Munster-Tübingen, No. 68 (repr.).

*Bibliography:*
J. Lassaigne, 1947, p. 120 (repr.); P. Courthion, 1972, p. 251, fig. G.

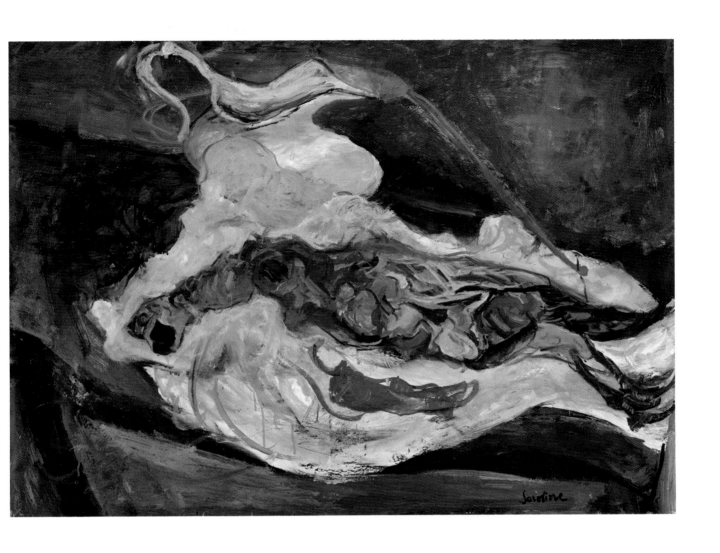

# Chaim Soutine

## 127
## *English Girl*
(La jeune Anglaise)

Oil on canvas. H. 46 cm.; W. 55 cm.
Signed in black with brush, on lower left: Soutine.
RF 1963-97

This portrait is further evidence of Soutine's fascination with red and white, as in the picture entitled *Choir Boy*. And, as noted by M. Bundorf, "As an exception to the portraits painted by Soutine, the model here has an almost pretty face, equilibrated by the mass of her hair. Her arms and bust are a bit on the thin side. However, no feeling of disquietude emanates from this portrait — quite the contrary. Soutine seems to have experienced a certain enjoyment in painting this girl, and to have sought to convey her charm and youthfulness" (1966 catalogue, No. 139). This present work is in fact reminiscent of a series of graceful portraits of female models that he painted during this period, including *Girl in Red* (Courthion, catalogue 259-C, Evelyn Sharp Collection); the *Portrait of Madame Castaing* (Courthion, catalogue 270-E, photograph D, New York, Pierre Matisse Gallery; *Maria Lani* (Courthion, catalogue 272-A); and *The Polish Girl*, purchased by René Gimpel (Courthion, catalogue 270-F, photograph G.). However, this portrait may possibly have been earlier than the date usually assigned to it, since a *Portrait of an Englishwoman* was displayed in 1924 in the exhibition of French art that marked the opening of the California Palace of the Legion of Honor in San Francisco, and it could well have been this one.

There is another portrait of this model in identical attire (oil on wood, 56 cm. × 34 cm., Drouot auction, 15 June 1938, No. 85, reproduction).

The present portrait was painted on the back of a canvas that bears traces of an earlier painting. It is a matter of record that Soutine did not like brand-new canvasses: Germaine Moncray (*Jardin des Arts*, No. 142, September 1966, pages 72-73) has described how Soutine obliged an innkeeper at Recloses, near Fontainebleau, to hand over to him a religious painting from her dining room so that he could clean it and replace the original scene with the picture of a choir boy.

Elie Faure, who was several times Soutine's host at his estate near Bordeaux, has recounted his excursions to second-hand shops, and Madeleine Castaing has described how she and her husband devoted many long hours to finding old paintings, which Soutine spent days on end cleaning before using them for his own paintings. He clearly derived a certain pleasure from destroying existing works. He displayed an obsessive craving to destroy all his works from the Céret period, but no period of this creative career was spared, not even when this destruction was not carried out systematically. C.G.

*Collections:*
Paul Guillaume; Mrs. Jean Walter.

*Exhibitions:*
1942, Geneva, Galerie Georges Moos, *Exposition d'art français depuis 1900*, No. 60; 1952, Venice, No. 24; 1962, Mexico City, *Cien años de Pintura en Francia de 1850 a nuestros días*, No. 133 (repr.); 1966, Paris, No. 139 (repr.).

*Literature:*
P. Courthion, 1972, p. 265, fig. I.

# Chaim Soutine

## 128
## *Choir Boy*
(Enfant de chœur)

Oil on canvas. H. 63.5 cm.; W. 50 cm.
Signed with brush in red, on lower right: Soutine.
RF 1963-96

Soutine's choir boy series was either contemporary with his various paintings of animal carcasses or dated only shortly thereafter. It corresponded with his attraction to red tones, which he caused to vibrate with whites, as he did also in *The Little Pastry Cook* (No. 119) and in *The Room-Service Waiter* (No. 129).

In this type of portrait, the glowing color of the vestimentary trappings that denote the boy's membership in an institution or a profession does nothing to conceal the awkward character of the models, whom Soutine unconsciously transposes into memories of his unhappy childhood. Here, with its unduly elongated face and the distorted hands emerging from the sleeves of the surplice, the portrait becomes animated and takes on a special form. The subject's eyes gaze directly at the beholder, and reveal an amused look of complicity with the outside world. Soutine deployed all his artistic craftsmanship here in the study of the surplice, whose white colors reflect many varied tones and are set off by the red robe and the midnight blue background.

Soutine painted several portraits of choir boys. Sometimes, they are portrayed seated (New York, Jack H. Poses Collection); at other times, standing and full length (Paris, Madame Castaing Collection, and Geneva, Charles Im Obersteg Collection); or, again, in three-quarter view, in the same manner as *Praying Men*, painted at Cagnes; examples are those at the Félix Vercel Gallery, Paris, and the more majestic one in the present collection, which takes possession of the canvas with all the authority of figures in classical portraits.                                C.G.

*Literature:*
*Formes*, No. 5, May 1930 (color repr.); *Les Arts à Paris*, No. 17, May 1930; J. Lassaigne, 1947, p. 119 (repr.); M. Wheeler, *Chaim Soutine*, New York, 1950, p. 74 (repr. p. 85); W. George, 1959 (repr.); W. George, *Arts*, 1959; *Goya*, September-October 1959, No. 32, repr. p. 99; M. Castaing and J. Leymarie, Paris, 1963, pl. 9; W. George, "Présence et primauté d'Eugène Delacroix," *L'Héritage de Delacroix*, exhibition, 1964, unpaginated; H. Serouya, Paris, 1967, pl. 12; R. Negri, *L'Arte Moderna*, Milan, 1967, p. 220 (repr.); M. Hoog, *Peinture moderne*, Paris, 1969, p. 158; P. Courthion, 1972, p. 259, fig. G and pl. p. 82; R. Cogniat, 1973, pl. p. 45; B. Scott, "Soutine and Some Others," *Apollo*, No. 138, August 1973 (repr. p. 142); *Goya*, July-August 1973, No. 115, repr. p. 33.

Soutine,
*Large Choir Boy*,
Paris,
Madeleine Castaing
Collection.

# Chaim Soutine

## 129
## *The Room-Service Waiter*
(Le garçon d'étage)

Oil on canvas: H. 87 cm.; W. 66 cm.
Signed with brush in red, on upper right: Soutine.
RF 1963-50

At Châtelguyon, where he went with the Castaings to take the cure, Soutine had an opportunity to observe bell boys and restaurant waiters. What kind of fellow feeling linked Soutine to these uniformed men? In the world of this childhood, servants had been held in contempt. He felt himself to be a kindred spirit because of the rejection from which he had suffered throughout his younger years and because of the difficulties of his insertion at the time when he was painting uniforms and dead birds, in the years from 1922 to 1928.

Soutine did several portraits of this hotel valet, including one entitled *The Headwaiter* (Soutine exhibition, Paris, Musée de l'Orangerie, No. 39, reproduction, private collec-

tion, Paris) and *Valet in Red Waistcoat* (33 cm. × 46 cm., United States, private collection). The faces in all three of these portraits display the same empty, impenetrable, not to say inscrutable expression. In the present portrait, the ill-fitting uniform conveys the appearance of an array of dislocated forms. The flat color of the clothing, the face whose skin pigmentation resembles the color of the texture of the waistcoat, the shapeless hands — all these are revelatory of the artist's intentions.

The deep blue background, which is echoed in the bow tie, creates a feeling of derision that is frequent in Soutine's works. C.G.

*Collections:*
H. Bing, Paris; Paul Guillaume; Mrs. Jean Walter.

*Exhibitions:*
1945, Paris, No. 29; 1952, Venice, No. 34; 1959, Paris, No. 89; 1966, Paris, No. 141 (repr.); 1981, Munster-Tübingen, No. 79 (repr.).

*Literature:*
W. George, 1959 (repr.); *Goya*, September-October 1959, No. 32, repr. p. 94; W. George, "Présence et primauté d'Eugène Delacroix," *L'héritage de Delacroix*, 1964, unpaginated; P. Courthion, 1972, p. 95, p. 267, fig. A, commentary B; R. Cogniat, 1973, p. 50 (repr.); E. G. Güse, "Chaim Soutine," *Die Kunst*, December 1983, p. 840 (color repr.); *Art International*, vol. 26, No. 5, November-December 1983, F. Whitford, "E. G. Güse, C. Soutine," p. 62 (color repr.).

# Chaim Soutine

## 130
## *The Groom*
(Garçon d'honneur)

Oil on canvas. H. 100 cm.; W. 81 cm.
Signed on lower right: signature slanted along the leg,
in blue paint blended with a touch of white: Soutine.
RF 1960-48

The title of this picture (conferred on it at a fairly recent date) should not be interpreted too literally, nor should it call forth any specific commentary. As in the portraits of bellbops and floor waiters, what is shown here is one of those young male figures whose formal attire (or livery) forms a contrast with their loutish or unattractive faces. In the present portrait, the physiognomy is virtually inscrutable, and the eyes are downcast. The contrast between the model and his clothing is further heightened by the caricatural depiction of his hands, which are worthy of those of a comic strip character; the proportions of his extremities are absurd, like those of a puppet or a jumping-jack. The setting is undefined, and no seating unit is suggested, nor is there any accessory. Unusual in Soutine's work, however, is the situating of the figure solely by the shadow of the head and arm against the background, unless this happens to be an alteration. The pervasive feeling is one of resignation and dejection rather than of sadness.

Waldemar George, one of the best-informed first-hand observers of Soutine's works in progress, dates this painting at 1928. The picture looks unfinished. The roughly-applied brushwork combines flat areas with those in which the paint was dribbled or splashed on. The work brings to mind that of Fautrier, whose early pictures, contemporary with this painting, display the same striving for "disfigurement," achieved via the same freedom of technique. The two artists had several admirers in common (including J. Castel and W. George) and were probably acquainted; whatever the case, Fautrier had ample opportunity to view Soutine's paintings.                    C.G.

*Collections:*
Paul Guillaume; Mrs. Jean Walter.

*Exhibitions:*
1959, Paris No. 90; 1966, Paris, No. 142 (repr.); 1982, Lucerne, No. 105 (repr.).

*Literature:*
W. George, 1959 (repr.); P. Courthion, 1972, p. 268, fig. C; P. Mathonnet, "L'homme bourreau de soi-même," *Journal de Genève*, 2 October 1982 (repr.).

# Chaim Soutine

## 131
## *Landscape with Figure*
(Paysage avec personnage)

Oil on canvas: H. 60 cm.; W. 80 cm.
Signed on lower left: Soutine.
RF 1963-87

This landscape, which depicts a site outside Paris, is composed of specific countryscape elements that interested Soutine at the time, including trees, a cluster of houses and a hillside with one or several roadways and pathways. Here, he chose the site of the intersection of a path and a road. Unlike the roads depicted at Cagnes, this one is neither twisting nor uneven, but rises in a straight line, abiding by the rules of receding lines and perspective. The roadsides are mordantly outlined, and the houses cling to the pattern of the slope in a natural arrangement. The artist employed a swift, brisk brushstroke, applying the paint in arabesques to depict undergrowth and trees; various figures disrupt his solitude. This painting sums up the poetics of Soutine, who, even when he is in quest of order and structure, presents a work in which the surging thrust of the brush creates a consistently expressive force.

C.G.

*Collections:*
Paul Guillaume; Mrs. Jean Walter.

*Exhibitions:*
1959, Paris, No. 103, 1966, Paris No. 144 (repr.).

*Literature:*
*Goya*, September-October 1959, No. 32, repr. p. 98; P. Courthion, 1972, p. 228, fig. D.

# Chaim Soutine

## 132
## *Large Blue Tree*
(Le gros arbre bleu)

Oil on canvas. H. 83 cm.; W. 80 cm.
Slanting signature on lower right: Soutine.
RF 1963-85

Whereas the portrayal of human figures is of infrequent occurrence in the works of the Céret period, in the Cagnes paintings one or several figures emerge, along with occasional details, such as hats on heads (*The Village*, No. 118). After 1930, the figures take on greater consistency, and make it possible to identify the presence of a man, a woman or a child. These details are fraught with meaning. Soutine undoubtedly encountered many difficulties in his human relationships, and his quest for "other people" lay at the back of his mind throughout his artistic career. A small anecdotal scene occupies the lower left part of the *Large Blue Tree*; it depicts a man in conversation with a woman seated on a bench; it is hard to decipher the exact forms, since the heads are absorbed by the colored mass of the landscape. But these two forms, in a dominant blue color, parallel to the roadway, equilibrate the composition by counterbalancing the rightward movement of the tree and the house.

A feeling of anguish is released by this painting, in which all the forms are juxtaposed: road, thickets, tree, house and sky. No air circulates. Time seems to have come to a standstill. Certain observers have interpreted this painting as representing the prelude to a storm, but that is an interpretation that recurs in connection with a number of Soutine's later works, and it does not tally with the accounts given by people who knew him. For example, Gerda Groth, who, under the name of Mlle Garde, shared Soutine's existence for three years beginning in 1937, notes in her memoirs (*loc. cit.*) the artist's assertion that he could paint only in the summer season, and then only in fine weather. In all likelihood, the artist's inner anguish fuelled this stifling climate, due among other things to his poor state of health, to his obsession with painting and to his doubts regarding his work, and also, last but not least, to the persecutions that he sensed were lying in wait on the eve of World War II.                                    C.G.

*Collections:*
Paul Guillaume; Mrs. Jean Walter.

*Exhibitions:*
1952, Venice, No. 27; 1959, Paris, No. 37; 1966, Paris, No. 145 (repr.).

*Literature:*
R. Negri, *L'Arte Moderna*, Milan, 1967, p. 205 (color repr.); P. Courthion, 1972, pp. 204-205, fig. D; Mlle Garde (G. Groth), *Mes années avec Soutine*, 1973, p. 22.

# Chaim Soutine

## 133
## *The White House*
(La maison blanche)

Oil on canvas. H. 65 cm.; W. 50 cm.
Unsigned.
RF 1963-92

This landscape stands out as unusual in Soutine's work. The white house rises up in sturdy verticality, and, for once, the house overshadows the trees. An effect of perspective emerges from the two paths that intersect in the foreground and that, merging, continue on the left as a road leading to a small cluster of houses and curving to follow the hill line. The sky is assigned a carefully equilibrated amount of space. Rendered in the same tones as the rest of the landscape, it helps to confer an impression of serenity. The house is clearly delineated in relation to the buildings in the middle ground at the top of the road. Soutine's concern with marking depth of field is one more reason for assigning the date of 1933, proposed by W. George, to this work which is so profoundly different from the landscapes painted in Céret and Vence in the years 1918-1923; however, P. Courthion proposes the date of 1919.     C.G.

*Collections:*
Paul Guillaume; Mrs. Jean Walter.

*Exhibitions:*
1952, Venice, No. 26, 1959, Paris, No. 102; 1966, Paris, No. 143 (repr.); 1973, Paris, No. 62; 1982, Lucerne, No. 96 (repr.).

*Literature:*
W. George, 1959 (repr.); P. Courthion, 1972, p. 41 (pl.), p. 190, fig. E; R. Cogniat, 1973, p. 16 (repr.).

# Maurice Utrillo

Paris, 1883-Dax, 1955

## 134
### *The Butte Pinson Hilltop*
(La Butte Pinson)

Oil on cardboard, on wood backing. H. 48 cm.; W. 37 cm.
Signed on lower right in black ink: Maurice Utrillo, V.
RF 1963-104

Utrillo initiated his artistic apprenticeship by painting landscapes of the countryside around Montmagny, the site of the Butte Pinson, and scenes of Montmartre. His mother, Suzanne Valadon, and his grandmother liked the region north of Paris, and spent their holidays at Pierrefitte. Because of her personal preferences, and in order to remove her son from the disastrous influence of Montmartre, Madame Valadon induced her husband, Paul Mousis, whom she had married in 1896, to build a house on this hilltop, where they eventually settled, at the same time keeping a studio at 12, Rue Cortot, in Montmartre. Under the guidance of his mother, who advised him on his color combinations, Utrillo did a series of views of the Butte Pinson from 1905 to 1907; these included, among others, *Rooftops at Montmagny* (Paris, Centre Georges Pompidou, Musée National d'Art Moderne), in the same range of yellow, green and blue; *La Butte Pinson*, in the Knollys Eardly Collection (England, Pétridès, No. 63), in which the signpost is placed nearer the center and the motif is denser; and one in the Musée de l'Annonciade (Saint-Tropez, Gramont Bequest, Pétridès, No. 64).

The painting shown here was signed in black ink, as was No. 135, and was not listed in the Pétridès catalogue. For a short period of time (1905-1908), Utrillo used dark colors. In the present scene, the buildings, which were an essential theme of his later work, are concealed behind a curtain of trees and wooden fences.                C.G.

*Collections:*
Paul Guillaume; Mrs. Jean Walter.

*Exhibitions:*
1966, Paris, No. 109 (repr.); 1981, Paris, No. 6.

*Literature:*
G. Coquiot, *Maurice, Utrillo, V.*, 1925, p. 13; not listed in the P. Pétridès catalogue.

# Maurice Utrillo

## 135
### *Notre-Dame Cathedral*
(Notre-Dame)

Oil on cardboard. H. 65 cm.; W. 49 cm.
Signed on lower right in black paint: Maurice, Utrillo, V.
RF 1963-103

The year 1895 witnessed the exhibition of Monet's series of paintings of the cathedral of Rouen, at the Durand-Ruel Gallery. Shortly thereafter, other artists began tackling this subject. Like Matisse and Marquet (*Notre-Dame Cathedral*, Paris), and Delaunay (*Cathedral of Laon*), Utrillo, after working from motifs devoid of intrinsic beauty —views of the suburbs or of little streets in Paris— undertook more ambitious subjects which, like certain artists who had preceded him, he interpreted from his personal approach. His concerns were basically similar to those of Monet, who had undertaken the *Cathedral* series only after doing those of the *Haystacks* and the *Poplar Trees*.

Utrillo devoted several works to Notre-Dame, one of which is quite similar to the one shown here (Pétridès, No. 598), while others show variations (Pétridès, Nos. 88, 112, 199).

In the present picture, the cathedral facade occupies the whole of the painted surface except for a few houses on the left, which suggest the beginning of a street. What Utrillo is interested in here is neither the daylight nor the sculptured adornments; rather, it is the achieving of the fullest effect out of an orderly sequence of patterns. The absence of background depth suggests both a massive affirmation of a certainty and the artificial appearance of a stage set. The reddish doors curiously disrupt the rather muted harmony of the greens and blues.

The sides of the painting were given a succession of different backgrounds and the picture remained unfinished. C.G.

*Collections:*
L. Libaude, Paris; Paul Guillaume (in 1929); Mrs. Jean Walter.

*Exhibitions:*
1935, Antwerp, Contemporary Art; 1937, Paris, No. 5; 1966, Paris, No. 110 (repr.); 1980, Athens, No. 41 (color repr.); Tbilisi-Leningrad, No. 50 (repr.); 1983, Paris, No. 10.

*Literature:*
*La Renaissance*, April 1929, No. 4, p. 181 (repr.), pp. 182, 183, 185; W. George, *Arts*, 1959; P. Pétridès, 1959, vol. 1. No. 200 p. 250 (repr. p. 251); P. Pétridès, 1978, *Ma chance et ma réussite*, p. 94.

# Maurice Utrillo

## 136
## *The Great Cathedral, or The Cathedral of Orléans*

(Grande cathédrale ou Cathédrale d'Orléans)

Oil on parqueted plywood. H. 72 cm.; W. 54 cm.
Signed on lower right: Maurice, Utrillo, V.
RF 1963-105

*The Cathedral of Orléans* is dated 1913 by Pétridès (page 404), although J. Fabris and Y. Bourel have assigned it the date of 1909. It was at that time that Utrillo had begun mixing his paint with glue, plaster or cement in order to achieve the highly characteristic whites that he used down to the war years. The model was possibly a postcard view. The straight line that limns the base of the monument, poised somewhat like a maquette on a beige background, is still visible. The large forms were traced with a ruler and compass, but this painting does not correspond to the painstaking work that Utrillo devoted to rendering architectural forms. This is an unfinished work;

the preparations for the background are still visible in the lower part.

The signature had originally been overpainted onto the picture, before being cleaned off and replaced by a signature written in ink. Tabarant reports that Libaude, to whom Utrillo was under contract, scolded the artist for writing his name in overly large script, and that Suzanne Valadon, who usually acted as a go-between, scratched off the painted signature and substituted another one in black ink. A large number of paintings that passed through Libaude's hands underwent the same fate.                C.G.

*Collections:*
L. Libaude, Paris; Paul Guillaume; Mrs. Jean Walter.

*Exhibitions:*
1929, Paris; 1935, Paris, No. 429; 1939, Amsterdam, Stedelijk Museum, *The School of Paris*, No. 128 (repr.); 1946, Paris, No. 87; 1959, Paris, No. 48 (repr.); 1966, Paris, No. 111 (repr.); 1983, Paris, No. 9.

*Literature:*
Tabarant, *Utrillo*, 1926, p. 88; W. George, *La Renaissance*, No. 4, April 1929, (repr. p. 181); W. George, undated, p. 153 (repr.); P. Pétridès, vol. 1., 1959, No. 404, p. 468 (repr. p. 469).

# Maurice Utrillo

## 137
## *The House of Berlioz*

(La maison de Berlioz)

Oil on parqueted plywood. H. 91.5 cm.; W. 121 cm.
Signed and dated on lower right: Maurice-Utrillo, V. 13 September 1914.
RF 1963-100

The title of this painting comes from the fact that the house depicted, which stood at the corner of Rue Saint-Vincent and Rue du Mont-Cenis, was lived in from 1834 to 1837 by Berlioz and his wife, the English actress Harriet Smithson. In 1911, Braque had a studio there. The house was razed in World War I and replaced by an apartment building. Utrillo depicted its two facades, seen from different viewpoints.

His technique here seems to be anterior to the date indicated on the painting. In all probability, this picture was started in 1911 or 1912, and work on it was resumed in 1914. The sky evokes the art of Sisley, whom Utrillo especially admired, its blueness softened with yellow and ochre, echoed in each chimney ledge. On the walls of the house, the dark undercoats emerge in contrast, with a surface stroke. As noted by M. Bundorf: "In this work, we once again see Utrillo's concern with linear design, reflected by his attention to the partitioning off of masses, to marking the outlines of buildings and the edges of wall angles with broad black lines. Only the small patches of foliage projecting beyond the enclosure wall enliven this cold composition of wide, barren expanses" (1966 catalogue, No. 114).

This is one of Utrillo's most austere works, one of the few paintings in which the geometrization of forms, the flattening of volumes and the quasi monochromy enable comparison with analytic, rigorously contemporary Cubism (cf. *Histoire de l'Art*, published by Gallimard in La Bibliothèque de la Pléiade, Paris, volume III, page 576). One of the few other examples is his painting entitled *Rue Montmartre* (Pétridès, volume 1, No. 154), which, precisely, belonged to A. Lefèvre, one of the major Cubist art collectors.

The flag flying over the low facade on the right was probably added when Utrillo took back the painting to sign it. Utrillo consistently shared his life and his emotions with whatever painting was in progress. The year 1914 was one of great upheaval for the artist, who had just been deprived of his accustomed family circle. Utter, whom, his mother had married on 1 September of that year, had departed for the front. Suzanne Valadon left Paris to take work on a farm (Edmond Heuzé, foreword to *L'Œuvre complet de Maurice Utrillo*, Paris, 1959, page 38). The years of the war had a sorry effect on him, and, more than ever, he sought refuge in alcoholism and painting.                    C.G.

*Collections:*
Paul Guillaume; Mrs. Jean Walter.

*Exhibitions:*
1918, Paris, Galerie Paul Guillaume, *Peintres d'aujourd'hui*, No. 30; 1966, Paris, No. 114 (repr.); 1983, Paris, No. 23.

*Literature:*
G. Charensol, "Paul Guillaume, curieux homme et homme curieux," *Plaisir de France*, December 1966; P. Pétridès, vol. 2, 1962, No. 439 p. 31 (repr.).

Utrillo, *Street in Montmartre*,
formerly in A. Lefèvre Collection.

# Maurice Utrillo

## 138
## *Rue du Mont-Cenis*
(Rue du Mont-Cenis)

Oil on parqueted cardboard. H. 76 cm.; W. 107 cm.
Signed and dated on lower right:
Maurice, Utrillo, V. 13 December 1914.
RF 1963-101

The Rue du Mont-Cenis was Utrillo's source of inspiration for many paintings. When he was living at Mr. Gay's, his bedroom window looked out upon this street, and his faithfulness to this subject reflects the comprehension he enjoyed on the part of the owner of the bistro called Le Casse-croûte.

This view of the Rue du Mont-Cenis, depicted in autumn, is a studio painting. The setting was constructed with a ruler; the perspective of the houses follows the slope of the street. Utrillo was striving to achieve new effects with his materials, using a very thick paint with a high content of the plaster that was being manufactured in Montmartre at the time. The colorings are autumnal. The yellow veers toward green and dominates, together with brown. The flag seems to have been added later, because there are visible traces of the shutter, whose lower part is now covered.

This painting bears the date of 13 December 1914, a day that may have marked an important event in Utrillo's life. The work had originally been signed in paint, as had No. 136, and traces of this earlier signature remain. It was scraped off and was covered over by the new signature, written in ink, which is considerably posterior to the first one.                                                     C.G.

## 138-A
## *Rue du Mont-Cenis*
(Rue du Mont-Cenis)

Oil on canvas. H. 72 cm.; W. 106 cm.
Signed on lower right: Maurice Utrillo, V.
RF 1960-54

Although the main lines of the composition are the same as in No. 138, these two works are nevertheless quite different. The clearly awkward insertion of the elements and the laboriousness of the brushwork make one reluctant to ascribe to Utrillo's hand the full execution of this painting.
                                                     M.H.

*Collections:*
Paul Guillaume; Mrs. Jean Walter.

*Exhibitions:*
1943, Paris, Galerie Charpentier, *L'Automne*, No. 266 (repr.); 1966, Paris, No. 112 (repr.); 1983, Paris, No. 21.

*Literature:*
Not listed in the P. Pétridès catalogue.

*Collections:*
Paul Guillaume; Mrs. Jean Walter.

*Exhibitions:*
1946, Paris, No. 86; 1966, Paris, No. 113 (repr.); 1983, Paris, No. 22.

*Literature:*
No listed in the P. Pétridès catalogue.

138

138 bis

# Maurice Utrillo

## 139
### *Church at Clignancourt*
(Eglise de Clignancourt)

Oil on canvas. H. 73 cm.; W. 100 cm.
Signed on lower right: Maurice Utrillo, V.
RF 1963-99

Emotional reasons frequently moved Utrillo to deal with certain themes that he took up again and again. One evening, he confided to G. Coquiot: "I was born in Paris on 25 December 1883, during the night of the Nativity, at 3, Rue du Poteau, next door to the church of Notre-Dame de Clignancourt. That church is neither very beautiful nor very ancient, and it just sits there all by itself. All the same, I'm deeply attached to it, and I painted it especially for my mother, who's keeping the picture" (*op. cit.*).

This work was painted in the studio. The ruled lines emerge in the outline of the edifice, and perspective, marked by the rows of houses, seems to have been abided by. Human figures stand out here and there, scattered over the space. Utrillo has striven to single out the foundations of the church. It was a matter of indifference to him that the structure lacked any outstanding character: in its architecture, he discerned stable lines, a pretext for a clear arrangement of design and the possibility for simple effects of perspective, occasionally akin to academism. As noted by Waldemar George, a critic who was well acquainted with Utrillo: "The *Church at Clignancourt* marks Utrillo's progression toward a linear style, toward a static view. In the place of his youthful ardour and fecund disorder, there is now the need for clarity" (*op. cit.*).     C.G.

*Collections:*
Paul Guillaume; Mrs. Jean Walter.

*Exhibitions:*
1959, Paris, No. 64; 1960, Paris, No. 97; 1966, Paris, No. 115 (repr.); 1980, Athens, No. 42 (color repr.); 1981, Tbilisi-Leningrad, No. 51 (repr.); 1983, Paris-Liège-Marcq-en-Barœul, No. 30.

*Literature:*
G. Coquiot, *Maurice, Utrillo, V.*, Paris, 1925, p. 11; W. George, undated, p. 156; P. Pétridès, 1962, vol. II, No. 465, p. 50 (repr. p. 51).

# Maurice Utrillo

## 140
### *Saint-Pierre Church*
(Eglise Saint-Pierre)

Oil on parqueted cardboard. H. 76 cm.; W. 105 cm.
Signed on lower right: Maurice, Utrillo, V.
RF 1963-102

The Saint-Pierre church, perched at the top of the Montmartre heights, was a frequent source of Utrillo's inspiration, and his variations on this theme escape monotony through the richness of the angles of the artist's viewpoint and through the coloring matter.

In this view, the artist chose to depict the monument in its anonymity. The point of departure was probably a postcard view, judging from the symmetry of the design and its right-angled lines. The artist's concern did not lie with setting off the edifice itself; rather, he was interested in rendering the sundry elements of its composition. There is the bituminous element of the sidewalk and street paving, done in fine horizontal strokes, in which light tones are interspersed with dark tones so as to bring out differences in levels and imperfections in the ground. A more thickly and more flatly applied paint characterizes the walls of the facing houses, as well as those of the church and of Sacré-Cœur basilica, shown in the background. Here and there, it is interrupted by trickled paint, as seen on the wall of the entrance gate set off by black grillwork, or, as is the case in the house on the right, the undercoat shows through, revealing the state of dilapidation of the plaster coating. The presence of several windows might have helped to enliven these facades, but the opacity of the brown tones makes them into blind openings. The plant element, in its alternation of tonalities, produced by the sun's effort to pierce the thickness of the foliage, is the only movement in this landscape. The sky, which occupies practically half of the composition, is done with a compact brush stroke and, instead of creating depth of field, it reduces the perspective.

With this painting, Utrillo was gradually progressing toward color. A few hesitant attempts had been made with the green tones of the *Church of Clignancourt* (No. 139). Here, they are diversified with the addition of grey, green and yellow tones.　　　　　　　　　　　　C.G.

*Collections:*
Paul Guillaume; Mrs. Jean Walter.

*Exhibitions:*
1946, Paris, No. 88; 1959, Paris, No. 63 (repr.); 1966, Paris, No. 116 (repr.); 1983, Paris, No. 29.

*Literature:*
P. Pétridès, 1962, vol. II, No. 442, p. 32 (repr. p. 33).

# Maurice Utrillo

## 141
## *Town Hall with Flag*
(La mairie au drapeau)

Oil on canvas. H. 98 cm.; W. 130 cm.
Signed and dated on lower left in black ink: Maurice. Utrillo. V. 1924.
RF 1960-53

The first-hand reports by Utrillo's friends and dealers concur with regard to establishing the sources of inspiration for his paintings. When his health allowed and when the scene moved him, Utrillo worked from the motif. In 1909, his health began to deteriorate, and he stayed in sanatoriums, or lived in a hotel room or in his studio under the surveillance of a close friend or relative. His mother, Suzanne Valadon, and his stepfather, André Utter, brought him postcards designed to let him continue painting and to diversify his subjects. A painting depicting this same motif, dated 1924, belonged to Lucie Valore, when she was married to Robert Pauwels (Galliéra auction, 10 June 1970, reproduction No. 124). Although it closely resembles the scene shown here, the human figures are arranged differently. According to Pétridès, *Town Hall with Flag* represents the village of Maixe (Meurthe-et-Moselle). The body of the pigment is characteristic of Utrillo's whites, although less thickly applied than in his white period. He had a certain fascination for rendering masonry and stonework, and in various places, he used a black brush to draw in the outlines of materials —stones or bricks. On the left there is a group of men and women in conversation, garbed in 1925 style: mid-calf skirts, soft hats, broad-edged boots, long jackets for the men. As in a photograph, their activity seems to have been suddenly interrupted, and two of the women, captured in motion, stand facing each other. Utrillo has created a contrast between the left part, enlivened by human figures, and the righthand side, which looks unfinished.

The signature on this painting is not Utrillo's usual signature. Its location near the center, the "V" of Valadon, and the form of the "4" are unusual. In all likelihood, this signature was affixed hastily by the artist's mother at the time the sale was transacted. C.G.

---

*Collections:*
Paul Guillaume; Mrs. Jean Walter.

*Exhibitions:*
1966, Paris, No. 118 (repr.); 1980, Athens, No. 43 (color repr.); 1981, Tbilisi-Leningrad, No. 52 (repr.); 1983, Paris-Liège-Marcq-en-Barœul, No. 42.

*Literature:*
F. Carco, *Maurice Utrillo*, Paris, 1921, p. 63 (repr.); W. George, undated, p. 156; P. Pétridès, 1962, vol. II, No. 1091, p. 432 (repr. p. 433).

# Maurice Utrillo

## 142
## *The Bernot House*
(La maison Bernot)

Oil on canvas. H. 100 cm.; W. 146 cm.
Signed and dated on lower right in black ink: Maurice, Utrillo, V, February 1924.
RF 1960-52

The Bernot house stands at a turning point in the Rue du Mont-Cenis, in Montmartre.

This same motif, featuring a few variations in the rendering of the roof, is represented in a drawing (charcoal, pastels and colored crayons, dated March 1924, auction at Sotheby's, London, 8 July 1965, No. 47, reproduction).

The brushwork in this townscape is quite different from that used in the preceding paintings. Heavy black lines bring out the architectural design, and enabled transcription from the postcard scene that was probably the basis for the artist's inspiration.

In this painting, Utrillo provides an animated version of a Montmartre street, both in his use of bright colors and in the human figures, which are portrayed almost as caricatures based on the stereotypes that he repeated on various occasions, including figures of women and bohemian artists. Utrillo, who painted this picture during a stay in France's Ain region, "recollects the humblest details and, with his brush, arranges them in a precise, beguiling array in order to better savour the melancholy feeling that sweeps over him" (Francis Carco, *Maurice Utrillo*, Paris, 1921). C.G.

*Collections:*
Paul Guillaume; Mrs. Jean Walter.

*Exhibitions:*
1945, Paris, Galerie Charpentier, *Paysages de France*, No. 187 (repr.); 1957, Paris, Galerie Charpentier, *Cent Chefs-d'œuvre de l'Art français, 1750-1950*, No. 99; 1959, Paris, No. 91 (repr.); 1966, Paris, No. 117 (repr.); 1983, Paris-Liège-Marcq-en-Barœul, No. 41.

*Literature:*
W. George, undated, p. 156; P. Pétridès, 1962, vol. 2, No. 1060, p. 418 (repr. p. 419).

# Kees Van Dongen

Delfshaven, 1877-Monaco, 1968

## 143

## *Portrait of Paul Guillaume*

(Portrait de Paul Guillaume)

Oil on canvas. H. 100 cm.; L. 74 cm.
Signed on the right in black: Van Dongen.
RF 1963-53

The friendship between Paul Guillaume and Kees Van Dongen was already on a long-time footing when the artist painted this portrait of the art dealer. In fact, in March 1918, Guillaume had mounted a special exhibition of twenty-five of the artist's works, the catalogue for which featured a foreword by Guillaume Apollinaire. Here, Van Dongen gives free rein to his talent as a painter of society figures, thanks to which he won renown after World War I. This *Portrait of Paul Guillaume* belongs on the impressively long list of portraits of prominent individuals of "that between-wars society for whose passing show... Van Dongen... had undeniably been the brilliant ballet master" (G. Diehl, *Van Dongen*, Paris, 1968, page 7), whom he was wont to entertain at glittering parties in his residence at 5, Rue Juliette-Lamber. It was probably at this latter address that he painted this portrait of the art dealer, representing not so much Modigliani's *Nova Pilota* (No. 61) as the socially prominent figure who is depicted by the "official" painter of the Paris "smart set." Paul Guillaume, in a blue suit — this same blue is repeated in the bow tie and is subtly used by the artist in the reflections of the model's hair and in the background of the painting —

displays the emblem of the Legion of Honor on his lapel. He had been awarded this distinction on 7 April 1930, in recognition of his activities both as an art publisher and an art critic, and was officially initiated into membership on 23 April 1930 by Ambroise Vollard. It is hence reasonable to assume that the execution of this portrait followed soon after the bestowing of the distinction. Here, Van Dongen shows himself to be both brilliant and sparing in his means (the model's suit is brought out quite simply by a few swift brushstrokes overlaid upon the colored mass that depicts the clothing). This is doubtless one of those portraits for which he required only four or five sittings, thereby earning the vast admiration of his models. Whatever the case, this portrait also reveals the somewhat facile easiness and the complete mastery that Van Dongen displayed in his contemporary portraits of such widely differing personalities as *Boni de Castellane* (1928, private collection), *Paul Painlevé* (1931) and *Anna de Noailles* (1931, Amsterdam, Stedlijk Museum). Van Dongen's activity as a portrait painter continued until late in his life (portraits of *Utrillo*, 1948, private collection, and *Brigitte Bardot*, 1954, private collection).

H.G.

*Collections:*
Paul Guillaume; Mrs. Jean Walter.

*Exhibitions:*
1966, Paris, No. 63 (repr.); 1980, Athens, No. 44 (color repr.); 1981, Tbilisi-Leningrad, No. 53 (color repr.).

*Literature:*
G. Charensol, "Guillaume, curieux homme et homme curieux," *Plaisir de France*, December 1966, p. 15 (repr.).

# Biography

## Cézanne, Paul
Aix-en-Provence, 1839-1906

After having been virtually ignored during his lifetime, Cézanne was recognized posthumously as being one of the outstanding figures in the history of painting.

He was the scion of an affluent family, and his father, after attempting to dissuade young Paul from pursuing his vocation, provided the wherewithal that enabled him to continue painting for a long time, except during a period of a few years. Cézanne's career is generally regarded as divided into four periods:

After spending his youth in Aix-en-Provence, where he formed a friendship with Emile Zola, he came to Paris, enrolled in a private academy, and frequented the Louvre; he devoted his talent to romantic painting, showing a predilection for dramatic landscapes and animated scenes. He applied dark colors violently onto the canvas.

As the result of contacts with the Impressionists, especially with Pissarro, Cézanne's palette lightened, and he began to use silvery lighting effects, refined tones and more peaceful patterns of composition. However, he remained rather isolated within the group.

After 1880-1882, Cézanne's representation of nature, particularly of southern French landscapes, acquired a grandiose, serene character, while in his still lifes and figures, he revolutionized the usual methods of rendering volume and space. This is generally described as Cézanne's classical period.

After 1890, his landscapes became energized with powerful lyricism, and, whatever the subject matter (landscape, bathers, still life, individual portrait or figure), Cézanne adopted a wholly new vision from which traditional perspective was definitively banished and in which forms became nearly illegible. All the artists of the succeeding generation turned this revolution to their advantage.

Paul Guillaume owned many Cézanne paintings, but sold most of them to collectors or museums, mainly in the United States. Most of the Cézannes in the Musée de l'Orangerie represent personal purchases made by Mrs. Walter.

## Derain, André
Chatou 1880-Garches 1954

Derain was the son of a pastry chef in the Parisian suburb of Chatou. After a start as an engineering student, he soon abandoned this curriculum in order to devote himself to painting. He became acquainted with Matisse in a private art academy in which Eugène Carrière was a corrector, and, in 1900, he met Maurice de Vlaminck, with whom he began a long and stormy friendship. During the summer of 1905, Derain joined Matisse in Collioure; this period yielded canvasses displaying extremely strident colors and, at the Salon d'Automne, these contributed to the famous scandal of the "cage of wild beasts," the Fauves. Already steeped in a broad artistic culture, Derain proceeded to discover African art, and developed a passionate admiration for Cézanne's work and for early painting, whence the qualifying adjectives assigned to certain "periods" in his production (Negro, Byzantine, Cézannian, etc.). He also formed friendships with Braque, Picasso and Modigliani, and undertook his first sculptures. He thenceforth enjoyed the backing of D. H. Kahnweiler, the art dealer for the Cubists.

Beginning in 1912, Derain's art was marked by the archaistic stylization of his designs and by austerity in his choice of colors. The 1914-1918 war years obliged him to interrupt his painting. However, in 1916, Paul Guillaume was able to mount Derain's first major one-man show. This event marked the onset of a lasting friendship between the two men. When Derain again took up his brushes, he adopted a more elegant manner of designing, but remained faithful to dark hues, notably browns, greys and blacks, which he handled with great mastery.

Derain became a dominant figure on the Paris art scene, and the painters of the succeeding generation denounced this new evolution of the artist, an evolution in which they claimed to discern reminiscences of early painting, and Derain's rejection of his initial venturesomeness. For the members of the new generation, this may have been a way of setting up their defense against Derain's strong personality, whose ascendancy over younger artists was incontrovertible.

At the start of his career, Derain became interested in book-illustrating (his first venture into this activity occurred in 1902), and he produced a considerable body of work in the way of both engravings and sculptures. He also designed several stage- and ballet sets, notably for Diaghilev's Ballets Russes, for the Ballets de Monte Carlo and for the festival of Aix-en-Provence.

# Gauguin, Paul

Paris, 1848-Atouana (The Marquesas), 1903

Gauguin was the grandson of the socialist militant Flora Tristan, and spent part of his boyhood in Peru, where he made an initial contact with non-Western art forms. After returning to France, he signed on as a trainee in the Merchant Service, and began an uneventful career as an employee of an exchange agent, an activity that provided him with an ample livelihood. At the time, Gauguin was merely an amateur painter interested in avant-garde art. Pissarro introduced him to Impressionism, and in 1883, Gauguin resolved to devote himself full-time to painting. For Gauguin, this decision ushered in an existence that would be marked by financial destitution and perpetual wanderings, which led him first to Brittany, and then to Martinique and Panama. Once back in France, he returned to Brittany, and swiftly emerged as the leader of a group opposed to Impressionism. His heavily delineated forms were surrounded with colors applied in flat tints, and traditional depth and modelling were banished. He undertook a period of residence in Arles with Van Gogh, an experiment that wound up in a dramatic finish. Ever dissatisfied in his quest for a primitive world, and eager for new sources of inspiration, Gauguin sailed for Tahiti, where he lived for eighteen months before returning to France and then setting out again for Oceania; he died amidst poverty and isolation just as the Paris art world was beginning to grant recognition to his grandiose. powerfully poetic work.

# Laurencin, Marie

Paris, 1883-1957

Although belonging to a middle-class family, Marie Laurencin was obliged to make her own way early in life. After completing her secondary studies, she hesitated between poetry and painting. Encouraged by Braque, and having become Apollinaire's Egeira, she frequented the Bateau-Lavoir, the ramshackle building in Montmartre that housed, notably, Picasso, Modigliani and Van Dongen; she exhibited with Robert Delaunay and the Cubists, with whom she briefly joined forces, although without much conviction, for her talents lay elsewhere. From the Cubist experience, she brought to her art a certain economy of statement, true rigorousness and the rejection of traditional perspective. Her somewhat pale chromatism also derived from this same influence, but with it she excelled in producing felicitous harmonies of pinks and blues blended with greys. Laurencin's paintings are consistently well-constructed.

In 1916, she married the German amateur painter Otto von Waëtjen, and spent the war years in exile in Spain, not returning to Paris until 1921. Laurencin thereupon swiftly regained her place in the Paris art world. She designed several sets for Diaghilev's Ballets Russes and for the Comédie-Française. She enjoyed a friendship with Paul Guillaume and his wife, and became one of the most sought-after portraitists of fashionable society; in addition, she designed fabrics and wallpapers, as well as producing a considerable number of engravings.

# Matisse, Henri
Le Cateau-Cambrésis, 1869-Nice, 1954

Matisse attended the classes of Gustave Moreau at the Paris School of Fine Arts, where his fellow students included Rouault, Marquet and Manguin. Moreau—an intelligent, liberal-minded teacher—realized his student's forceful personality, and after Moreau's death, Matisse proceeded to carve out his own career independently, quickly discarding academic tradition. After a brief period of Neo-Impressionism, he opted for brilliant colors and complete freedom of artistic expression. When the Fauve scandal occurred, at the 1905 Salon d'Automne in which he was exhibiting, Matisse emerged as the leader of the group. He undertook travels to Algeria, Germany, Russia and Morocco. Art students from every country flocked to the atelier that he directed.

From 1914 on, Matisse lived during the greater part of every year on the Mediterranean coast; his prestige was steadily enhanced, more so abroad than in France. His life story is inextricably identified with the story of his ceaseless activity, interspersed with the occasional travels that enriched his vision.

In 1918, Paul Guillaume held his first exhibition of Matisse, for whom he became one of the principal dealers in the 1920s. He even purchased works at auction, and many of the Matisse works that are now in the United States passed through Guillaume's hands.

By 1903, Matisse had begun doing sculpture and was producing his first engravings; from then on, he continued to diversify his ways of expression increasingly and with equally felicitous results (stage sets, sculptures, book illustrations, tapestries, cut papers). This rich array of activities found its crowning expression in the Dominican chapel in Vence, in which all the decorations are by Matisse, who devoted the bulk of his time to this undertaking from 1948 to 1951.

The technical masterfulness, the formal beauty and the poetic richness of Matisse's works, as well as his ability to diversify his art, to which these works testify, earned him an outstanding place in twentieth-century art and explain his prestige in the eyes of the artists of succeeding generations.

# Modigliani, Amedeo
Livorno, 1884-Paris, 1920

Modigliani's brief but pathetic career emerges like a resume—indeed, like the very symbol—of that of many twentieth-century artists. After leaving his native Italy at a fairly young age (in 1906) to settle in Paris, he experienced the picturesque but poverty-stricken existence of the down-and-out artist, doing sketches in the cafés of Montmartre and Montparnasse, where he sold his works in order to eke out a living. He mingled with the avant-garde circles, did sculpture with the Romanian Brancusi, who had also recently moved to Paris. Modigliani became interested in African sculpture and archaic arts, as was Paul Guillaume, whom he met in 1914 through the poet Max Jacob. Guillaume noted as follows: "In 1914, throughout 1915 and during part of 1916, I was Modigliani's sole customer."

Modigliani's painting was initially influenced by Fauvism, but soon acquired a sheerly personal atmosphere, belonging to no school. Portraits and full-length figures were virtually his only subjects. Each of his figures is outlined in clear, sinuous strokes; he gradually and increasingly stylized the form, to which he imparted a prodigious elegance. Modigliani's career was extremely brief: his health undermined by poverty and alcohol, he died in 1920, just as his work was beginning to win public recognition thanks to the dealers Paul Guillaume and Zborovsky.

# Monet, Claude
Paris, 1840-Giverny, 1926

At the very first Impressionist exhibition held in Nadar's studio in 1874, Claude Monet emerged as the leading figure in this innovating movement. In fact, it was because of the title of one of his paintings, *Impression, soleil levant (Impression, Sunrise)*, that a critic, primarily in a spirit of derision, coined the word Impressionism, which would endure and enjoy soaring heights of fame and fortune.

After spending the early part of his life in Le Havre, where he was encouraged by Boudin, Monet studied in Paris at the Académie Suisse, where he met Pissarro, and also in Gleyre's atelier, where he formed friendships with Renoir, Bazille and Sisley. He divided his time between the Normandy coasts and the Paris area, and his subject matter at this time was quite varied. His themes included, along with landscapes and still lifes, a few major compositions featuring human figures. In 1870, Monet traveled to England with Pissarro and met Paul Durand-Ruel, the dealer who would later be handling his works. He exhibited in the Impressionist shows in 1874, 1876, 1877 and 1882, and more exclusively devoted his energies to landscapes. In 1880, Monet had his first one-mane show, marking the end of the difficult period of his life and the beginning of his popularity. He undertook further travels through France and to other countries, proceeding to Holland, Norway, London and Venice. After living in Argenteuil and Vetheuil, he settled in Giverny in 1882.

Monet's initial "series" paintings date from 1890-1894, including *Haystacks, Poplar Trees* and *Rouen Cathedral*. He set up several canvasses simultaneously and, under the changing hours of daylight and during the different seasons, he investigated the variations of light on a given motif. In his garden at Giverny, he installed a water-lily pond and painted his *Nymphea* compositions, the greatest of which were donated to the French government in 1922, through Clemenceau's intervention, and were hung in the Musée de l'Orangerie. Although claiming to be a "realist," Monet set about devising a colored environment in which the references to nature are increasingly rare and the forms ever less precise. He thereby paved the way for the questing of the abstract painters. The artists of succeeding generations made no mistake about it. Kandinsky, for example, stated that it was by looking at Monet's *Haystacks* that he had realized what "modern" painting could be.

# Picasso, Pablo
Málaga, Spain, 1881-Mougins, 1973

After an initial period of study in Spain, Picasso moved to Paris in 1900. At the outset, he was influenced by the caricatural, strident art of Toulouse-Lautrec and Forain, and painted people in everyday situations, followed by virtually monochromatic compositions, typical of his blue and pink periods. In his quest for increasingly stylized forms, influenced by Cézanne and, doubtlessly, also by African art and the ancient arts that had recently regained their popularity, Picasso, together with his friend Braque, oriented his approach toward a style that has gone down in history as Cubism. His painting entitled *Les Demoiselles d'Avignon* constituted its starting point. In this work the forms are discordant in structure and are becoming geometrical, a prelude to becoming increasingly unreadable, and the colors are reduced to a camaieu. Concurrently, Picasso took up the cut-paper technique and became interested in sculpture.

But Picasso moved in a state of perpetually ongoing change, and frequently gave proof of his ability to paint pictures of utterly different types within a few days of one another. After 1914, without rejecting what Cubism had brought him, he resorted to using more distinctly emergent colors, in which objects became more distinguishable. A major share of his artistic concern was thenceforth devoted to stage-set designing. There ensued another mutation, geared to linear, pared down artistic expression, and after 1929, he resumed a form of expressionism of which the most typical example is *Guernica*, inspired by the Spanish civil war. Picasso remained continuously and prodigiously active as a stage-set designer, engraver, sculptor and ceramist, and ceaselessly added to a body of work that is marked by his disquietude as a questing artist and by his never-ending need to create.

Although Paul Guillaume by no means ignored Picasso's Cubist period, of which he owned a few paintings, he was primarily concerned with Picasso's production from the period at which he had made the artist's acquaintance, during the 1920s, and, curiously, also with the works that had preceded *Les Demoiselles d'Avignon*.

# Renoir, Pierre-Auguste
Limoges, 1841-Cagnes-sur-Mer, 1919

Renoir, who came from a poverty-stricken family, began as a porcelain painter, before progressing to the decoration of window blinds and earning enough money to pay his tuition at the Ecole des Beaux-Arts, where he enrolled in 1862. At the same time, he painted in the Louvre, and also in Gleyre's atelier, the initial stronghold of the Impressionist group. In the Fontainebleau forest, he painted outdoors with Monet, Bazille and Sisley. He exhibited at the official Salon in 1864, but after that date his works were refused. In 1869, he was in Bougival with Monet; during the Franco-Prussian war in 1870, he was mobilized in Bordeaux and later assigned to Tarbes.

Renoir adopted light colors sometime around 1872. He did not confine himself to either easel painting or landscapes, and undertook large-sized compositions depicting human figures, the best-known being *Le Moulin de la Galette*. Throughout his career, without discontinuing his landscapes, he found his preferred subjects in portraits and full-length figures.

Renoir exhibited with the Impressionists in 1874, 1876, 1877 and 1882; in 1878, he was again allowed to exhibit at the official Salon. His art evolved, his subject matter became more sophisticated, and his works from this period attest to dazzling technical mastery. From a trip to Algeria in 1881, he brought back vividly colored paintings in which the light fairly vibrates.

In 1882, Renoir travelled to Italy, where he looked at the works of Raphael, notably. He felt the need for discipline, devoted his skills to lines and forms, and adopted cruder colors. This "Ingresque" period began around 1883.

Within a few years' time, he resumed using fuller, less sharply defined outlines. He undertook further travels before settling in Cagnes, near Nice, in 1903. Renoir's last paintings, which testify to his adaptation to change, were handled in warm color harmonies in which red predominated. In addition to his familiar subjects (nudes, human figures, still lifes), he resumed painting landscapes, which he had abandoned over a certain length of time.

# Rousseau, Henri,
called the Douanier Rousseau
Laval, 1844-Paris, 1910

Henri Rousseau, who was actually a minor civil servant in the employ of the Paris toll house authority rather than a customs agent, devoted his leisure time to painting, in addition to dabbling in both music and literature. From 1885 on, he exhibited regularly at the Salon des Indépendants, and in 1893, he requested early retirement in order to give himself full-time to his passion for painting. The so-called Douanier Rousseau, a self-taught artist whose work cannot be identified with any school of painting, occasionally drew his inspiration from certain academic painters or from illustrated magazines. The exotic backgrounds in certain of his scenes are largely the result of his visits to the Paris Zoological Gardens, since he had never been to Mexico, contrary to what the public was encouraged to fondly imagine and to what had been believed by the poet Guillaume Apollinaire, his great admirer.

The Douanier Rousseau's work, evidence of a broad range of inspiration clearly marked by unity of style, includes urban landscapes of Paris and its suburbs, portraits, compositions involving several figures, as well as jungle scenes. In every case, Rousseau combined painstakingly minute execution with rigorousness of style and amazing poetic inventiveness, in addition to a sharply attuned sense of color harmonies. In the early part of the twentieth century, he began to win recognition and to enjoy the devoted admiration of many avant-garde artists, including notably Signac, Brancusi, Picasso, Robert and Sonia Delaunay and Kandinsky. It seems that the young Paul Guillaume had never actually met Rousseau, but had gathered first-hand information about him from Apollinaire.

# Sisley, Alfred
Paris, 1839-Moret-sur-Loing, 1899

Alfred Sisley was born in Paris to English parents who had planned a business career for their son. After moving to England to learn the rudiments of trade, Sisley became more interested in Turner and Constable than in commercial dealings. He returned to Paris determined to become a painter and, in 1862, enrolled in Gleyre's atelier. He enjoyed friendships with Monet, Renoir and Bazille. He painted with them in Fontainebleau, admired the artists of the Barbizon School, and engaged in plein air painting.

In 1870, the Franco-Prussian war spelled the financial ruin of his family. Thenceforth, Sisley shared the struggles and poverty-stricken existences of his fellow artists. He exhibited with the Impressionists in 1874, 1876, 1877 and 1882. He also sought to show his works at the official Salon, but his application was rejected. Despite assistance from the critic T. Duret and the dealer Durand-Ruel, Sisley's existence remained precarious, and his paintings did not win recognition until after his death.

Sisley made several trips to England, but painted mostly in the area around Paris (Argenteuil, Louveciennes). In 1882, he settled in Moret-sur-Loing.

# Soutine, Chaim
Smilovichi, Lithuania, 1894-Paris, 1943

The son of a poverty-stricken Lithuanian village tailor, Soutine was fascinated by painting at an early age. After working in Minsk and, later, in Vilno (Vilnius), he moved to Paris at the age of seventeen. Aside from a brief period of attendance at the Ecole des Beaux-Arts, he was self-taught, in addition to gleaning insights from contacts with the Fauvists and with his friends Chagall and Modigliani. Soutine found quarters at the "Ruche," the building in the Vaugirard district of Paris made available to needy artists by the sculptor Alfred Boucher; many of the "Ruche" residents were from central or eastern Europe. From 1919 to 1922, he lived in southern France, in Cagnes and Céret, before returning to Paris. After years of near-starvation, he at length won fame and fortune when Paul Guillaume discovered him and introduced him to Dr. Alfred Barnes, the founder of the Barnes Foundation at Merion, Pennsylvania, who purchased about one hundred of Soutine's works in 1923 (cf. catalogue commentary, page 119).

Soutine's restless, uneasy disposition often moved him to destroy his paintings, and after 1933 he virtually discontinued working. His work shows little development. However, his mobile landscapes were largely produced in the years prior to 1922; after that date, he primarily expressed himself in sanguinolent still lifes and in a series depicting motionless, twisted faces, for which the paint is applied by means of brushwork that makes it look both thickly laid on and liquid, in which contours are sometimes swallowed up by flowing surges of warm hues. As a Jew, Soutine was hunted by the Nazis during the Occupation of France; he had to go into hiding, and died of a stomach ulcer that could not be treated in time.

# Utrillo, Maurice
Paris, 1883-Dax, 1955

Utrillo was the natural son of Suzanne Valadon, who herself had become a highly original painter after posing for Puvis de Chavannes, Renoir and other artists. He was advised to take up painting as a means of overcoming the alcoholism to which he fell victim at a very young age. In the beginning, he received instruction from his mother, who quickly realized the originality of her son's talent and encouraged him to continue.

Virtually all of Utrillo's work was devoted to the depiction of landscapes. At the outset, he was influenced by the Impressionists, notably by Sisley, but swiftly developed his own individual style. His preferred sites were the streets of Paris and its suburbs, which he painted from life; not until later on did he use postcard scenes to fix his compositions. His earliest landscapes, generally devoid of figures, were handled in darker colors, and the brushwork is conspicuously visible; beginning about 1909, his paint was applied in smoother, thick touches, occasionally enhanced by the addition of plaster, and he adopted a color range in which grey and white predominated, to the almost total exclusion of any other color. Not until about 1916 did he adopt brighter, more varied colors. He was starting to become known, and a certain monotony occasionally pervaded his paintings, while a rather facile legend caught the public fancy, that of the instinctive, alcoholic artistic genius, whereas, actually, Utrillo's art, especially in his finest periods, emerges as something that is quite sure of itself.

# Van Dongen, Kees
Delfshaven, 1877-Monaco, 1968

After briefly attending Rotterdam's School of Decorative Arts, the young Dutchman Van Dongen moved to Paris in 1897. In Montmartre, he eked out a precarious existence like many of the young painters of his generation, becoming largely self-taught, visiting the official Salons and the art galleries. He first gained recognition for his drawings, which were published in satirical magazines (notably *L'Assiette au Beurre*) to which Villon, Vallotton, Marcoussin, Kupka and Juan Gris were also contributors. After a transient Pointillist period, Van Dongen became one of the most violent converts to Fauvism, to which he remained faithful longer than the others. Actually, he occupied a somewhat special place within that movement, evincing a predilection for colors with a shot effect, and for harsh lighting effects that hardened the features of his models: the latter included a considerable array of distinguished figures from the entertainment world, and Van Dongen was beginning to become known. Starting in about 1913, his colors became less strident, and it was at this time that he started bestowing his characteristic long-limbed shapes upon his human and animal figures. Van Dongen's first exhibitions were organized by Ambroise Vollard, Kahnweiler, Bernheim-Jeune, and, in 1915, by Paul Guillaume.

In the 1920s, Van Dongen resumed using broader brushstrokes and a more naturalistic representation. He became the official portraitist of the members of Paris' high society and its demi-monde, for whom he gave fabulous parties in his studio. Writers, diplomats, businessmen and stage performers vied for the distinction of sitting for him. Of these people, he produced strictly objective images, executing with great ease an amazing series of portraits many of which verge on caricature.

# Bibliography:

Publications and articles listed
in abbreviated form in the catalogue.

*L'Atelier de Renoir,* 2 volumes, Paris, 1931
Abe, Yoshio and Marchesseau, Daniel
*Marie Laurencin,* Tokyo 1980
Barnes, Albert C. and de Mazia, Violette
*The Art of Renoir,* Philadelphia, Pennsylvania, 1944
Barr, Alfred H. Jr.
*Matisse, his Art and his Public,* New York, 1951
Basler, Adolphe
*Henri Rousseau, sa vie et son œuvre, Paris, 1927*
*Basler, Adolphe*
*André Derain,* Les Albums d'Art Druet XXI, Paris, 1929
Basler, Adolphe
"M. Paul Guillaume et sa collection de tableaux", *L'Amour de l'Art,* July 1929, pp. 252-256, p. 274
Basler, Adolphe
*Modigliani,* Paris, 1931
Bouret, Jean
*Henri Rousseau,* Neuchâtel, 1961
Brion, Marcel
*Cézanne,* Paris, 1974
Cachin, Françoise and Ceroni, Ambrogio
*Tout l'œuvre peint de Modigliani,* Milan, 1970, Paris, 1972
Castaing, Marcellin and Leymarie, Jean
*Soutine,* Paris and Lausanne, 1963
Cogniat, Raymond
*Soutine,* Paris, 1973
Courthion, Pierre
*Henri Rousseau, Le Douanier,* Geneva, 1944
Courthion, Pierre
*Soutine, peintre du déchirant,* Lausanne, 1972
Daix, Pierre and Boudaille, Georges
*Picasso 1900-1906, catalogue raisonné de l'œuvre peint,* Neuchâtel and Paris, 1966
Dale, Maud
*Modigliani,* New York, 1929
Daulte, François
*Auguste Renoir, catalogue raisonné de l'œuvre peint,* Volume 1: Figures, Lausanne, 1971
Descargues, Pierre
*Modigliani,* Paris, 1954
Diehl, Gaston
*Derain,* Paris, undated [1964]
Drucker, Michel
*Renoir,* Paris, 1944
Drucker, Michel
*Renoir,* Paris, 1955
Elgar, Frank
*Rousseau,* Paris, 1980
Fermigier, André

*Picasso,* Paris, 1969
George, Waldemar
"Trente ans d'art indépendant" in *L'Amour de l'Art,* February 1926
George, Waldemar
*Soutine,* Paris, 1928
George, Waldemar
*La grande peinture contemporaine à la collection Paul Guillaume,* Paris, undated [1928 or 1929]
George, Waldemar
"La grande peinture contemporaine à la collection Paul Guillaume", in *La Renaissance,* April 1929, No. 4
George, Waldemar
"Derain," *Médecines, Peintures,* Paris, undated (1935)
George, Waldemar
*Art et Style,* No. 52, "Soutine," third quarter 1959
*Arts,* 4-10. February 1959, "Galerie vivante de la peinture contemporaine, la donation Walter est indispensable au Louvre"
Georges-Michel, Michel
*Les Montparnos,* Paris, 1923 (republished 1929, 1957)
Georges-Michel, Michel
*De Renoir à Picasso, les peintres que j'ai connus,* Paris, 1959
Gimpel, René
*Journal d'un collectionneur marchand de tableaux,* Paris, 1963
Gindertael, Roger V.
*Modigliani et Montparnasse,* Milan, 1967, Paris, 1976
Grey, Roch
*Henri Rousseau,* Rome, 1924
Grey, Roch
*Henri Rousseau,* Paris, 1943
Hilaire, Georges
*Derain,* Geneva 1959
Henry, Daniel (Pseudonym of Daniel Henry Kahnweiler)
*André Derain,* Leipzig, 1920
Keay, Carolyn
*Henri Rousseau, Le Douanier,* London, 1976
Kolle, Helmud
*Henri Rousseau,* Leipzig, 1922
Lanthemann, Joseph
*Modigliani, 1884-1920. Catalogue raisonné, sa vie, son œuvre complet, son art,* Barcelona, 1970
Lanthemann, Joseph and Parisot, Christian
*Modigliani inconnu, suivi de précisions et documents inédits,* Brescia, 1978
Lanthemann, Joseph
*Catalogue raisonné de l'œuvre dessiné de Soutine,* Monte-Carlo, 1981
Larkin, David
*Henri Rousseau,* Paris, 1975
Lassaigne, Jacques
*Cent chefs-d'œuvre des peintres de l'Ecole de Paris,* Paris, 1947
Lassaigne, Jacques
*Soutine,* Paris, 1954
Lassaigne, Jacques
*Tout Modigliani. La peinture,* Paris, 1982
Le Pichon, Yann
*Le monde du Douanier Rousseau,* Paris, 1981
Leymarie, Jean

*Renoir,* Paris, 1978
Mann, Carol
*Modigliani,* London, 1980
Marchesseau, Daniel
*Catalogue raisonné de l'œuvre gravé de Marie Laurencin,* Tokyo, 1981
Meier-Graefe, Julius
*Renoir,* Leipzig, 1929
Monod-Fontaine, Isabelle
*Matisse. Œuvres de Henri Matisse, collection du Musée national d'Art moderne,* Paris, 1979
Moravia, Alberto, Lecaldano, Paolo and Daix, Pierre
*Tout l'œuvre peint de Picasso. Périodes bleue et rose,* Paris, 1980
Nicholson, Benedict
*Modigliani,* London-Paris, 1948
Palau i Fabre, Josep
*Picasso vivant 1881-1909,* Paris, 1981
Pétridès, Paul
*L'œuvre complet de Maurice Utrillo,* Paris 1959-1962
Pfannstiel, Arthur
*Modigliani,* preface by Louis Latourettes, followed by a catalogue raisonné, Paris, undated [1929]
Pfannstiel, Arthur
*Modigliani et son œuvre, étude critique et catalogue raisonné,* Paris, undated [1956]
Picon, Gaëtan and Orienti, Sandra
*Tout l'œuvre peint de Cézanne,* Paris, 1975
Robida, Michel
*Renoir. Portraits d'enfants,* Paris, 1959
Rewald, John
The name of J. Rewald followed by a number refers the reader to Lionello Venturi's revised edition of the Cézanne catalogue. Mr. Rewald kindly supplied us with unpublished data concerning a number of the Cézanne works in the Walter-Guillaume Collection.
Salmon, André
*Henri Rousseau dit Le Douanier,* Paris, 1927
Salmon, André
*André Derain,* Paris, 1929
San Lazzaro, Giovanni di
*Modigliani, peintures,* Paris, 1947
Schneider, Pierre, Carrá, Massimo and Deryng, Xavier
*Tout l'œuvre peint de Matisse 1904-1928,* Paris, 1982
Serouya, Henry
*Soutine,* Paris, 1967
Sutton, Denys
*Derain,* London, 1959
Tobien, Félicitas
*Paul Cézanne,* Ramerding, 1981
Vallier, Dora
*Henri Rousseau,* Paris, 1961
Vallier, Dora
*Tout l'œuvre peint d'Henri Rousseau,* Paris, 1970
Venturi, Lionello
*Cézanne, son art, son œuvre,* Paris, 1936, 2 volumes.
Vollard, Ambroise
*Tableaux, Pastels et Dessins de Pierre-Auguste Renoir,* 2 volumes, Paris, 1918
Zervos, Christian
*Pablo Picasso,* Paris, Cahiers d'Art, 1932-1978, 33 volumes.

# Exhibitions listed in abbreviated form

1920
Venice, Twelfth Biennial, *Mostra individuale di Paul Cézanne*
1926
Paris, Grand Palais, *Trente ans d'art indépendant 1884-1914*
1929
Paris, Galerie Bernheim-Jeune, *La grande peinture contemporaine à la Collection Paul Guillaume*
Paris, Galerie Pigalle, *Cézanne Exhibition*
1931
New York, Marie Harriman Gallery, *Henri Rousseau*
Paris, Galerie Bernheim-Jeune, *Cézanne*
1932
Paris, Galerie Georges Petit, *Picasso*
1933
Basel, Kunsthalle, *Henri Rousseau*
New York, Galerie Durand-Ruel, *Derain*
1935
Paris, *Les Expositions des Beaux-Arts et de la Gazette des Beaux-Arts. Les étapes de l'art contemporain. Peintres instinctifs.*
Paris, Petit Palais, *Hommage du Musée de Grenoble à Paul Guillaume*
Springfield, Massachusetts, Springfield Museum, *French Paintings and Prints.*
1936
Paris, Orangerie des Tuileries, *Cézanne*
New York, Valentine Gallery, *Ten Paintings by Twentieth-Century French Masters*
1937
Paris, Galerie Paul Rosenberg, *Henri Rousseau, 1844-1910*
Zürich, Kunsthaus, *Les Maîtres populaires de la Réalité*
Paris, Petit Palais, *Les Maîtres de l'art indépendant 1895-1937*
1939
London, Wildenstein Gallery, *Homage to Cézanne*
Lyon, Palais Saint-Pierre, *Exposition Cézanne*
1944
Paris, Musée d'Art Moderne de la Ville de Paris, *Henri Rousseau, le Douanier*
1945
Paris, Galerie de France, *Rétrospective Soutine 1894-1943*
1946
Paris, Galerie Charpentier, *Cent chefs-d'œuvre des peintres de l'Ecole de Paris*
1950
Venice, Twenty-fifth Biennale, *Rousseau Retrospective Exhibition*
New York, Museum of Modern Art-Cleveland, Museum of Art, *Chaïm Soutine*
1951
New York, Sidney Ianis Gallery, *Henri Rousseau*
1952
Venice, Twenty-sixth Biennale, *Thirty-five Works of Soutine*
1954
Paris, Musée National d'Art Moderne, *Derain*
1957
Paris, Galerie Charpentier, *Cent chefs-d'œuvre de l'art français, 1750-1950*

London, Wildenstein Gallery, *André Derain.*
1958
Paris, Galerie Maeght, *Derain*
Marseilles, Musée Cantini, *Modigliani*
Paris, Galerie Charpentier, *Cent tableaux de Modigliani*
1959
Paris, Galerie Charpentier, *Cent tableaux par Utrillo.*
Paris, Galerie Charpentier, *Cent tableaux de Soutine*
1960
Paris, Galerie Charpentier, *Cent tableaux des Collections particulières de Bonnard à de Staël*
1961
Paris, Galerie Charpentier, *Henri Rousseau dit Le Douanier*
1963
London, Tate Gallery - Edinburgh, Arts Festival, *Fifty-seven works by Soutine, Retrospective organized by the Arts Council of Great Britain*
1964
Rotterdam, Musée Boymans-Van Beuningen, *De Lusthof der Naieven*
Paris, Musée National d'Art Moderne, *Le monde des naïfs*
Salzburg, Residenzgalerie, *Die Welt der Naiven Malerei*
Marseilles, Musée Cantini, *Derain*
1966
Paris, Orangerie des Tuileries, *Collection Jean Walter-Paul Guillaume*
1967
Edinburgh, The Royal Scottish Academy-London, *An André Derain Exhibition of Paintings, Drawings, Sculpture and Theatre Designs*
1973
Paris, Orangerie des Tuileries, *Soutine*
1974
Tokyo-Kyoto-Fukuoka, *Cézanne Exhibition*
Paris, Orangerie des Tuileries, *Cézanne dans les musées nationaux*
1976
Rome, Villa Medici, *André Derain*
1977
Paris, Grand Palais, *André Derain*
1978
Paris, Grand Palais, *Vingt-deux chefs-d'œuvre des musées soviétiques et français*
Paris, Musée Jacquemart-André, *La Ruche et Montparnasse, 1902-1930*
1980
Athens, National Art Gallery, *Impressionists and Post-Impressionists in the French Museums from Manet to Matisse*
Paris, Musée d'Art Moderne de la Ville de Paris, *Hommage à André Derain, 1880-1954*
1981
Tbilisi, Fine Arts Museum of Georgia-Leningrad-Hermitage Museum, *Impressionists and Post-Impressionists in the French Museums from Manet to Matisse*
Paris, Palais de Tokyo, Musée d'Art et d'Essai, *Visages et Portraits de Manet à Matisse,* no catalogue.
Münster, Landesmuseum-Tübingen, Kunsthalle-Lucerne, Kunstmuseum, *Chaïm*

*Soutine 1893-1943*
Paris, Musée d'Art Moderne de la Ville de Paris, *Amedeo Modigliani, 1884-1920*
Marcq-en-Barœul, Septentrion, Fondation Anne et Albert Prouvost, *A. Derain*
1982
Prague, Waldstein Manege, *Od Courbeta K Cézannovi,* Berlin, East Germany, Staatliche Museen, National Galerie, *Von Courbet bis Cézanne*
Liège, Musée Saint-Georges-Aix-en-Provence, Musée Granet, *Cézanne*
1983
Paris, Palais de Tokyo, Musée d'Art et d'Essai, *La nature morte et l'objet de Delacroix à Picasso,* no catalogue.
Paris, Musée Jacquemart-André - Liège, Musée Saint-Georges-Lille, Fondation Septentrion, Marcq-en-Barœul, *Centenaire de la naissance de Maurice Utrillo (1883-1955)*
1984-1985
Paris, Galeries Nationales du Grand Palais-New York, Museum of Modern Art, *Henri Rousseau.*
1985
London, Hayward Gallery-Paris, Grand Palais-Boston, Fine Arts Museum, *Renoir.*

# Index of proper names

The numbers listed as *page numbers* refer to pages in the introduction. Those listed as *catalogue numbers* refer to the numbers assigned to the various works. Names of authors of bibliographical references are not indexed, nor are the names of artists referring to their works.

# Contents

Provenance of photographs

Réunion des Musées Nationaux
and
Baltimore, Maryland, The Baltimore Museum of Art, The Cone Collection,
formed by Dr. Claribel Cone and Miss Etta Cone of Baltimore, p. 132
Berne, Hahnloser, p. 184
Cambridge, Mass., Harvard University, The Fogg Art Museum, Bequest-
Collection of Maurice Wertheim, class of 1906, p. 150
Chicago, Illinois, The Art Institute, p. 122
Grenoble, Ifot, pp. 5, 74
Merion, Penn., The Barnes Foundation, pp. 156, 264
Milan, Civica Galleria d'Arte Moderna, p. 7
Moscow, Pushkin Museum, p. 54
Ottawa, The National Gallery of Canada, p. 199
Paris, Bibliothèque Nationale, Service photographique, p. 58
Paris, Durand-Ruel, pp. 184, 191, 194, 196, 213, 218, 222
Paris, Galerie Berggruen, p. 154
Paris, Giraudon, pp. 9, 30, 272
Paris, Musée de l'Homme, pp. 7, 8, 10
Toledo, Ohio, The Toledo Museum of Art, p. 6
Troyes, André Godin, pp. 57, 58
Zürich, Institut für Kunstwissenschaft, p. 240


Layout
Jean-Pierre Vespérini

Adaptation for English edition by Hans Hunziker

Iridium photocomposition
L'Union Linotypiste

Photogravure
N.S.R.G.

Printer
Société Nouvelle de l'Imprimerie Moderne du Lion, Paris, 1987

Translation: Barbara Shuey


Dépôt légal : Janvier 1987
ISBN 2-7118-0.262-0 (French edition, RMN)
ISBN 2-7118-2.076-9 (English edition, RMN)
8040.143